D0065353

BLOOM'S

HOW TO WRITE ABOUT

Shakespeare's Comedies

PAUL GLEED

Introduction by Harold Bloom

BLOOM'S
LITERARY CRITICISM
An imprint of Infobase Publishing

Bloom's How to Write about Shakespeare's Comedies

Bloom's Literary Criticism
An imprint of Infobase Publishing
132 West 31st Street
New York NY 10001

Library of Congress Cataloging-in-Publication Data

Gleed, Paul.
  Bloom's how to write about Shakespeare's comedies / Paul Gleed ; introduction by Harold Bloom.
      p. cm. — (Bloom's how to write about literature)
  Includes bibliographical references and index.
  ISBN 978-1-60413-705-7 (hardcover)
  1. Shakespeare, William, 1564–1616—Comedies. 2. English drama (Comedy)—History and criticism. 3. Criticism—Authorship. I. Bloom, Harold. II. Title. III. Title: How to write about Shakespeare's comedies.
  PR2981.G54 2010
  822.3'3—dc22
                    2010015950

Bloom's Literary Criticism books are available at special discounts when purchased in bulk quantities for businesses, associations, institutions, or sales promotions. Please call our Special Sales Department in New York at (212. 967-8800 or (800) 322-8755.

You can find Bloom's Literary Criticism on the World Wide Web
at http://www.chelseahouse.com

Text design by Annie O'Donnell
Cover design by Ben Peterson
Composition by Mary Susan Ryan-Flynn
Cover printed by Art Print, Taylor PA
Book printed and bound by Maple Press, York PA
Date printed: September 2010
Printed in the United States of America

10 9 8 7 6 5 4 3 2 1

This book is printed on acid-free paper.

All links and Web addresses were checked and verified to be correct at the time of publication. Because of the dynamic nature of the Web, some addresses and links may have changed since publication and may no longer be valid.

CONTENTS

SERIES
INTRODUCTION

BLOOM's How to Write about Literature series is designed to inspire students to write fine essays on great writers and their works. Each volume in the series begins with an introduction by Harold Bloom, meditating on the challenges and rewards of writing about the volume's subject author. The first chapter then provides detailed instructions on how to write a good essay, including how to find a thesis; how to develop an outline; how to write a good introduction, body text, and conclusion; how to cite sources; and more. The second chapter provides a brief overview of the issues involved in writing about the subject author and then a number of suggestions for paper topics, with accompanying strategies for addressing each topic. Succeeding chapters cover the author's major works.

The paper topics suggested within this book are open-ended, and the brief strategies provided are designed to give students a push forward in the writing process rather than a road map to success. The aim of the book is to pose questions, not answer them. Many different kinds of papers could result from each topic. As always, the success of each paper will depend completely on the writer's skill and imagination.

HOW TO WRITE ABOUT SHAKESPEARE'S COMEDIES: INTRODUCTION

by Harold Bloom

S HAKESPEARE'S TEN comedies are so rich and varied that they can be written about in myriad ways. My own experience of teaching them for more than a half century and writing about them in several different contexts prompts me to suggest that a study of his comic characters works very well.

The greatest of Shakespeare's comedians is Sir John Falstaff, the dominant presence of the *Henry IV* plays. I cannot abide *The Merry Wives of Windsor*, because its "Falstaff" is an impostor who attempts to usurp that greatness but in vain. He is merely a travesty of the immortal Falstaff.

In the pure comedies, the superb protagonists are Rosalind of *As You Like It*; Bottom in *A Midsummer Night's Dream*; Feste, Malvolio, and Viola in *Twelfth Night*; and Berowne in *Love's Labour's Lost*. *The Merchant of Venice* has darkened with the centuries, though Portia remains its redemptive joy. I have to assume that Shakespeare intended Shylock to be a comic villain, on the model off Barabas in Christopher Marlowe's *The Jew of Malta*. History across four hundred years now renders that impossible.

I will give some brief hints here about the seven figures: Rosalind, Bottom, Feste, Malvolio, Viola, Berowne, and Portia. All dramas, of whatever genre, depend on the audience achieving a perspective on the protagonists that enables us to see them as they cannot see themselves. Shakespeare's Rosalind is the grand exception: All perspectives are at home in her, and so we cannot see anything crucial in which she has not long preceded us. That allows her ironic perspectives on us, as though we were the players and she the auditor.

Rosalind's freedom from our irony allies her to the giants of consciousness in Shakespeare: Falstaff, Hamlet, Cleopatra, and, on the negative side, Iago and *King Lear*'s Edmund. Shakespeare's own consciousness is so capacious that he can create masters of knowing, and his genius is so adroit that he can sustain our interest even when our own quest for knowledge is baffled.

Bottom, ostensibly the clown or fool in *A Midsummer Night's Dream*, allows us to see what he cannot, yet never to his imaginative diminishment. Nothing daunts him or causes him humiliation. Were he to have been changed into a Kafkan waterbug, like the donkeyhood imposed on him, he remains Bottom: charmed and charming, compassionate, boisterous, an emblem of human dignity and value overmatching whatever sorrow could come to him.

In the world of *Twelfth Night*, everyone is a zany: the wise clown Feste, the day-dreaming Malvolio, and most of all the infinitely beguiling Viola. And yet this zaniness attracts us: It grants Feste wisdom, though it socially destroys poor Malvolio, and lands Viola on the shore of her desire, the absurd Orsino.

The dazzling Berowne of *Love's Labour's Lost* is language drunk, and the play is a great feast of language. That plethora calls our perspectivism into question. In this comedy, language and reality so interfuse that we, too, realize that we are made up out of words.

Portia, high spirited and perpetually delightful, is too good for her play, but she refuses to know that. A kind of slummer, she is content with the second best, in her friends and in her suitor Bassanio. Portia triumphs over Shylock, but Christian Venice allows no other outcome.

Perspectivism allows us to ask, in writing about Shakespearean comedy, "Does it have to turn out this way rather than that?"

HOW TO WRITE
A GOOD ESSAY

By Laurie A. Sterling and Paul Gleed

WHILE THERE are many ways to write about literature, most assignments for high school and college English classes call for analytical papers. In these assignments, you are presenting your interpretation of a text to your reader. Your objective is to interpret the text's meaning in order to enhance your reader's understanding and enjoyment of the work. Without exception, strong papers about the meaning of a literary work are built upon a careful, close reading of the text or texts. Careful, analytical reading should always be the first step in your writing process. This volume provides models of such close, analytical reading, and these should help you develop your own skills as a reader and as a writer.

As the examples throughout this book demonstrate, attentive reading entails thinking about and evaluating the formal (textual) aspects of the author's works: theme, character, form, and language. In addition, when writing about a work, many readers choose to move beyond the text itself to consider the work's cultural context. In these instances, writers might explore the historical circumstances of the time period in which the work was written. Alternatively, they might examine the philosophies and ideas that a work addresses. Even in cases where writers explore a work's cultural context, though, papers must still address the more formal aspects of the work itself. A good interpretative essay that evaluates Charles Dickens's use of the philosophy of utilitarianism in his

1

novel *Hard Times*, for example, cannot adequately address the author's treatment of the philosophy without firmly grounding this discussion in the book itself. In other words, any analytical paper about a text, even one that seeks to evaluate the work's cultural context, must also have a firm handle on the work's themes, characters, and language. You must look for and evaluate these aspects of a work, then, as you read a text and as you prepare to write about it.

WRITING ABOUT THEMES

Literary themes are more than just topics or subjects treated in a work; they are attitudes or points about these topics that often structure other elements in a work. Writing about theme therefore requires that you not just identify a topic that a literary work addresses but also discuss what the work says about that topic. For example, if you were writing about the culture of the American South in William Faulkner's famous story "A Rose for Emily," you would need to discuss what Faulkner says, argues, or implies about that culture and its passing.

When you prepare to write about thematic concerns in a work of literature, you will probably discover that, like most works of literature, your text touches upon other themes in addition to its central theme. These secondary themes also provide rich ground for paper topics. A thematic paper on "A Rose for Emily" might consider gender or race in the story. While neither of these could be said to be the central theme of the story, they are clearly related to the passing of the "old South" and could provide plenty of good material for papers.

As you prepare to write about themes in literature, you might find a number of strategies helpful. After you identify a theme or themes in the story, you should begin by evaluating how other elements of the story—such as character, point of view, imagery, and symbolism—help develop the theme. You might ask yourself what your own responses are to the author's treatment of the subject matter. Do not neglect the obvious, either: What expectations does the title set up? How does the title help develop thematic concerns? Clearly, the title "A Rose for Emily" says something about the narrator's attitude toward the title character, Emily Grierson, and all she represents.

WRITING ABOUT CHARACTER

Generally, characters are essential components of fiction and drama. (This is not always the case, though; Ray Bradbury's "August 2026: There Will Come Soft Rains" is technically a story without characters, at least any human characters.) Often, you can discuss character in poetry, as in T. S. Eliot's "The Love Song of J. Alfred Prufrock" or Robert Browning's "My Last Duchess." Many writers find that analyzing character is one of the most interesting and engaging ways to work with a piece of literature and to shape a paper. After all, characters generally are human, and we all know something about being human and living in the world. While it is always important to remember that these figures are not real people but creations of the writer's imagination, it can be fruitful to begin evaluating them as you might evaluate a real person. Often you can start with your own response to a character. Did you like or dislike the character? Did you sympathize with the character? Why or why not?

Keep in mind, though, that emotional responses like these are just starting places. To truly explore and evaluate literary characters, you need to return to the formal aspects of the text and evaluate how the author has drawn these characters. The 20th-century writer E. M. Forster coined the terms *flat* characters and *round* characters. Flat characters are static, one-dimensional characters that frequently represent a particular concept or idea. In contrast, round characters are fully drawn and much more realistic characters that frequently change and develop over the course of a work. Are the characters you are studying flat or round? What elements of the characters lead you to this conclusion? Why might the author have drawn characters like this? How does their development affect the meaning of the work? Similarly, you should explore the techniques the author uses to develop characters. Do we hear a character's own words, or do we hear only other characters' assessments of him or her? Or, does the author use an omniscient or limited omniscient narrator to allow us access to the workings of the characters' minds? If so, how does that help develop the characterization? Often you can even evaluate the narrator as a character. How trustworthy are the opinions and assessments of the narrator? You should also think about characters' names. Do they mean anything? If you encounter a hero named Sophia or Sophie, you should probably think about her wisdom (or lack thereof), since *sophia* means "wisdom" in Greek. Similarly, since the name Sylvia is derived from the word *sylvan*, meaning "of the wood," you might want to evaluate that character's relationship with nature. Once again, you might look to the title of the work. Does Herman Melville's "Bartleby, the Scrivener" signal anything about Bartleby himself? Is Bartleby adequately defined by his job as scrivener? Is this part of Melville's point? Pursuing questions such as these can help you develop thorough papers about characters from psychological, sociological, or more formalistic perspectives.

WRITING ABOUT FORM AND GENRE

Genre, a word derived from French, means "type" or "class." Literary genres are distinctive classes or categories of literary composition. On the most general level, literary works can be divided into the genres of drama, poetry, fiction, and essays, yet within those genres there are classifications that are also referred to as genres. Tragedy and comedy, for example, are genres of drama. Epic, lyric, and pastoral are genres of poetry. *Form,* on the other hand, generally refers to the shape or structure of a work. There are many clearly defined forms of poetry that follow specific patterns of meter, rhyme, and stanza. Sonnets, for example, are poems that follow a fixed form of 14 lines. Sonnets generally follow one of two basic sonnet forms, each with its own distinct rhyme scheme. Haiku is another example of poetic form, traditionally consisting of three unrhymed lines of five, seven, and five syllables.

While you might think that writing about form or genre might leave little room for argument, many of these forms and genres are very fluid. Remember that literature is evolving and ever changing, and so are its forms. As you study poetry, you may find that poets, especially more modern poets, play with traditional poetic forms, bringing about new effects. Similarly, dramatic tragedy was once quite narrowly defined, but over the centuries playwrights have broadened and challenged traditional definitions, changing the shape of tragedy. When Arthur Miller wrote *Death of a Salesman,* many critics challenged the idea that tragic drama could encompass a common man like Willy Loman.

Evaluating how a work of literature fits into or challenges the boundaries of its form or genre can provide you with fruitful avenues of investigation. You might find it helpful to ask why the work does or does not fit into traditional categories. Why might Miller have thought it fitting to write a tragedy of the common man? Similarly, you might compare the content or theme of a work with its form. How well do they work together? Many of Emily Dickinson's poems, for instance, follow the meter of traditional hymns. While some of her poems seem to express traditional religious doctrines, many seem to challenge or strain against traditional conceptions of God and theology. What is the effect, then, of her use of traditional hymn meter?

WRITING ABOUT LANGUAGE, SYMBOLS, AND IMAGERY

No matter what the genre, writers use words as their most basic tool. Language is the most fundamental building block of literature. It is essential that you pay careful attention to the author's language and word choice as you read, reread, and analyze a text. Imagery is language that appeals to the senses. Most commonly, imagery appeals to our sense of vision, creating a mental picture, but authors also use language that appeals to our other senses. Images can be literal or figurative. Literal images use sensory language to describe an actual thing. In the broadest terms, figurative language uses one thing to speak about something else. For example, if I call my boss a snake, I am not saying that he is literally a reptile. Instead, I am using figurative language to communicate my opinions about him. Since we think of snakes as sneaky, slimy, and sinister, I am using the concrete image of a snake to communicate these abstract opinions and impressions.

The two most common figures of speech are similes and metaphors. Both are comparisons between two apparently dissimilar things. Similes are explicit comparisons using the words *like* or *as*; metaphors are implicit comparisons. To return to the previous example, if I say, "My boss, Bob, was waiting for me when I showed up to work five minutes late today—the snake!" I have constructed a metaphor. Writing about his experiences fighting in World War I, Wilfred Owen begins his poem "Dulce et decorum est," with a string of similes: "Bent double, like old beggars under sacks, / Knock-kneed, coughing like hags, we cursed through sludge." Owen's goal was to undercut clichéd notions that war and dying in battle were glorious. Certainly, comparing soldiers to coughing hags and to beggars underscores his point.

"Fog," a short poem by Carl Sandburg, provides a clear example of a metaphor. Sandburg's poem reads:

The fog comes
on little cat feet.

It sits looking
over harbor and city
on silent haunches
and then moves on.

Notice how effectively Sandburg conveys surprising impressions of the fog by comparing two seemingly disparate things—the fog and a cat.

Symbols, by contrast, are things that stand for, or represent, other things. Often they represent something intangible, such as concepts or ideas. In everyday life we use and understand symbols easily. Babies at christenings and brides at weddings wear white to represent purity. Think, too, of a dollar bill. The paper itself has no value in and of itself. Instead, that paper bill is a symbol of something else, the precious metal in a nation's coffers. Symbols in literature work similarly. Authors use symbols to evoke more than a simple, straightforward, literal meaning. Characters, objects, and places can all function as symbols. Famous literary examples of symbols include Moby Dick, the white whale of Herman Melville's novel, and the scarlet *A* of Nathaniel Hawthorne's *The Scarlet Letter*. As both of these symbols suggest, a literary symbol cannot be adequately defined or explained by any one meaning. Hester Prynne's Puritan community clearly intends her scarlet *A* as a symbol of her adultery, but as the novel progresses, even her own community reads the letter as representing not just *adultery*, but *able, angel,* and a host of other meanings.

Writing about imagery and symbols requires close attention to the author's language. To prepare a paper on symbolism or imagery in a work, identify and trace the images and symbols and then try to draw some conclusions about how they function. Ask yourself how any symbols or images help contribute to the themes or meanings of the work. What connotations do they carry? How do they affect your reception of the work? Do they shed light on characters or settings? A strong paper on imagery or symbolism will thoroughly consider the use of figures in the text and will try to reach some conclusions about how or why the author uses them.

WRITING ABOUT HISTORY AND CONTEXT

As noted above, it is possible to write an analytical paper that also considers the work's context. After all, the text was not created in a vacuum. The author lived and wrote in a specific time period and in a specific cultural context and, like all of us, was shaped by that environment. Learning more about the historical and cultural circumstances that surround the author and the work can help illuminate a text and provide you with productive material for a paper. Remember, though, that when you write analytical papers, you should use the context to illuminate the text. Do not lose sight of your goal—to interpret the meaning of the literary work. Use historical or philosophical research as a tool to develop your textual evaluation.

Thoughtful readers often consider how history and culture affected the author's choice and treatment of his or her subject matter. Investigations into the history and context of a work could examine the work's relation to specific historical events, such as the Salem witch trials in 17th-century Massachusetts or the restoration of Charles II to the English throne in 1660. Bear in mind that historical context is not limited to politics and world events. While knowing about the Vietnam War is certainly helpful in interpreting much of Tim O'Brien's fiction, and some knowledge of the French Revolution clearly illuminates the dynamics of Charles Dickens's *A Tale of Two Cities*, historical context also entails the fabric of daily life. Examining a text in light of gender roles, race relations, class boundaries, or working conditions can give rise to thoughtful and compelling papers. Exploring the conditions of the working class in 19th-century England, for example, can provide a particularly effective avenue for writing about Dickens's *Hard Times*.

You can begin thinking about these issues by asking broad questions at first. What do you know about the time period and about the author? What does the editorial apparatus in your text tell you? Similarly, when specific historical events or dynamics are particularly important to understanding a work but might be somewhat obscure to modern readers, textbooks usually provide notes to explain historical background. With this information, ask yourself how these historical facts and circumstances might have affected the author, the presentation of theme, and the presentation of character. How does knowing more about the work's specific historical context illuminate the work? To take a well-known example, understanding the complex attitudes toward slavery during the time Mark Twain wrote *Adventures of Huckleberry Finn* should help you begin to examine issues of race in the text. Additionally, you might compare these attitudes to those of the time in which the novel was set. How might this comparison affect your interpretation of a work written after the abolition of slavery but set before the Civil War?

WRITING ABOUT PHILOSOPHY AND IDEAS

Philosophical concerns are closely related to both historical context and thematic issues. Like historical investigation, philosophical research can provide a useful tool as you analyze a text. For example, an investigation into the working class in Dickens's England might lead you to a topic on the philosophical doctrine of utilitarianism in *Hard Times*. Many other works explore philosophies and ideas quite explicitly. Mary Shelley's famous novel *Frankenstein*, for example, explores John Locke's tabula rasa theory of human knowledge as she portrays the intellectual and emotional development of Victor Frankenstein's creature. As this example indicates, philosophical issues are more abstract than investigations of theme or historical context. Some other examples of philosophical issues include human free will, the formation of human identity, the nature of sin, or questions of ethics.

Writing about philosophy and ideas might require some outside research, but usually the notes or other material in your text will provide you with basic information, and often footnotes and bibliographies suggest places you can go to read further about the subject. If you have identified a philosophical theme that runs through a text, you might ask yourself how the author develops this theme. Look at character development and the interactions of characters, for example. Similarly, you might examine whether the narrative voice in a work of fiction addresses the philosophical concerns of the text.

WRITING COMPARISON AND CONTRAST ESSAYS

Finally, you might find that comparing and contrasting the works or techniques of an author provides a useful tool for literary analysis. A comparison and contrast essay might compare two characters or themes in a single work, or it might compare the author's treatment of a theme in two works. It might also contrast methods of character development or analyze an author's differing treatment of a philosophical concern in two works. Writing comparison and contrast essays, though, requires some special consideration. While they generally provide you with plenty of material to use, they also come with a built-in trap: the laundry list. These papers often become mere lists of connections between the works. As this chapter will discuss, a strong thesis must make an assertion that you want to prove or validate. A strong comparison/contrast thesis, then, needs to comment on the significance of the similarities and differences you observe. It is not enough merely to assert that the works contain similarities and differences. You might, for example, assert why the similarities and differences are important and explain how they illuminate the works' treatment of theme. Remember, too, that a thesis should not be a statement of the obvious. A comparison/contrast paper that focuses only on very obvious similarities or differences does little to illuminate the connections between the works. Often, an effective method of shaping a strong thesis and argument is to begin your paper by noting the similarities between the works but then to develop a thesis that asserts how these apparently similar elements are different. If, for example, you observe that Emily Dickinson wrote a number of poems about spiders, you might analyze how she uses spider imagery differently in two poems. Similarly, many scholars have noted that Hawthorne created many "mad scientist" characters, men who are so devoted to their science or their art that they lose perspective on all else. A good thesis comparing two of these characters—Aylmer of "The Birth-mark" and Dr. Rappaccini of "Rappaccini's Daughter," for example—might initially identify both characters as examples of Hawthorne's mad scientist type but then argue that their motivations for scientific experimentation differ. If you strive to analyze the similarities or differences, discuss significances, and move beyond the obvious, your paper should move beyond the laundry list trap.

PREPARING TO WRITE

Armed with a clear sense of your task—illuminating the text—and with an understanding of theme, character, language, history, and philosophy, you are ready to approach the writing process. Remember that good writing is grounded in good reading and that close reading takes time, attention, and more than one reading of your text. Read for comprehension first. As you go back and review the work, mark the text to chart the details of the work as well as your reactions. Highlight important passages, repeated words, and image patterns. "Converse" with the text through marginal notes. Mark turns in the plot, ask questions, and make observations about characters, themes, and language. If you are reading from a book that does not belong to you, keep a record of your reactions in a journal or notebook. If you have read a work of literature carefully, paying attention to both the text and the context of the work, you have a leg up on the writing process. Admittedly, at this point, your ideas are probably very broad and undefined, but you have taken an important first step toward writing a strong paper.

Your next step is to focus, to take a broad, perhaps fuzzy, topic and define it more clearly. Even a topic provided by your instructor will need to be focused appropriately. Remember that good writers make the topic their own. There are a number of strategies—often called "invention"—that you can use to develop your own focus. In one such strategy, called *freewriting*, you spend 10 minutes or so just writing about your topic without referring back to the text or your notes. Write whatever comes to mind; the important thing is that you just keep writing. Often this process allows you to develop fresh ideas or approaches to your subject matter. You could also try *brainstorming*: Write down your topic and then list all the related points or ideas you can think of. Include questions, comments, words, important passages or events, and anything else that comes to mind. Let one idea lead to another. In the related technique of *clustering*, or *mapping*, write your topic on a sheet of paper and write related ideas around it. Then list related subpoints under each of these main ideas. Many people then draw arrows to show connections between points. This technique helps you narrow your topic and can also help you organize your ideas. Similarly, asking journalistic questions—Who? What? Where? When? Why? and How?—can lead to ideas for topic development.

Thesis Statements

Once you have developed a focused topic, you can begin to think about your thesis statement, the main point or purpose of your paper. It is absolutely imperative that you craft a strong thesis; otherwise your paper will likely be little more than random, disorganized observations about the text. Think of your thesis statement as a kind of road map of your paper. It tells your reader where you are going and how you are going to get there.

In order to craft a good thesis, you must keep a number of things in mind. First of all, as the title of this subsection indicates, your paper's thesis should be a statement, an assertion about the text that you want to prove or validate. Often beginning writers formulate a question that they attempt to use as a thesis. For example, a writer exploring the character of Shylock in *The Merchant of Venice* might ask, Although the Venetian Christians tell us that Shylock is a villain, does Shakespeare himself appear to agree? While a question like this is a good strategy to use in the invention process to help narrow your topic and find your thesis, it cannot serve as the thesis statement because it does not tell your reader what you want to assert about Shylock. A writer might shape this question into a thesis by instead proposing an answer to that question: Although the Venetian Christians tell us that Shylock is a villain, there is enough evidence in the play to suggest that Shakespeare has a much more complex, even sympathetic view of his character. We can see this not only in Shylock's statements of vulnerability and weakness, but also in the dubious, hypocritical conduct of the play's Christians. Notice that this thesis provides an initial plan or structure for the rest of the paper—the writer will spend some time establishing how the Venetian community perceives Shylock, then move into a discussion of scenes where Shylock's words reveal him to be a victim in his own right, and then finally into a section treating the portrait of the apparently "good" Christians of Venice who are really no better than Shylock. Notice, too, that the thesis statement does not necessarily have to fit into one sentence.

Secondly, remember that a good thesis makes an assertion that you need to support. In other words, a good thesis does not state the obvious. If you tried to formulate a thesis about *The Taming of the Shrew* by saying, Shrew is about gender relations, you have done nothing but state the obvious. This example gives the reader merely a theme, and a thesis is much more than a theme or subject. The thesis is what you have to say about your theme, of course. In other words, while your essay certainly can be about gender in *The Taming of the Shrew*, it must make a precise point about witchcraft. Of course, the theme of gender in *Shrew* is a rich one and might stimulate many good thesis statements. For example: While many modern productions of Shrew set out to present a feminist interpretation of the play, one in which Kate winks knowingly as she ironically speaks her closing lines, there seems little evidence in the text for this modern reinvention of the play. Instead, it seems most likely that the play's comic resolution is intended as a celebratory return to the patriarchal order that Kate has threatened throughout the play.

As the comparison with the road map also suggests, your thesis should appear near the beginning of the paper. In relatively short papers (three to six pages) the thesis almost always appears in the first paragraph. Some writers fall into the trap of saving their thesis for the end, trying to provide a surprise or a big moment of revelation. (As if to say, "TA DA!!! I've just proved that Shylock is a sympathetic figure and you didn't even see it coming!") While surprise endings may be thrilling in a murder mystery novel, they are utterly self-destructive in an academic essay. Placing a thesis at the end of an essay can seriously mar the paper's effectiveness. If you fail to clearly define your essay's point and purpose at the beginning, it makes it difficult for your reader to assess the clarity of your argument and understand the points you are making. Your argument should not come as a surprise to the reader at the end. When you do this, you have forced your reader to re-read your essay in order to assess its logic and effectiveness.

Finally, you should avoid using the first person ("I") as you present your thesis. Though it is not strictly wrong to write in the first person, it is difficult to do so gracefully. While writing in the first person, beginning writers often fall into the trap of writing self-reflexive prose (writing *about* their paper *in* their paper). Often this leads to the most dreaded of opening lines: "In this paper I am going to discuss. . . ." Not only does this self-reflexive voice make for very awkward prose, it frequently allows writers to boldly announce a topic while completely avoiding a thesis statement.

Outlines

As with most things in life, essay writing is made easier by some advance planning. Many students avoid making plans because they feel it wastes time or that "it's just not my style." While there certainly is something to be said for spontaneity—a great deal, in fact—making a plan will not prevent you from having "eureka" moments as you write. Nor will making an outline mean that you spend an extra hour or so in the company of that essay you would so dearly love to see completed. In fact, it is almost certain that making an outline will allow you and your essay to bid each other good night significantly sooner than you otherwise might have. Think of it this way. If somebody asked you to get in a car and drive from Carlisle, Pennsylvania, to Washington, D.C., wouldn't you want a map and detailed directions? You would certainly get to Washington quicker—and with far less stress—than if all you knew was that you wanted to get to the capital. Think of all the wrong turns you would make without your map and directions. Writing an essay is exactly the same. Making an outline not only means that you will get to your desired destination sooner, but also that you will probably steer clear of the single-lane, standstill traffic jam known as writer's block.

However, not all outlines are created equal. While some planning is better than none when it comes to essay writing, better planning is best. One useful method is based on an adaptation of the brainstorming technique mentioned in the "Preparing to Write" section. Let us say that we will be writing an essay on Caliban in Shakespeare's *The Tempest*. All you have right now is a theme, something that interested you enough while you read to make you pick it as a topic. Take a sheet of paper and brainstorm on Caliban, not editing or ordering your thoughts in any way. This should take a while and ideally should be done with *The Tempest* in hand, thumbing through the pages and looking at your margin notes and underlining. Write down everything that might go into an essay on Caliban. The result should be a page of brief notes, lots of points, details and thoughts. Study the list carefully, thinking about possible arguments that could be developed from your material. After some reflection, you decide on the following thesis: The Tempest encourages us to view Caliban as a tragic figure, a victim of Prospero's colonial project. Here is what your brainstormed notes may look like:

Caliban tried to rape Miranda
> Prospero's famous line about Caliban: "This thing of darkness I / Acknowledge mine." But what does this line mean?
> Caliban's mother ruled the island before Prospero's arrival
> At first Caliban and Prospero got along
> Prospero and Miranda need Caliban
> Caliban is repeatedly referred to as "slave"
> Prospero keeps Caliban in line by hurting and punishing him
> Caliban knows the island and seems to be in tune with it

Caliban is actually very eloquent and makes several strong arguments against Prospero's rule—act 1, scene 2 and act 4, scene 1 especially.
> Prospero seems really shocked and angry (are these the right words?) by Caliban's attempt to kill him, even though Pros-

pero is so much more powerful and not really in any danger. I wonder why this is?

Count up the number of points you have, then take a clean piece of paper. Write down numbers for each of your points, plus two more. For example, there are 10 points above, so in this instance, you would write 12 numbers on the second piece of paper. If you had thirty points, write 32 numbers, and so on. For the example above, the paper would look like this.

1.
2.
3.
4.
5.
6.
7.
8.
9.
10.
11.
12.

The next step is the most important—and perhaps most difficult—one. Alongside number one, write something like "Introduction/clear statement of thesis," while next to the final number write "conclusion." In this case, as we know, our argument is that *The Tempest* encourages us to view Caliban as a tragic figure, a victim of Prospero's colonial project. We need to pick a strong first point now to follow from this initial thesis statement. What is our most compelling piece of evidence that Caliban is anything but the monstrous savage that the Europeans take him for? This will be subjective; different writers might pick different starting points. The important thing is that you believe the chosen point is your strongest piece of evidence and you are confident in it. Let us say that you picked the point about Caliban's eloquence and the powerful speeches he makes against his mistreatment. You would scratch this out from your notes and write it alongside number two on your second sheet. After this, you are no longer concerned about the strength of the points, but rather how they tie in or connect to and support your point about Caliban's eloquence. The intention is to produce a list of points that moves from idea to idea logically and seamlessly. Think of it as a bit of a puzzle. Here is *one* solution that works:

1. Introduction and thesis: *The Tempest* encourages us to view Caliban as a tragic figure, a victim of Prospero's colonial project.
2. Caliban's eloquent appeals against his treatment (1.2 and 4.1 in particular)
3. Caliban is repeatedly referred to as "slave"
4. Prospero keeps Caliban in line by hurting and punishing him
5. Caliban's mother ruled the island before Prospero's arrival
6. Caliban knows the island and seems to be in tune with it
7. At first Caliban and Prospero got along
8. Caliban tried to rape Miranda
9. Prospero and Miranda *need* Caliban
10. Prospero's shock and anger at Caliban's betrayal
11. "This thing of darkness. . ."
12. Conclusion

You now know exactly where you are going in this essay and exactly how you are going to get there. Each point moves logically to the next. Here, for example, points two, three, and four all address the abuses of Caliban and his intelligent response to them. It is easy to make a transition from here into points five through nine, all of which describe the emergence of the colonial relationship, charting the move from encounter to conflict. These points, then, suggest the foundation of the relationship between Prospero and Caliban, while points 10 and 11 build on this to show how complex and tragic, how harmful to all parties, the relationship between these two antagonists has become. This essay will certainly provide ample support and exploration of the thesis's claim about the tragic quality of Caliban. Keep in mind that each point does not necessarily represent a paragraph or any other fixed amount of page space. For example, you could spend several pages on point number two, assessing Caliban's intellectual resistance through a close reading of some of his speeches, while only dedicating a few lines to point number six.

Some students may wish to develop an outline even more, adding more detail and specificity to it. For example, it might be beneficial to know which quotes you will be using and when, so make sure your outline includes a list of act, scene, and line numbers to refer to as you write. A more elaborate version of an outline for the same essay could look something like this:

1. Introduction and thesis
   - Prospero often seen as the central tragic figure in *The Tempest*
   - The tragedy of the play is also traditionally viewed as being one of "time"
   - However, Caliban is in fact a figure of the same tragic power as Prospero because they are both victims of the colonial system

2. Caliban's sophistication
   - Introduce the idea of a sympathetic Caliban
   - Is modern interest in Caliban simply a result of a contemporary distrust of colonialism?
   - On the contrary, Shakespeare seems to have worked hard to make Caliban a sympathetic and complex figure
   - Caliban claims his right to the island is superior to Prospero's (1.2.334)
   - Caliban is able to recognize that he has not benefited from the supposed "civilizing" process of colonialism (1.2.364–5)

3. The mistreatment of Caliban
   - Introduce the idea that sympathy for Caliban comes not only from his intelligence but from his mistreatment
   - Instances of Caliban being treated as a "slave"

- Prospero's justification for the ill-treatment of Caliban does not hold up to scrutiny (4.1.188–9)

4. A reconsideration of the relationship between Prospero and Caliban
   - Caliban seems essentially "good" (1.2.335)
   - If Caliban's "nature" is not flawed, it must be the "nurture" provided by Prospero
   - Eventually, Prospero recognizes that he and Caliban are victims of the same political power system
   - "This thing of darkness . . ." (5.1.277). A close reading of this line and its implications. For example, is it Prospero claiming "responsibility" for the moral failures of Caliban?
   - A better reading might be that Prospero recognizes not responsibility but rather equality; they are both victims

5. Conclusion
   - Recap the concept of a "shared" tragedy for both Prospero and Caliban
   - Their tragedy is rooted in the political/social bonds of colonialism that enslave both to the mutually destructive logic of that system

At the end of this chapter is a sample essay based on this outline, so you can see one version of how this paper might look. The most important thing, nonetheless, is to know that this road map will save you time and produce a better essay, one that flows well and builds its argument logically and carefully.

Body Paragraphs

Once your outline is complete, you can begin drafting your paper. Paragraphs, units of related sentences, are the building blocks of a good paper, and as you draft you should keep in mind both the function and the qualities of good paragraphs. Paragraphs help you chart and control the shape and content of your essay, and they help the reader to see your organization and your logic. You should begin a new paragraph whenever you move from one major point to another. In longer, more complex essays, you might use a group of related paragraphs to help support major points. Remember that in addition to being adequately developed, a good paragraph is both unified and coherent.

Unified Paragraphs

Each paragraph must be centered on one idea or point, and a unified paragraph carefully focuses on and develops this central idea without including extraneous ideas or tangents. For beginning writers, the best way to be assured that you are constructing unified paragraphs is to include a topic sentence in each paragraph. This topic sentence should convey the main point of the paragraph, and every sentence in the paragraph should relate back to that topic sentence. Any sentence that strays from the central topic does not belong in the paragraph and needs to be revised or deleted. Consider the following paragraph about love in *As You Like It.*

> It seems, then, that Shakespeare cannot rightly be called a cynic when it comes to love but rather a realist. Rosalind's pragmatic advice to Orlando centers on realizing that the idealism and optimism of love's first bloom is unsustainable. Instead, she argues, it is vital to the health of a relationship to understand that frustrations and acrimony are inevitable in a partnership, and that there really is a thin line between love and hate, a division that will likely be straddled often in the lifetime of a relationship. It is important, too, to see that Orlando is able to reestablish his brotherly love for Oliver by the play's close. This is only one part, of course, but an important part nonetheless, of the play's fairy-tale push to a blissful comic resolution.

The paragraph begins well enough. Notice, though, the break that takes place on "It is important . . ." The shift from Rosalind and Orlando to

Orlando and Oliver is jarring, and the final reference to the "fairy-tale push" of the play's resolution seems to develop naturally but is actually a significant thematic departure. Monitor your own thinking and movement within each paragraph; just as the overall essay needs to flow and transition smoothly, so too does each paragraph.

Coherent Paragraphs

In addition to shaping unified paragraphs, you must also craft coherent paragraphs, paragraphs that develop their points logically with sentences that flow smoothly into one another. Coherence depends on the order of your sentences, but it is not strictly the order of the sentences that is important to paragraph coherence. You also need to craft your prose to help the reader see the relationship between the sentences. Let us imagine that a writer revised the above paragraph to create a unified passage, but the text he settled on now highlights a different problem:

> It seems, then, that Shakespeare cannot rightly be called a cynic when it comes to love, but rather a realist. Rosalind's pragmatic advice to Orlando centers on realizing that the idealism and optimism of love's first bloom is unsustainable. Instead, she argues, it is vital to the health of a relationship to understand that frustrations and acrimony are inevitable in a partnership, and that there really is a thin line between love and hate, a division that will likely be straddled often in the lifetime of a relationship. Petrarchan love poetry creates impossible romantic goals. Orsino, in *Twelfth Night*, shows that such people are simply in love with being in love.

This paragraph demonstrates that unity alone does not guarantee paragraph effectiveness. The argument is hard to follow because the author fails both to show connections between the sentences and to indicate how they work to support the overall point.

A number of techniques are available to aid paragraph coherence. Careful use of transitional words and phrases is essential. You can use transitional flags to introduce an example or an illustration *(for example, for instance)*; to amplify a point or add another phase of the same idea *(additionally, furthermore, next, similarly, finally, then)*; to indicate a conclusion or result *(therefore, as a result, thus, in other words)*; to signal a contrast or a qualification *(on the other hand, nevertheless, despite this, on the contrary, still, however, conversely)*; to signal a comparison *(likewise, in comparison, similarly)*; and to indicate a movement in time *(afterwards, earlier, eventually, finally, later, subsequently, until)*.

In addition to transitional flags, careful use of pronouns aids coherence and flow. If you were writing about *The Wizard of Oz*, you would not want to keep repeating, the phrase "the witch" or the name "Dorothy." Careful substitution of the pronoun "she" in these instances can aid coherence. A word of warning, though: when you substitute pronouns for proper names, always be sure that your pronoun reference is clear. In a paragraph that discusses both Dorothy and the witch, substituting "she" could lead to confusion. Make sure that it is clear to whom the pronoun refers. Generally, the pronoun refers to the last proper noun you have used.

While repeating the same name over and over again can lead to awkward, boring prose, it is possible to use repetition to help your paragraph's coherence. Careful repetition of important words or phrases can lend coherence to your paragraph by helping remind readers of your key points. Admittedly, it takes some practice to use this technique effectively. You may find that reading your prose aloud can help you develop an ear for effective use of repetition.

To see how helpful transitional aids are, compare the paragraph below to the preceding paragraph about love in *As You Like It*. Notice how the author works with the same ideas but shapes them into a much more coherent paragraph whose point is clearer and easier to follow. The result is a paragraph that is both unified and coherent:

It seems, then, that Shakespeare cannot rightly be called a cynic when it comes to love but rather a realist. Rosalind's pragmatic advice to Orlando centers on realizing that the idealism and optimism of love's first bloom is unsustainable. Instead, she argues, it is vital to the health of a relationship to understand that frustrations and acrimony are inevitable in a partnership, and that there really is a thin line between love and hate, a division that will likely be straddled often in the lifetime of a relationship.

This wisdom is a direct response to Orlando's embrace of the ideals of Petrarchan love poetry, including its commonplaces of the lover-poet's suffering and the mistress's cruelty. Indeed, Orlando becomes an example of a particular kind of male figure in Shakespearean comedy, twinned with Orsino of *Twelfth Night*. These men are simply in love with being in love.

Introductions

Introductions and conclusions present particular challenges for writers. Generally, your introduction should do two things: capture your reader's attention and explain the main point of your essay. In other words, while your introduction should contain your thesis, it needs to do a bit more work than that. You are likely to find that starting that first paragraph is one of the most difficult parts of the paper. It is hard to face that blank page or screen, and as a result, many beginning writers, in desperation to start somewhere, start with overly broad, general statements. For example, the mere sight of an opening line like Throughout history Shakespeare's plays have been considered the greatest ever written will likely create in the experienced reader a feeling of exasperation. Not only will she have seen this type of opening in scores and scores of essays before (perhaps even several times in the pile of essays she's currently working through), the phrase, frankly, *just does not make sense.* Very few things have applied throughout history or throughout time; there was a time when Shakespeare was utterly unheard of because he had not been born! While some instructors do encourage students to start broadly and proceed to a more narrow focus—and this can work well—it is a risky strategy. Potentially, it creates a funnel effect: a wide chunk of writing at the start of an essay that then narrows into the desired focus of the paper. But why not just get right to the point? There is a great rule to remember: If you have a sentence, paragraph, or page of writing that could be erased entirely from the paper without anyone noticing it is missing, that sentence, paragraph, or page probably should not be there in the first place. Academic writing is a very economical genre of writing, and, generally speaking, every line and paragraph should be playing a part in supporting your thesis and developing your arguments—moving forward. So it makes sense to hit the ground running in an introduction, starting with a powerful quotation from your text, precise questions that will moments later allow you to arrive at your thesis statement by answering them, or even the thesis itself. Each of these methods will draw the reader into a paper, enveloping him or her immediately in the issues and problems at hand. Basically, in whatever way you feel is best, get right to the principle text or texts of your essay. See how not a moment is wasted in the following introduction, and after initially establishing the key topic—components of two Shakespeare plays that are not actually "part" of the play we are watching—the introduction quickly poses questions and follows up with an answer that functions as the essay's thesis statement:

> The "induction" scene from *The Taming of the Shrew* and the play-within-the-play in *A Midsummer Night's Dream* are both fascinating departures from the dramas they are part of. However, while the humiliation of Christopher Sly by an aristocratic hunting party brings forth many of the themes that will be central to the play, its relationship to the text as a whole is more questionable than Bottom's play in *Dream*. What effect does the "disappearance" of Sly from the play have on the action in Padua? What are the metaphysical implications of a framing device that does not frame? By comparing the Sly episodes with the play-within-the-play from *Dream*, two distinct "types" of metatheatrical devices become clearly visible. While Bottom's play offers an alternate ending and threatens to darken the outcome of Shakespeare's play, the Sly action fundamentally calls into question the "reality" of the play it introduces.

Conclusions

If many writers struggle with introductions, the act of starting a paper, we frequently also struggle with conclusions, the appropriate "wrapping up" of the work. Both introductions and conclusions should receive special attention from the writer because they mark important moments of engagement with the reader. Just as the introduction is our opportunity to make a good first impression on the reader, to give her an early sense of the paper's quality—and teachers marking large stacks of papers, unfortunately but almost inevitably, have often learned to form early opinions about the essays they read—the conclusion is an opportunity to leave your reader with a pleasant aftertaste. Of course, there are two main reasons writers struggle with conclusions. For one, by the time the writer gets to a conclusion she is exhausted and often desperate to be done. The rest of the paper is complete, but the conclusion has yet to be formulated and is still demanding attention. Second, conclusions are difficult to write. Sometimes students simply give up and come to a sudden stop. It is as if they feel that they have said all they wanted to say, so any additional writing would be a waste of time. This tends to be one hallmark of an extremely weak paper. A safe but rather boring and mechanical solution to the conclusion problem is what could be called the "sports highlights" approach. While a soccer match might have lasted ninety minutes, for example, the highlights on the evening news may be just a few seconds. The segment will show the score and probably the goals. It may also show a near miss or two. A basic, competent conclusion does something similar. It restates the thesis (the score) and recalls the key pieces of evidence that helped you to support that argument (the most memorable action). More creative conclusions might also suggest related problems outside the essay's scope but potentially of interest to your reader (see the last few sentences of the example at the end of this section). The conclusion might also be seen as an opportunity to become lyrical or poetic in the final lines (again, see the example), the verbal equivalent of fireworks at the end. What a good conclusion will not do is any of the three following things: First, it will not begin with the phrase In conclusion . . . . The fact that it is the last one or two paragraphs of your essay should be enough to clue most readers in to the fact that you are now concluding your essay. Second, do not introduce big new ideas in the conclusion—it is too late. If a good idea arrives late in the writing process, revise the paper and put the idea where it fits best in the work (sometimes students will even find that they have an idea good enough to become a new thesis statement altogether. This is fine as an unexpected development, but you must recast and revise the body of the essay so that it appears this argument was what you had in mind all along). Finally, do not feel the need to end with a moral. Students often channel memories of childhood stories by ending an essay along the lines of Thus, we see Kate as the victim of vicious suppression. But how many women, 400 years after *The Taming of the Shrew* was written, continue to suffer psychological and physical abuse at the hands of men no less savage and out of place in the modern world than Petruccio? While the final sentiments of this conclusion are noble, they have shifted the essay away from *Shrew* and into the ethical world of the author's life and social concerns. This "moral swing" has been noted by a number of commentators on student work, and writers should guard against it.

Here is a conclusion that serves its purpose. The thesis for this essay is Although As You Like It appears to be a wholehearted comedy, ending in not one but four marriages, the play is nonetheless busy questioning, even undermining the commonplaces of the comic genre:

As we have seen, then, As You Like It is a play that creates strong tensions between form and content. While it is finally a comedy, it is a comedy in part about the very limits of comedy. It is clear that all four of the final pairings, to varying degrees, are faulty and, despite the nuptial ceremonies, do not necessarily promise "happily ever after." Moreover, the impossibility of Frederick's conversion, along with the exaggerated convenience of Rosalind's resolution of the play's otherwise intractable problems of romance, further add to the sense of Shakespeare writing a play that asks its audience not only to question the structure of the play but its own theatrical expectations and desires. The play, of course, represents just one stage in Shakespeare's examination of comedy, however. How will he develop the genric innovations of As You Like It in the comedies ahead of him? What traces of future plays can we find in this much-loved comedy? What is certainly evident here, however, is that Shakespeare was drawn to the idea of providing what the audience anticipated, while at the same time offering it plays that tested the very boundaries of theatrical form.

Citations and Formatting

Using Primary Sources

As the examples included in this chapter indicate, strong papers on literary texts incorporate quotations from the text in order to support their points. It is not enough for you to assert your interpretation without providing support or evidence from the text. Without well-chosen quotations to support your argument you are, in effect, just saying to the reader, "take my word for it." It's important to use quotations thoughtfully and selectively. Remember that the paper presents *your* argument, so choose quotations that support *your* assertions. Do not let the author's voice overwhelm your own. With that caution in mind, there are some guidelines you should follow to ensure that you use quotations clearly and effectively.

Integrate Quotations

Quotations should always be integrated into your own prose. Do not just drop them into your paper without introduction or comment. Otherwise, it is unlikely that your reader will see their function. You can integrate textual support easily and clearly with short phrases that identify the speaker. For example:

```
According to Antonio, "In nature there's no blemish but
the mind."
```

While here the identification appears before the quotation, you can also use tags after or in the middle of the quoted text, as the following examples demonstrate:

```
"In nature there's no blemish but the mind," suggests
Antonio.
```

You can also use a colon to formally introduce a quotation:

```
It is at this point that Antonio gives us one of the
most concise visions of tolerance found anywhere in
Shakespeare's work: "In nature there's no blemish but
the mind."
```

When you quote brief sections of poems (three lines or fewer), use slash marks to indicate the line breaks in the poem:

```
Antonio's frustration at what he believes to be
Sebastian's betrayal is the catalyst for a powerful
outburst against superficial beauty that masks moral
```

weakness: "But, O, how vile an idol proves this god! / Thou hast, Sebastian, done good feature shame. / In nature there's no blemish but the mind."

It is important to realize that not all of Shakespeare's dialogue is written in verse or poetic lines. Sometimes his characters speak in prose, too. Often the distinction is an important one, loaded with different implications. For example, lower class characters are more likely to speak in prose rather than verse, or the use of prose may suggest a moment of intimacy where a character feels he or she can shed the niceties of poetic speech and just talk. Whatever the reason, prose is easily identified by the fact that each line does *not* begin with a capital letter. When quoting prose lines from Shakespeare's plays, there is no need for the slash marks. So, for example, a few lines after Antonio's moving outburst in *Twelfth Night*, Sir Toby Belch (an aristocrat, but a drunk and waster, too—thus the prose) has the following forgettable line worth citing only as a way of demonstrating how to quote small amounts of prose dialogue:

Sir Toby then quips: "Come hither, Knight. Come hither, Fabian. We'll whisper o'er a couplet or two of most sage saws."

Longer quotations (more than four lines of prose or three lines of poetry) should be set off from the rest of your paper in a block quotation. Double space before you begin the passage, indent it ten spaces from your left-hand margin, and double space the passage itself. Because the indentation signals the inclusion of a quotation, do not use quotation marks around the cited passage. Use a colon to introduce the passage:

Antonio's frustration at what he believes to be Sebastian's betrayal is the catalyst for a powerful outburst against superficial beauty that masks moral weakness:

But, O, how vile an idol proves this god!
Thou hast, Sebastian, done good feature shame.
In nature there's no blemish but the mind.
None can be called deformed but the unkind.

```
Virtue is beauty, but the beauteous evil
Are empty trunks o'er-flourished by the devil.
```

```
For Antonio, it is fidelity and honesty that are the
true markers of beauty, not the "empty" features of a
handsome face.
```

It is also important to interpret quotations after you introduce them. Explain how they help to advance your point. You cannot assume that your reader would interpret the quotations the same way that you do. The line that begins "For Antonio . . ." is an attempt to start this process.

Quote Accurately

Always quote accurately. Anything within quotations marks must be the author's *exact* words. There are, however, some rules to follow if you need to modify the quotation to fit into your prose.

1. Use brackets to indicate any material that might have been added to the author's exact wording. For example, if you need to add any words to the quotation or alter it grammatically to allow it to fit into your prose, indicate your changes in brackets:

   ```
   Viola confesses that "As [he] is a man, [his]
   state is desperate for [his] Master's love."
   ```

2. Conversely, if you choose to omit any words from the quotation, use ellipses (three spaced periods) to indicate missing words or phrases:

   ```
   Orsino announces that "When that is known . . .
   / A solemn combination shall be made / Of our
   dear souls"
   ```

3. If you delete a sentence or more, use the ellipses after a period:

   ```
   It is at this point that Antonio gives us one
   of the most concise visions of tolerance found
   anywhere in Shakespeare's work: "In nature
   ```

```
there's no blemish but the mind. . . . Virtue
is beauty, but the beauteous evil / Are empty
trunks o'er-flourished by the devil."
```

Punctuate Properly

Punctuation of quotations often causes more trouble than it should. Once again, you just need to keep these simple rules in mind.

1. Periods and commas should be placed inside quotation marks, even if they are not part of the original quotation:

   ```
   Shakespeare, in Kevin Webster's pithy phrase,
   was "rooted in his moment, not born of the
   eternal."
   ```

   The only exception to this rule is when the quotation is followed by a parenthetical reference. In this case, the period or comma goes after the citation (more on these later in this chapter):

   ```
   Shakespeare, in Kevin Webster's pithy phrase,
   was "rooted in his moment, not born of the
   eternal" (135).
   ```

2. Other marks of punctuation—colons, semicolons, question marks, and exclamation points—go outside the quotation marks unless they are part of the original quotation:

   ```
   What does Webster mean when he writes that
   Shakespeare was "rooted in his moment, not born
   of the eternal"?
   ```

   ```
   The fastidious Webster asks, "Are you certain
   you have cited me properly?"
   ```

Documenting Primary Sources

Unless you are instructed otherwise, you should provide sufficient information for your reader to locate material you quote. Generally, literature papers follow the rules set forth by the Modern Language Association. These can be found in the *MLA Handbook for Writers of Research Papers* (sixth edition). You should be able to find this book in the reference section of your library. Additionally, its rules for citing both primary and secondary sources are widely available from reputable online sources. One source is the Online Writing Lab [OWL] at Purdue University. OWL's guide to MLA style is available at http://owl.english.purdue.edu/owl/resource/557/01/. The Modern Language Association also includes answers to frequently asked questions about MLA style on this helpful Web page: http://www.mla.org/style_faq. Generally, when you are citing from literary works in papers, you should keep a few guidelines in mind.

Parenthetical Citations

MLA asks for parenthetical references in your text after quotations. When you are working with prose (short stories, novels, or essays) include page numbers in the parentheses:

> Shakespeare, in Kevin Webster's pithy phrase, was "rooted in his moment, not born of the eternal" (135).

When you are quoting poetry, include line numbers:

> Shakespeare's Sonnet 18 has developed the reputation of a classic love poem. Many readers, then, are surprised to learn that the following oft-quoted lines are addressed to a man: "Shall I compare thee to a summer's day? / Thou art more lovely and more temperate" (1-2).

Shakespeare's plays—and early modern drama more generally—also have a specific format for citations. Included in the parenthetical reference, in this order, are the act, scene, and line numbers. The first of the two line numbers indicates where the quote begins, while the second tells the reader the number of the last line you quoted. It should look like this:

> The entire meaning of *The Taming of the Shrew* can be changed by an ironic reading of Kate's last speech. Does she really mean it, for example, when she states

that "Thy husband is thy lord, thy life, thy keeper, / Thy head, thy sovereign . . ." (5.2.150–51).

Works Cited Page

These parenthetical citations are then linked to a separate works cited page at the end of the paper. The works cited page lists works alphabetically by the authors' last names:

Shakespeare, William. *The Taming of the Shrew. The Norton Shakespeare.* Ed. Stephen Greenblatt, et al. New York: Norton, 1997: 133–203.

The *MLA Handbook* includes a full listing of sample entries, as do many of the online explanations of MLA style.

Documenting Secondary Sources

In order to assure that your paper is built entirely upon your own ideas and analysis, instructors often ask that you write interpretative papers without any outside research. If, on the other hand, your paper requires research, you must document any secondary sources you use. You need to document direct quotations, summaries, or paraphrases of others' ideas, and factual information that is not common knowledge. Follow the guidelines above for quoting primary sources when you use direct quotations from secondary sources. Keep in mind that MLA style also includes very specific guidelines for citing electronic sources. OWL's Web site provides a nice summary: http://owl.english.purdue.edu/owl/resource/557/09/.

Parenthetical Citations

As with the documentation of primary sources, described above, MLA guidelines require in-text parenthetical references to your secondary sources. Unlike the research papers you might write for a history class, literary research papers following MLA style do not use footnotes as a means of documenting sources. Instead, after a quotation, you should cite the author's last name and the page number:

According to one recent biography of Shakespeare, "the dramatist borrowed heavily from a variety of sources,

but the originality of each and every play is still
without doubt" (Kazinski 216).

If you include the name of the author in your prose, then you would
include only the page number in your citation. For example:

As Robert Kazinski observes of Shakespeare, "the
dramatist borrowed heavily from a variety of sources,
but the originality of each and every play is still
without doubt" (216).

If you are including more than one work by the same author, the parenthetical citation should include an identifiable word or words from
the title in order to indicate which of the author's works you cite. For
example:

As Mary Rudolph puts it, "the final notes of A *Midsummer*
Night's Dream, with Puck's evocation of dead men and
ominous owls, mar the comic resolution of the play and
encourage us to reconsider the preceding events from
the play in this new, dark light—the dream becomes a
faintly awkward and uncomfortable nightmare" (*Midnight*
134).

Similarly, if you summarize the particular ideas of your source, you
must provide documentation:

It has been observed that Puck's somber speech at the
close of the play is potent enough to challenge the
comic character of the play (Rudolph 134).

Works Cited Page
As with the primary sources discussed above, the parenthetical refer-
ences are keyed to a separate works cited page at the end of the paper.
Here is an example of the text of a works cited page that uses the exam-
ples cited above. You can find a complete list of sample entries in the
MLA Handbook or from a reputable online summary of MLA style.

WORKS CITED

Kazinski, Robert. *Shakespeare from Afar.* New York: NY
    Press, 2006.

Rudolph, Mary. *Another Book about Shakespeare.* London:
    Cockney Press, 1993.

———. *Shakespeare at Midnight.* New York: NY Press, 2005.

Plagiarism

Failure to document carefully and thoroughly can leave you open to charges of stealing the ideas of others, which is known as plagiarism, and this is a very serious matter. Remember that it is important to use quotation marks when you use distinct language used by your source, even if you use just one or two words. With the previously cited quotation from Mary Rudolph in mind, it would be plagiarism if you wrote the following: Because of Puck's dark, ominous speech at the play's close, the comic ending of the play is marred and the dream of the play becomes an uncomfortable nightmare. See how the words and ideas of Rudolph plainly make up the core of this sentence. Instead, you should write in such a way as to acknowledge the source of the thoughts and language in your writing, such as: Critics have observed that Puck's lines about shadowy night creatures might even make the play something other than a comedy. But what does it become? Is there enough in the play, perhaps, to transform it so far as to become "a faintly awkward and uncomfortable nightmare" (Rudolph 134)?

Some cases of plagiarism are the result of students simply not understanding how to quote from secondary sources. This can be avoided simply by assuming a non-negotiable position on the matter: If the words are not yours, put them in quotation marks and tell the reader who wrote them. Paraphrasing the arguments of others is fine, but again you must acknowledge the source, such as: Mary Rudolph has written convincingly about the distorting effect of Puck's speech about lions, corpses, and owls, suggesting that the play at this point is transformed from dream to nightmare.

Closely related to all of this is the question of how to use secondary sources. A lot of accidental plagiarism is the result of students wanting to use outside opinions and ideas but not knowing what to do with them. The two most effective ways of using outside sources—both of which have built-in guards against accidental plagiarism—are either as evidence to support your argument or as a challenge to your ideas that you must defeat. In the first case, you are basically saying, here is someone who thinks the same as I do: Mary Rudolph makes a fine point when she argues that *A Midsummer Night's Dream* finally may be seen as more nightmare than dream (134). In the second, you challenge the author: While Mary Rudolph has suggested that the play is more nightmare than dream (134), this seems like an exaggeration. . . . The first strategy can become a little static if used too often, but the second can add energy and original insights to your paper.

However, many cases of plagiarism are simply the result of dishonesty and laziness. Be aware that plagiarism can haunt a student years after the event, perhaps even preventing him or her from getting into certain schools or programs down the road. While it has become all too easy to plagiarize using the internet, web based methods for catching plagiarists are developing quickly as well. Perhaps the greatest weapon instructors have against plagiarism, however, is a well trained eye; many instructors will have read hundreds if not thousands of student essays and will have become adept at noticing the tell-tale signs of plagiarism. It is certainly possible that you may know people who have plagiarized and gotten away with it, but their luck is sure to run out sooner rather than later.

Finally, while it is not necessary to document well-known facts, often referred to as "common knowledge," any ideas or language that you take from someone else must be properly documented. Common knowledge generally includes the birth and death dates of authors or other well-documented facts of their lives. An often-cited guideline is: if you can find the information in three sources, it is common knowledge. Despite this guideline, it is, admittedly, often difficult to know if the facts you uncover are common knowledge or not. When in doubt, document your source.

Sample Essay

Richard Kline

Eng 210

Professor Gleed

"THIS MISSHAPEN KNAVE":

THE TRAGEDY OF CALIBAN IN SHAKESPEARE'S *THE TEMPEST*

At the close of *The Tempest,* Prospero tells us that, despite his complete victory over his enemies, "Every third thought shall be my grave" (5.1.314). Indeed, Prospero is a profoundly melancholy figure at the close of the play, bereft of his books, magic, and those many long years passed away in banishment. Because we are used to associating Prospero with his creator, Shakespeare, understanding the great speeches of the former to be the latter's farewell to the stage, it is all too easy to understand the play simply as a tragedy of time, of growing old, and of things changing. While this is clearly a powerful current in *The Tempest,* the text's sadness, its tragedy, is wider still. The play roots its tragedy not only in the fact that men must grow old, but in the power struggles and relationships that characterize human society. The key figure here is Caliban, Prospero's island slave and would-be revolutionary. For all its charm and magic, for all the traditional association of Prospero with Shakespeare, the play encourages us to see Caliban as no less of a tragic figure than Prospero. Moreover, as a victim of Prospero's colonial project, Caliban's tragedy becomes intimately twinned with Prospero's, suggesting that a clear understanding of each figure can only be achieved through a reading of their relationship. Caliban, no less than Prospero, is at the heart of the play's wistful tragic qualities.

It would be possible for critics to argue that foregrounding Caliban in this way, however, is simply the product of a twenty-first century sensibility, one accustomed to the undesirable consequences of colonialism in all its forms. However, while it is unquestionably true that this present generation of critics is keenly drawn to the theme of colonialism in *The Tempest* for contemporary reasons, Shakespeare writes into his treatment of Caliban a tragic depth that cannot simply be the product of hindsight on our part. The figure of Caliban could certainly have been a mere brute, a murderous beast that threatened Prospero's plotting. This would have been enough from a narrative point of view. But for Shakespeare's thematic purposes, for his tragic ambitions in this romance, much more was required. We see powerful evidence of this investment, for example, in Caliban's eloquent insights into the nature of his plight.

First, Caliban argues that Prospero's rule over the island and its inhabitants is illegitimate. Instead, he posits an alternative line of descent, one in which he is the natural heir to power. "This island's mine," he tells Prospero, "by Sycorax my mother, / Which thou tak'st from me" (1.2.334). Perhaps more perceptive and persuasive still, Caliban argues that Prospero's influence has been corruptive and that the process of "civilizing" Caliban has finally been destructive rather than beneficial: "You taught me language, and my profit on't / Is I know how to curse" (1.2.364–65). Language becomes a metaphor for civilization, and Caliban's argument suggests not only that he resents Prospero's power but that he has compelling moral and ideological reasons for doing so.

But, of course, Caliban also has more immediately painful reasons to resent the new order. Shakespeare makes it clear that Caliban exists in forced servitude (the word *slave* appears numerously throughout the text), and also that Prospero is a harsh, punitive taskmaster. Naturally, we cannot assume that the language of slavery stimulated the same responses in Renaissance audiences as it does in twenty-first century audiences and readers (in fact, it certainly did not), but the way in which Shakespeare vividly represents both the cruel, animal-like treatment of Caliban and his refined, intellectual resistance to that treatment establishes a social and psychological paradox that makes Caliban a clearly tragic figure.

Indeed, it is even more tragic because the relationship between Caliban and Prospero had not always been this way. The encounter between Prospero and Caliban follows a familiar pattern of infatuation and fascination, followed by conflict and violence; such was the pattern of a great many encounters between European explorers and indigenous peoples. Moreover, despite Prospero's claim that Caliban is "a born devil, on whose nature / Nurture can never stick . . ." (4.1.188–89), there is ample evidence that Caliban had welcomed his new neighbors at first with kindness. As Caliban recalls:

> When thou cam'st first,
> Thou strok'st me and made much of me, woulds't
> give me Water with berries in't, and teach me how
> To name the bigger light, and how the less,
> That burn by day and night; and then I loved thee,
> And showed thee all the qualities o'th' isle. . .
> .(1.2.335–40)

The relationship is a reciprocal one, built on mutual fascination and profit. In exchange for Caliban's local knowledge, Prospero shares his understanding of science and letters. Caliban's "nature" appears to be benign, even affectionate; it can only, therefore, be Prospero's "nurture" that turns Caliban into a drunken monster who tries to rape Miranda. Or, to be more precise, it is the nature of the relationship between them, established within the dynamics of a colonial encounter, that corrupts both of them. Indeed, perhaps the greatest proof of this inextricable bond of tragedy between Prospero and Caliban can be found in Prospero's faint, ambiguous, half-recognition of their shared fate.

We see Prospero's awareness of his profound tie with Caliban develop from a purely emotional instinct, fired by anger and rage, into a firmer but still opaque understanding. Prospero's awareness of Caliban seems to reach a new level when the magician interrupts his own show, staged for the benefit of Ferdinand and Miranda, because he recalls Caliban's plot against him. The anger he shows does not reflect the amount of danger he is in; rather, it signals the emotional depth of his bond with Caliban. This raw, uncertain sense of Caliban reaches it apex with Prospero's famous declaration (but declaration of what, exactly?): "This thing of darkness I / Acknowledge mine" (5.1.277–78). Critics have interpreted this statement various ways. For example, one point of view is that the line is Prospero's recognition of his responsibility for Caliban's crimes. In other words, Prospero has arrived at an understanding of the relationship that mirrors Caliban's assessment back in the first act. This is possible, but Prospero's comment may be less about guilt and responsibility than it is about a broader kinship or interconnectivity. To read the line as Prospero taking responsibility is, nonetheless, still to put Prospero *above* Caliban, still to put Prospero in the position of authority and Caliban in a position of subservience. A better model might be to see in Prospero's acknowledgment not a paternal, grudging claim of responsibility but rather recognition of himself in Caliban. After all, Prospero had sought initially to take revenge on his enemies as Caliban had sought revenge on Prospero. Francis Barker and Peter Hulme argue that Prospero takes from Caliban's failed mutiny a "final and irrevocable confirmation of the natural treachery of savages" (42). However, it is also possible to argue that what Prospero finally sees in Caliban is his frailty, a tragic frailty born of Caliban's humanity. The colonial project of Prospero is the immediate connection between the pair, but behind it is a bond of common weakness reaching into their shared natures.

What can be seen by assessing the relationship between Caliban and Prospero is that Prospero's tragedy is Caliban's tragedy, and Caliban's is Prospero's. Clifford Leech is only half right when he argues that the close of *The Tempest* witnesses "a kind of death for Prospero" (102). We can also read the fifth act as a powerful and emboldening epiphany, one that makes Prospero more aware of his own mortality but also significantly more alive to the life and humanity of others. Through moments of eloquence and insight, both characters attempt to unravel the complex chains that connect them.

What they discover is that the tragedy of power relations, here in the colonial context, rests on the fact that both those on the top and on the bottom are divided and joined by the same forces: the nature of power itself and the frailties and weakness of human beings. Caliban, then, as a component of Prospero himself, is far from a brute or monster but a figure whose tragic flaw is nothing more or less than the colonial system in which he exists.

WORKS CITED

Barker, Francis and Peter Hulme. "Discursive Con-Texts of *The Tempest." New Casebooks: The Tempest.* Ed. R.S. White. New York: St. Martin's Press, 1999: 32–49.

Leech, Clifford. "View Point on *The Tempest." Twentieth Century Interpretations of The Tempest.* Ed. Hallett Smith. Englewood Cliffs, N.J.: Prentice Hall, 1969: 100–02.

Shakespeare, William. *The Tempest. The Norton Shakespeare.* Ed. Stephen Greenblatt et al. New York: W. W. Norton, 1997.

HOW TO WRITE ABOUT SHAKESPEARE: AN OVERVIEW

FOR MANY students, the greatest obstacle to writing about Shakespeare is the process of reading Shakespeare. The root of the problem for many, not surprisingly, is Shakespeare's language, which is unfamiliar at times and can seem difficult to read. Like everything else, practice, patience, and a little effort will help. In the meantime, there are some things you can do that will make Shakespeare much more accessible to you. First, do not overestimate or make too much of the role Shakespeare's language should play in your encounter with his work. For many dedicated readers of Shakespeare, it is precisely the language, its poetic power and verbal creativity, that separates his work from the ordinary. Yet a fuller understanding or appreciation of the Shakespearean idiom is not something that needs to come immediately. Rather, at the core of the plays are themes, questions and ideas that pulse with the energy of humanity, and these are open and accessible to all. Do not let the language get in the way or become an obstacle to an appreciation of Shakespeare as a storyteller, as a representer and presenter of lives. Here are some considerations to bear in mind:

1. **Before you read, know the plot:** Shakespeare's language causes most problems for the student who does not already know the play's plot. If a reader does not know what is going on in the narrative, he or she will feel lost and confused trying to piece

it all together. Conversely, if the student has a sense of the plot, of roughly what will be happening at each point in the play, it is easy to push through unfamiliar language and still understand, in broader terms, what you have read. Plot summaries of the plays are widely available on the Web and in print. Ask your instructor, too, if he or she would not mind giving an overview of the whole plot for you before you read.

2. **Watch a movie:** As most people will not have the opportunity to see a Shakespeare play performed onstage at the same time they begin reading it in class, a film adaptation can be an excellent alternative option. There is an important caution to be offered here, though. All film versions of Shakespeare's plays change the text in some way. Whether it is a faithful adaptation that merely chops off a few minor scenes or offers interesting and original interpretations of a character or scene, or a film that radically overhauls its Shakespearean source, a movie should never be used as a substitute for the play. Good film versions of a play, however, allow students to see a version of the play performed, to hear the language spoken, and to witness the passion and drama of the text made real. A subsequent reading of the play is made easier and smoother by watching the movie (again, be careful to keep play and film separate in your thinking, as there will be differences. Also, do not accept the film's interpretation of the play as your own or as the only one available).

Shakespeare on film is actually a large and active area of study for contemporary scholars. There are many versions of the major plays (*Hamlet, Othello,* and *Macbeth,* for example), and these vary in quality and purpose. Watch as many as you can find of your chosen play before reading it. Often, unless the movie is newly released or has attained classic status, Shakespeare films can be difficult to track down. An Internet DVD rental membership offering access to a huge catalog of titles is probably the best way to find many of the films. Often you can find inexpensive used copies on Internet auction sites too. Alternately, for productions that stick closely to the original text, during the early 1980s, the British Broadcasting Corporation (BBC) set about filming the bulk of Shakespeare's canon, shooting most of the text scene for scene and adding little in the way of radical interpretation. Arguably the creative team involved aimed to interpret the plays as closely to the Renaissance mentality as possible. While the films offer little in terms of gloss or production values, they give an accurate account of the text, thereby making excellent tools for reading support.

3. **Use glosses but not obsessively:** Good editions of Shakespeare's plays come with glosses printed on the page. They are used when the editor of the play believes a word will be particularly unfamiliar to modern audiences, so a "translation" is provided either in the margins of the text or at the bottom of the page. Of course, glosses are helpful inclusions, and even advanced or experienced Shakespearean readers use them frequently. However, do not check every word; do not look at every gloss. Checking the glosses too frequently drastically slows your reading pace and may prove to be unnecessary. If you read a speech and its overall sense is initially elusive, check the glossed words, phrases, and lines to see if they offer any help or insight. If you have an overall sense of the speech, it might be better to keep reading and become absorbed in the rhythm and flow of the text.

4. **Talk to teachers and participate in discussions:** Perhaps the greatest resource you have at hand will be your instructor. If you have questions about any aspect of the play, ask. Become involved, too, in class discussions about the plays—just as Shakespeare's language is clearest when spoken, so are his themes most accessible when debated. Classroom discussion is often the best place to elicit and define a special and important aspect of Shakespeare's drama: its contemporary relevance. While some instructors might not encourage it in a paper, a fascinating discussion could be started, for example, by asking what life might be like for Othello and Desdemona today. What

has changed over the centuries for interracial couples? Starting or playing a part in these conversations can make Shakespeare seem alive. If no such opportunities arise in class, chat about it elsewhere with other students in the class. It is fascinating to reflect on how much we are alike and different from the lives of those who came long before us.

Certainly, Shakespeare—like all artists—is of his moment, writing for his contemporaries about his own world. But equally, as we have seen, Shakespeare's contemporaries were not as far removed from us, from our troubles and fears, our hopes and joys, as the archaic language and footnote-laden lines of a Shakespeare volume suggest. Readers of the future will most likely need glosses to explain the references and allusions that populate contemporary literature. Cultures are based on a "language" of their own, a system of shared knowledge, assumptions, and beliefs that distinguish them from others. There are also the more superficial codes such as manners and fashion that serve as an expression and embodiment of those cultural codes and precepts. Yet, just as a trip to a foreign country can offer uncertainties and a great many more thrills, so, too, does a journey to Shakespeare's England. It is a remarkable journey, rewarding us with many unfamiliar sights and sounds.

Topics and Strategies

Knowledge of important historical movements and backdrops will provide the writer with a valuable reservoir to draw from in virtually any essay on Shakespeare's drama. The chapters on individual plays point out specific historical contexts and suggest how research into those contexts could provide the backbone of an excellent essay. While specific knowledge of different events or trends will help, depending on the play, essays generally become more authoritative and impressive when they demonstrate sensitivity to the broad strokes of Shakespeare's world. Shakespeare's writings reflected the reality and concerns, historically and socially, of his era. Familiarity with these contextual currents can serve to strengthen and broaden the scope of your essay:

1. **The Elizabethan and Jacobean stage:** Some understanding
of the theatrical world of Shakespeare's time, its conventions
and how it was perceived, will assuredly help the writer as she
assesses texts written to be performed there. However, though
the stage was unquestionably important to English Renaissance
culture, it meant different things to different people. Critics today, like Shakespeare's contemporaries, hold a variety of
opinions about how exactly the theater worked, who controlled
it, and what effect it had on the wider society. For example,
modern critics are divided on the important issue of whether
the Renaissance stage served to support state authority or challenge it. In other words, was the theater a radical or a conservative institution? (The answer probably varies from play to play,
author to author, of course). Certainly it was heavily policed and
censored by the authorities and frequently defended by the government (which suggests the latter of the above scenarios), but
a great many things still found their way onto the stage that
implicitly called into question the role and function of the English state. As she works, the writer can also usefully consider the
question of political and social ideology, especially if the Shakespeare play in question is an overtly political one (and many of
the tragedies and all of the histories are explicitly political).

The central opponents of the stage, however, tended not
to be government officials but religious radicals who saw the
theater as a devilish hotbed of sin and deception. These critics
objected to such things as the practice of boy actors playing
women's roles, suggesting that such conventions toyed with
moral and physical convention. Shakespeare, however, seems
to have found this aspect of Elizabethan stagecraft great fun.
In many of his plays, writers can find and make use of Shakespeare's playful exploration of a boy playing a woman (with
the "woman" then further disguising "herself" as a man in a
number of cases).

The locations of the playhouses did little to discourage the
notion of theater as a seedy business. After all, the stages were
largely located south of the River Thames, away from the city

and nestled among brothels, taverns, and the many other pastimes of London's least fortunate. Many of the stages doubled as arenas for bloodthirsty entertainments such as cockfighting or bearbaiting (a "sport" in which a chained bear fought off the attacks of savage dogs for the pleasure of a paying audience). It should come as no surprise, then, that actors, writers, and others associated with the world of the theater were by no means the highly esteemed thespians of our time but had the reputation of vagabonds and "masterless" men who were loosely protected and supported by royal or aristocratic patronage. They were seen largely as wasters and borderline criminals by the society in which they lived.

What might the reader and essay writer take from this? Broadly, it should be clear that the Elizabethan and Jacobean stage was a contested area, one whose politics and influence were as uncertain to contemporaries as they are to modern scholars. These plays were often much more than entertainment and, consciously or not, exerted a powerful force on English political and social life. The task of the writer, then, is to judge the direction of any given play's "social energy," whether it be in matters of sexuality or statehood, and begin to unravel the complex and potentially explosive mix of intention and consequence.

2. **The New World and the ancient world:** Only a small number of Shakespeare's plays explicitly treat the discovery of the Americas or life beyond the borders of Europe, but it is impossible to overestimate the effect of the New World on Renaissance consciousness. As a reader, be aware that exploration of the New World forced Europeans to reflect on their own identities as well as the identities of the indigenous peoples they were newly encountering. Certainly, the tragic tale of European expansion into the Americas is well known, and most students will be familiar with the enormous suffering that resulted from the colonialist agenda. Less familiar, perhaps, are the philosophical debates that circulated in Europe, thousands of miles away from the front lines of colonialism and exploitation. At the loftiest level, the "discovery" of the New World forced thought-

ful people to ask exactly what it was that separated European civilization from the perceived wildness and disorder of indigenous life. Most entered into this debate, however, from the starting point of European superiority, unwilling to consider that there might be something to learn about human existence from these hitherto unknown populations and cultures. Invariably the encounter merely confirmed and cemented the righteousness of a European, Christian model of life. A few sympathetic souls, however, most notably the French essayist Michel de Montaigne, rejected the preconception of European superiority. Montaigne argued that the savagery of Europeans in the New World meant that the colonizers had little right to consider themselves more civilized than the native peoples they butchered, enslaved, and abused.

On a more pragmatic level, much of the intellectual energy invested in the New World took the form of economic calculation. Shakespeare's England, along with Spain, led the way in trying to establish profitable and powerful outposts in the New World. Certainly, as a result of the New World encounter, the economies of the Old World expanded and an age of consumerism and mercantilism was rapidly accelerated. So the energy of the New World infuses many aspects of life in Shakespeare's world, and the drama of the colonial encounter becomes an engine for powerful forces of social transformation.

For the student composing an essay on one of Shakespeare's tragedies, it is important to keep in mind the broad and far-reaching nature of change during the Renaissance, an important part of which was stimulated by the colonialist encounters with foreign and previously unknown peoples. It might also be helpful to touch on some recent changes in the way scholars talk and think about the Renaissance. Historians, in fact, now tend to prefer the term *early modern* to describe the century or so before and after Shakespeare's death. In part, this change of terminology comes out of a gathering consensus that the term *Renaissance*, or rather the image of wholesale rebirth and reinvention it conjures up, is misleading. These historians caution that not everyone experienced a renaissance and that the medieval world did not disappear instantly in a brilliant burst of collective genius. The truth is much more complex and muddled. Certainly there was an enormous outpouring of artistic, scientific, and intellectual innovation, and elites across Europe (especially in Italy) sought to reconnect with the great achievements and spirit of the ancient world. It is also true, however, that this creativity had significant geographic and class-based limitations. For many people, life continued as it had for centuries, as agrarian peoples remained rooted to the earth, the cyclical seasons, and the mysteries of the supernatural. The term early modern captures this duality nicely, especially with the addition of the qualifying adjective. The concept of the Renaissance encourages us to see the period in which Shakespeare lived as the birth of our contemporary world, a time that ushered in the world we now inhabit. Early modern is more judicious, however, pointing out that while it was in many ways the period that generated so many of the systems and ideas we continue to use, it was merely a stage of development rather than an explosion of civilization and culture.

This duality is important to remember as you write on any aspect of the period, particularly the plays of Shakespeare, which so beautifully crystallize this coexistence of change and continuity. Shakespeare himself, a country-born man who found success in the exploding metropolis of London, might even serve as a metaphor for his age. As you read and write, think about this twofold nature and look for ways in which Shakespeare—who clearly knew the court and the latest ideas well—represents the forces of change but also remembers his simpler, country origins in reflecting on the "old ways." Like his world, though, all Shakespeare's plays retain traces of continuing, long-established ways of life alongside glimpses of and insight into new ways of thinking and behaving. The writer would do well to look for the harmonies and tensions between these two modes of life as she examines the themes, characters, and ideas contained in each play.

3. **Queen Elizabeth I and King James I:** Arguably, no dynasty of English monarchs left a greater mark on Great Britain than

the Tudors. Beginning with the crowning of Henry VII in 1485 and ending with the death of Elizabeth I in 1603, the Tudor monarchs reigned over a period of epochal change for the English nation. Shakespeare lived during the final, tense years of Tudor England and continued his career into the reign of the first Stuart king, James I. Elizabeth and James, then, must be understood as key figures at the center of Shakespeare's world. However, while Shakespeare certainly sought to earn the approval of his monarch through writing, he also used his stage to participate in conversations about the nature of monarchical power and the latest affairs at court. The writer must first and foremost remember that the theater was not merely an art form that responded to events from a distance but a part of the Tudor and Stuart political system.

It is not really clear that we have an equivalent today. Perhaps film and television come closest, but the parallel is not a particularly strong one. These mediums (especially film) can be political, and they can mount powerful critiques of government and policies, though this is rare given the enormous budgets involved and the need for broad audience support. The key difference, perhaps, is the closeness of early modern theater to the seat of power. If the film industry today was based in Washington, D.C., and those involved in the production of movies were themselves watchful hangers-on around powerful people, and the government meddled directly and openly with the content of film, then the parallel might be an apt one. As it is, though, early modern theater differs markedly from anything in our time. The theater was policed by the government, but the theater, in delicate and subtle ways, in turn policed the government by offering a lively forum for veiled but serious political debate often leavened with the use of jokes or humor. The most powerful Elizabethans and Jacobeans may have watched theatrical performances, but the theater as an institution also watched them and frequently, though always discretely, mindful of the terrible consequences of speaking too plainly or boldly, made those same individuals the subject of its drama. Most powerful of all, the monarch was a magnetic subject for many playwrights, not least of all Shakespeare.

Shakespeare and Elizabeth I are bound together in our historical imagination, twin symbols of the mythological greatness of their age. In his film *Shakespeare in Love,* Tom Stoppard depicts the sovereign as a powerful devotee of the playwright, even playing a hand in orchestrating his love life. This is a fantasy, no doubt, but the stage linked the two figures tightly, and Elizabeth would have enjoyed Shakespeare's plays at private performances and Shakespeare's livelihood was boosted by the continuance of that pleasure. In the final years of Elizabeth's reign, there is evidence that Shakespeare's plays were significant components of an increasingly vexed conversation about the aging, fading queen.

Elizabeth had come to power in less than ideal circumstances. While she was daughter of Henry VIII, a still-much-loved king a decade after his death, her mother was Henry's disgraced and executed second wife, Anne Boleyn. Moreover, Elizabeth inherited a weakened state, one destabilized by two brief and unsuccessful reigns. The boy king, Edward VI, Henry's sickly son, had ruled between 1547 and 1553, during which time his handlers enacted a vigorously Protestant agenda. After his death, Henry's first daughter, Mary, began her short and destructive time in power. She married a Spaniard, King Philip, and in the process annoyed a great many Englishmen; Mary's subjects balked at the prospect of their country's great enemy inheriting the reigns of power. More harmful still, Mary aggressively reversed the Protestant policies of Edward and set about a bloody and murderous defense of Roman Catholicism against heretics. She executed large numbers of Protestant reformers, many of whom quickly became martyrs to the cause of the English Reformation. We can only imagine what effect this theological back and forth had on the populace of England, but Elizabeth learned a great deal from it.

One of her great triumphs as monarch was to nimbly walk the tightrope of religious difference in England, never adopting the extremes of her predecessors. Elizabeth was a Protestant queen, but her reign is characterized by a mood of relative religious tolerance, even while some around her pushed hard for a more hawkish model of reform. Still, for all her effective ambiguity in religious matters, the Roman Catholic Church saw her as an enemy, and the pope made vocal protests to encourage Catholic assassins against England's Protestant queen. Such attempts were, of course, never successful, though they became increasingly frequent in the final years of her reign.

Those final years were generally unstable and fraught with danger and intrigue. Her decision to never marry had been contested vigorously by England's political elites, but Elizabeth never wavered on this vital matter. During her childbearing years, there was no shortage of suitors, foreign and domestic, suitable and undesirable. She encouraged some, but accepted none; her rhetoric was as powerful as it was consistent: She saw herself as married to the people and viewed England as her spouse. Speculations never ceased, of course, and it appears that Elizabeth, never a wife, was several times a woman in love. Approaching the end of her reign, however, these strategies that once strengthened Elizabeth's position were working against her. A general unease appears to have infused English life at the close of the sixteenth century: Who would rule when Elizabeth dies?

The answer to that question—as a result of furtive negotiations carried on behind Elizabeth's back—was Scotland's king James VI, who became James I of England upon the queen's death. James does not cut as recognizable a figure as Elizabeth for us today, but for Shakespeare's fellow citizens, James, as a male monarch with an existing heir, was a welcome presence. The long-nagging problems of succession had been resolved without great pain, and James's monarchy, though not necessarily as remarkable as Elizabeth's, was marked by relative stability. James was an intellectual who wrote on numerous subjects but was particularly interested in political philosophy and theories of monarchy. His reign, however, was stained by a number of sexual and moral scandals, all of which, historians tend to agree, circumscribed the effectiveness of his rule. If the Tudors appear now to have been the most successful of English dynasties, the Stuarts, James's heirs, arguably suffered the greatest ill luck and misery in English royal history. Nonetheless, James was the last king Shakespeare knew.

Whether it is in passing allusions to Elizabeth (such as we find in *A Midsummer Night's Dream*), engagements with James' intellectual interests (the use of witchcraft in *Macbeth*, for example), or displaced and buried consideration of contemporary royal politics (as many have found in *Julius Caesar*), Shakespeare's plays are infused more with the presence of the monarchs of his lifetime, about which he could not openly write, than with those of former English rulers. The essay writer can find in the narratives of Richard II or Henry IV, for example, a great deal of conversation about Elizabeth I. Late in life, she identified herself with the embattled and deposed Richard II of Shakespeare's stage, yet another example of the degree to which the plays are alive with an energy drawn from the political, cultural, and social life of the author's time. No matter to what extent the student wishes to penetrate the historical and political context of the day, it is useful to be aware of Shakespeare's role as a chronicler of his time. Our task as writers is not so much to reconstruct Shakespeare's world through our essays but to respect and conduct into our own work the energy with which he wrote and observed the life around him.

4. **Shakespeare and anonymity:** After considerable discussion of Shakespeare's world and times, what about the man himself? What about his possible beliefs, opinions, dreams, fears, and personality traits? Such information could help the writer greatly; however, surprisingly, given Shakespeare's near monolithic status in our culture, we actually know little about the man behind the plays. This fact is made even more difficult to believe by the countless biographies of Shakespeare that have been published through the years, but it has undoubtedly added to the awe and power of Shakespeare's work, existing as it seems to, independent of a human author. As we have seen, Shakespeare's dialogic method, staging in his plays philosophical conversations that are not satisfactorily resolved by a single answer, means that Shakespeare as author fundamentally "disappears" into his plays, and there is little in our knowledge of the man to help us recover him intact. The bare facts, mostly

collected from mundane legal documents, take us more or less only this far: Shakespeare was born into a middle-class family in the country town of Stratford-upon-Avon. As a young man he married a somewhat older woman who, as a crosschecking of parish records reveals, was already pregnant. Shakespeare left behind his family in Stratford to seek—successfully—his fortune in London, first as an actor, then writer, then shareholder in a theatrical company. We do not know how often he returned to his wife and children while he was in London, nor very much of how he lived when in the city. By the time he retired, Shakespeare was wealthy enough to purchase one of the finest houses in his hometown of Stratford, where, coming full circle, he spent the final years of his life. As you can see, there is little in this silhouette of a man's life to illuminate the great works of literature he produced. It is ironic, poetically so, that we know his work so intimately but essentially know no more of his life than we could discover of any one of his countless, forgotten contemporaries. This speaks to the transience of human life and the longevity of art; it reminds us, too, that literature has a life of its own, independent of the author's intentions. Essay writers, therefore, may actually fare better in the playwright's absence, for there is no ultimate truth or real answer to uncover, rather endless possibilities.

It is thus left to each reader and writer to invent his or her own Shakespeare. As you do so, of course, you invent (and then reinvent) yourself as a Shakespeare scholar. The following chapters will offer a variety of approaches to the plays, some of which are traditional, some quite modern. For example, Shakespeare scholarship over the last few decades has been largely dominated by the desire to historicize the plays, to explore them in the historical context in which they were written. In many of the chapters, viable historical approaches to a given play are presented, to encourage writers to explore the interaction between Shakespeare's work and the material world that surrounded him. During the middle of the twentieth century, however, criticism tended to be more formalist in nature, examining the texts as self-contained worlds. Students, more or less free from the vagaries and fashions of the academy, can benefit from this view of the literary text as a world unto itself and can explore the psyches, motivations, and, personalities of Shakespeare's carefully crafted characters. Writers can engage in the seemingly academic matters of form and genre or make use of their 21st-century sensibilities and address about issues such as postcolonialism or homosexuality in Shakespeare's works. So much has been said and written about the plays already, but rest assured you will see, think or say something that is fresh and original as you encounter Shakespeare. The challenge before you is then to help you put those ideas where they belong: on paper for someone to read, consider, and enjoy.

Bibliography for "How to Write about Shakespeare: An Overview"

Bloom, Harold. *Shakespeare and the Invention of the Human.* New York: Penguin, 1999.

Fernie, Ewan, ed. *Reconceiving the Renaissance: A Critical Reader.* New York: Oxford University Press, 2005.

Greenblatt, Stephen. *Will in the World: How Shakespeare Became Shakespeare.* New York: W.W. Norton, 2004.

Guy, John. *The Tudors: A Very Short Introduction.* New York: Oxford University Press, 2000.

Hadfield, Andrew. *The English Renaissance: 1500–1620.* New York: Blackwell, 2001.

Hale, John. *The Civilization of Europe in the Renaissance.* New York: Simon and Schuster, 1993.

McDonald, Russ. *Shakespeare: An Anthology of Criticism and Theory, 1945–2000.* New York: Blackwell, 2004.

Morrill, John. *Stuart Britain: A Very Short Introduction.* New York: Oxford University Press, 2000.

Shapiro, James. *A Year in the Life of William Shakespeare: 1599.* New York: HarperCollins, 2006.

HOW TO WRITE ABOUT SHAKESPEARE'S COMEDIES

PICTURE THE scene: A woman is discovered in the woods by an obsessive stalker. He pleads his pathetic romantic case to her, and when she predictably turns him down, he prepares to rape her. Suddenly, the woman's partner emerges and triumphantly stops the terrible attack. However, he knows the rapist well. They have been best friends for many years, though they have been estranged of late because of tensions over this woman. The would-be rapist apologizes, and the hero is reminded of the intense friendship the pair once shared. He tells the rapist that he can go ahead and have his way with the woman. Fortunately, the attacker has come to his senses and does not take him up on the offer.

Now picture this scene: A woman does not want to get married, much to her wealthy father's chagrin. A down-on-his-luck adventurer arrives in town and eyes the woman as a lucrative prize. The father encourages the man to take his daughter off his hands. The woman wants no part of this, of course, but she is backed into a corner and unwillingly marries the man. He takes her away from her family and home to his own secluded estate where he tortures her until she is so beaten down she is willing to proclaim her husband to be "master" and will not resist his will on anything.

Or consider this scene: A Jewish man is routinely victimized on the streets of his town. He is, however, as wealthy as he is hated, so a Christian man asks him if he can borrow a considerable amount of money. The moneylender senses the possibility of revenge—the Christian is one of many who have abused him for so long—and sets a remarkably high prize on the forfeiture of the loan. If the Christian should fail to pay up, the Jew will slice out a pound of flesh from the man's chest and kill him. It turns out that the Christian cannot pay, and the moneylender prepares to publicly execute the man. As he prepares to slice out his pound of flesh, the Jew is stopped by a sharp young lawyer who has found a loophole in the contract between the two men. It turns out the Jew does not have the right to kill the man after all. Rather than let the defeated moneylender leave empty handed, however, the young lawyer and the Christian court quickly conspire to take revenge on him. They strip him of his money and, more painfully still, they command that he must convert from his Jewish faith to Christianity. The moneylender leaves silently, a broken, destroyed man.

These chilling, even repulsive tales make up the plots of three Shakespearean comedies: *The Two Gentlemen of Verona*, *The Taming of the Shrew*, and *The Merchant of Venice*, respectively. As can be gleaned from the incompatible nature of comedy with these seemingly tragic scenes of abuse and violence, one lesson for the beginning student of Shakespeare's comedies is that these plays can be problematic, frequently difficult to accommodate in our modern age, and often disappointing to anyone who wishes Shakespeare to be the liberal, universal genius he is often seen as. Far from simple or simplistic, these plays are deeply philosophical, sometimes offensive, and always look to do more than make the reader or spectator laugh or feel entertained.

The sense of Shakespearean comedy that circulates in popular culture is that the works are sparkly and light, frolicsome and merry. It is hard to see any of these elements, however, in the previously cited plot summaries, of course. As you progress through Shakespeare's comedies in this volume and in your own reading of the plays, you will find that Shakespeare has absolutely no interest in simple comedy, in merely "happy" or humorous events. Even his most purely comic play, *The Merry Wives of Windsor*, the only comedy that reaches for an unambiguously happy ending, turns out to be a politically charged assessment of contemporary marriage and class mobility (and contains what is intended to be the severe beating of an old woman for the audience's entertainment!).

Despite the many other issues and questions these plays engage, then, they are always studies of the comic form. Before you progress into any consideration of themes, characters, ideas, or any of the various elements that interconnect among the various plays, you should pause and reflect briefly on the meaning of *comedy*. We use the term today primarily to mean "funny." Shakespeare also often intends for there to be laughter in his comedies, too, but when the word *comedy* is used in literary circles, it often refers to the form or "shape" of the play. A tragedy has a distinct shape as does a comedy. These structures and patterns are part of how we assign a piece of art to a particular genre. A tragedy, for example, will see its characters face obstacles and difficulties, but in some meaning-ful, profound way the central characters will fail to triumph over these adversities. The presence of death, too, marks out a tragedy—often in a Shakespearean tragedy, the final curtain comes down on a stage full of corpses. The philosophical implications of tragedy can be stark and unsettling. A tragedy frequently suggests a chaotic or malign universe as a foundation for the play's action. Macbeth's vision of life as meaningless, "a tale / Told by an idiot, full of sound and fury, / Signifying nothing" (*Macbeth*, 5.5.25–27), is a particularly grim and unsettling articulation of what we might term the tragic spirit.

By contrast, the comic form sees it characters overcome obstacles and come together at the end of the play for some kind of communal feast or celebration, often a wedding. In its purest form, this feast will even include the play's blocking or impeding figures, the character or charac-ters who have caused trouble and created obstacles to the course of action throughout. This is evidenced in *The Merry Wives of Windsor:* When the outrageous Falstaff is punished for his attempts to seduce two married women, he learns from his mistakes and is welcomed to a feast for the wedding of one of the wives' daughters. The implication of the comic movement is a benign and optimistic one, a universe in which people get what they deserve and fortune intervenes, often in the most improbable ways, to make sure that the outcomes are happy. Shakespeare seems to have found the comedy in its purest form unappealing, something that suggested a basic framework or canvas for his work but also something that needed to be experimented with, questioned and interrogated in order to produce the kind of complex statements and moods he sought.

One of the most illustrative moments in Shakespeare's comedies takes place in the final 200 lines of *Love's Labour's Lost*. During the play, we have seen a king and his lords wooing a visiting princess and her ladies. After the expected mishaps and misunderstandings, the men and women come together for a final "showdown" that we anticipate will lead to a convenient pairing off of the lovers to be. However, a messenger arrives to tell the Princess that her father has died. She announces that she and her ladies will return home for a long period of mourning. Moreover, they set the somewhat fickle men a series of tasks to complete in their absence. The love of the women will be dependent on the successful completion of these tasks, but as the King and his lords have demonstrated themselves to be hardly the most diligent of men, we have every reason to suppose the lovers will never come together at any point in the future. This is arguably the oddest, most unexpected moment in all of Shakespeare. It is illustrative, however, because it is a template for frustrated comedy, something that Shakespeare will modify, moderate, and play with in the years that follow but never set aside. He remains fascinated by the shadows that can be seen on the brightest of days, by the failures and hardships experienced by some as others celebrate their greatest victories and triumphs nearby.

Tone, then, the mixture of light and dark crafted by Shakespeare in each play, is likely to always be a powerful influence on the essay writer. Even if you are not specifically addressing form in your essay, the issue of tone and mood infuses many of the topics you may be writing on. Two additional consistently appearing factors should also be foremost in the mind of the essay writer. The first is Shakespeare's predilection for debate, for giving space to different sides of an argument or issue in his plays while only rarely allowing a particular side to prevail or win the day. The second, and this is particularly true of the comedies, is Shakespeare's profound interests in ideas of mutability, of shifting change and instability. An awareness of these three key concepts—1. Shakespeare's mingling of light and dark to create mixed modes, 2. the presence of the debate format, though rarely allowing a single voice to dominate, and 3) a heavy investment in the changing and shifting nature of the world and the men and women who populate it—is vital to someone wishing to write insightful and penetrating essays on Shakespeare's comedies. All of these three concepts will, in a multitude of forms and ways, underpin, explicitly or implicitly, much of your own writings on Shakespeare's comedies.

Finally, this chapter identifies patterns and trends that run through the comedies as a whole. Plays are grouped together that overlap in each respective category (plays that talk about love, or plays that meditate on the shifting nature of human identity, for example), but do not go into significant detail here. If you see ideas or combinations of plays that interest you, you should go to the chapter for the individual plays where you will find additional information and more in-depth guidance.

Themes

The comedies are deeply invested in the politics of love, sexuality, and the domestic sphere. It is often said that Shakespeare depicts a "battle of the sexes," fought on a variety of fronts, with such different outcomes arising from the various rivalries that it is impossible to declare a winner of the overall "war." It is no surprise, either, that in the age of feminism and gender studies, these components of the plays have garnered vast amounts of attention from critics, directors, readers, and audiences alike. The majority of the themes discussed in this section will draw on this key "battle of the sexes" motif and look at ways in which the plays can be viewed as individual contributions to ongoing debates within Shakespeare's canon.

Sample Topics:

1. **Love:** Is Shakespeare a cynic or an optimist when it comes to love?

   Comedies that will be particularly helpful in answering this question include: *The Two Gentlemen of Verona, A Midsummer Night's Dream, Love's Labour's Lost, Much Ado about Nothing, As You Like It,* and *Twelfth Night.* Obviously, how you approach this kind of essay will depend on the texts you are working with, but be aware of two clear trends in Shakespeare's thinking on love. First, the earlier plays seem to suggest that love is an unstable and unreliable emotion, quickly given and quickly taken away again. Look for examples of this kind of fickle lover, especially in the earlier comedies. These figures in general are often the target of a strong vein of cynicism from Shakespeare, but can you find characters or ideas that seem more upbeat about the prospects of love? Perhaps plays such as *Much Ado about Nothing,* with arguably Shakespeare's happiest and best-matched couple in Beatrice and Benedick, or *As You Like It,* the stage for Shakespeare's masterful creation Rosalind and her endlessly wise meditations on the true nature of love may encourage you to reach for some kind of reformulation of "optimism" around pragmatism and realism in matters of the heart. Certainly, you will find in Shakespeare's comedies contempt for the kind of love that revels in its own anxieties and hardships to the point of becoming merely the performance of love. Look for the ways in which these romantic comedies, stage productions though they may be, reject artifice and showmanship in the name of love.

2. **Marriage:** What model of marriage appears to be Shakespeare's ideal?

Particularly helpful comedies for this topic include *The Comedy of Errors, The Taming of the Shrew, The Merry Wives of Windsor,* and *The Merchant of Venice.* Shakespeare's England was engaged in a heated and ongoing debate about the institution of marriage. They wondered whether marriage was best based on love or more material concerns such as wealth and political alliances. The Elizabethans contested whether the husband should be more inclined to see his wife as a partner rather than as a subordinate. They reflected on whether a marriage could or should be terminated, and under what circumstances such a move might be justifiable. They debated even the degree of physical violence a husband could reasonably be permitted to use in the name of domestic order. Many of these issues are directly picked up and handled by Shakespeare as he explores the nature of marriage while establishing the marriage bed as a key front in the "battle of the sexes." The combative term is appropriate, too, because many of the marriages that figure into Shakespeare's comedies are rarely peaceable. In *A Midsummer Night's Dream,* we learn that Theseus wooed his bride-to-be Hippolyta after taking the Amazon warrior as a prisoner of war. He promises that he will marry her, but the ferocious struggle between the play's only married couple, Titania and Oberon, suggests that such promises are unlikely to be kept. When you encounter marriages in the plays, be ready to assess the tensions and characterize the outcomes. Notice, too, that power struggles are rarely one sided in these marriages, so look for different, sometimes subtle, kinds of battle tactics. For example, although Kate apparently has little power in *The Taming of the Shrew*, it could be argued that her apparent (and potentially insincere) capitulation to the brutal Petruccio is the most strategically sound and effective retaliation or effort at resistance she could deliver. Assess where the balance of power lies and what forms resistance to it takes.

3. **Gender:** Is Shakespeare something of a feminist or a misogynist?

Plays that could be used for this kind of essay include *The Two Gentlemen of Verona, The Taming of the Shrew, The Comedy of Errors, Love's Labour's Lost, A Midsummer Night's Dream,* and *The Merry Wives of Windsor.* This question is, of course, potentially misleading. The first thing to remember is that Shakespeare lived centuries ago in a world with an entirely different mentality. The term *feminist* is unquestionably an anachronism, then, a twentieth-century ideology that does not fit the early modern context. Nonetheless, though a writer must attempt to show historical sensitivity as much as possible, she cannot help but bring to an essay the terms and mindset of her own time. So a question about Shakespeare and feminism, especially if couched in the more timeless language of respect and equality for women, for example, can be excellent fuel for an essay.

This question obviously invites a discussion of the marriage politics previously discussed, but it is an inclusive theme that draws in, to some degree, each of the comedies. However, it is the earlier comedies that seem most heavily invested in tensions between the sexes, often depicting scenes of cruelty to or the mistreatment of women. On the other hand, there are plays in which the women possess or manifest the power and emerge ambiguously or unambiguously victorious in their battles with men. It is the reoccurring acts of cruelty, however—the betrayal of Silvia at the close of *The Two Gentlemen of Verona;* the humiliation of Titania at the hands of her husband, Oberon; or the breakdown of Helena and Hermia's friendship in *A Midsummer Night's Dream*—that make us ask why these scenes are echoed throughout the plays with such frequency. Be aware that one play alone is unlikely to present answers that can be applied beyond that text, but if you begin to work within an awareness of two or three plays, then you can be more confident in making overarching, comparative claims. Does Shakespeare keep showing these scenes because such treatment of women unnerves or saddens him, because he feels for the women, or do you feel that such a claim implies too much questioning of and resistance to social norms on the dramatist's part?

4. **The green world:** Do Shakespeare's various "green worlds" all function in the same way?

Plays of particular importance here include *The Taming of the Shrew, A Midsummer Night's Dream, As You Like It,* and *Twelfth Night.* Shakespeare's comedies follow a reliable spatial pattern. Typically, they begin in a court setting, in a troubled world of some kind, and then proceed into a space critics refer to as the "green world," in which the rules of court no longer apply and regular order is somehow suspended. An example of this would be the escape to the forest of Ardenne in *As You Like It.* The space is magical, pastoral, an "anything goes" place where women can pretend to be men, lovers can be taught that a showy display of courtly love is a poor substitute for a more mundane but genuine affection, and a true villain can be reformed the second he sets foot in the forest. Other green worlds are less obvious, but nonetheless function as "wild," almost lawless spaces. Petruccio's country house in *The Taming of the Shrew* is a good example of this. As to the more quintessential green world spaces you will find in *A Midsummer Night's Dream, As You Like It,* and, later in Shakespeare's career, *The Winter's Tale* and *The Tempest,* there is a set of questions that could be posed. First, despite the differences between the court world and the green world, what parallels can be identified? For example, Prospero's island, it turns out, contains just as much political intrigue and talk of usurpation as Milan did. Likewise, look for ways in which the green world is, despite pastoral delights or the promise of magical resolutions, consciously darkened by the dramatist. Jaques' insistent mourning for the hunted deer in *As You Like It* or the nightmare of a snake slithering toward a lover's heart in *A Midsummer Night's Dream* provide haunting examples of this.

Characters

Although some of the earlier comedies are populated by sketches (relatively one-dimensional renderings that represent a certain problem or idea) rather than fully developed characters, the mature comedies give us some of Shakespeare's greatest and most memorable characters. Shylock, for example, has attracted vast amounts of critical interest over the generations, as have Rosalind, Beatrice and Benedick, and Viola. They are all complex creations, developing over the course of their respective plays and making decisions that are grounded in more than the needs of the play.

If you are writing essays on characters from a play such as *The Two Gentlemen of Verona* or *The Comedy of Errors*, however, recognize that to a large extent, your character analysis is likely to be a modified version of thematic analysis. For example, the Antipholi are not really characters but rather bodies placed in a situation by the dramatist and voices used to articulate the confusion that lurks at the heart of Shakespeare's philosophy of identity. If working with more concrete characters, the resulting essays can be nicely structured by a narrative of evolution. For example, Shylock starts the play as a brutal and hardhearted moneylender, and though he still possesses these qualities at the close of the play, his character has acquired an additional layer, one of sympathy as he recalls the harsh treatment he has received, makes the case for his equal humanity in a memorable speech, and gives us a glimpse into a lost married life. Finally, we come to see him in the context of the equally harsh and abusive Christians.

Sample Topics:

1. **The heroine:** What kind of female characters does Shakespeare craft in the comedies?

The works that provide especially good material here include *Two Gentlemen of Verona, The Taming of the Shrew, The Merry Wives of Windsor, Much Ado about Nothing, The Merchant of Venice, As You Like It,* and *Twelfth Night.* It is interesting to note that the majority of the most attractive characters in the comedies are women. In a surprising number of plays, the women in some way also acquire authority over the men of the play. In other works, though, they may not have much power, they are active and do not sit idly by. Sometimes the heroines are idealized, as seems to be the case with Beatrice (from *Much Ado about Nothing*) and Rosalind (from *As You Like It*), two witty, wise, and endearing women that more than hold their own. At other times, the female protagonists may be more problematic. Kate in *The Taming of the Shrew,* for example, appears to break down at the end of her play and abandon her struggle with Petruccio. Equally, however, it can be claimed that she holds her own in the most difficult of situations and does what is necessary to preserve what quality of life she can obtain. Viola, in *Twelfth Night,* seems to be consciously passive, willing to let the drama unfold around her rather than drive it toward her desired resolution, as Rosalind clearly does in *As You Like It.* Portia from *The Merchant of Venice* is a puzzle but seems to have aged badly and is little loved today, though traditionally she was seen as one of Shakespeare's finest female creations. For each and every one of these characters, her sex and gender, her status as a woman, is fundamentally important to her as an individual and to how she acts and what she accomplishes in her respective play. For this reason, many of the issues discussed in the preceding section on gender will have considerable resonance for writers attempting character analysis of Shakespeare's comic heroines.

2. **The blocking or impeding characters:** How does Shakespeare handle anticomic characters in comedies?

Useful plays here include *Much Ado about Nothing, The Merchant of Venice,* and *Twelfth Night.* Blocking characters are those that stand in the way of the comic resolution, actively working against or becoming obstacles to the comic thrust of the play. Traditionally, for example, a father might play this role in a romantic comedy, disapproving of a son or daughter's desired match and doing all he can to block it. We see such a traditional use of the blocking character in *A Midsummer Night's Dream*. Of course, Shakespeare extends his use of impeding or blocking characters beyond this commonplace and uses them to often great complexity in his comedies. Sometimes a writer can find surprising levels of sympathy for a figure that should, strictly speaking within the comic framework, receive little. Shylock is an obvious example of this, though look also at how Malvolio emerges as a sympathetic figure, too, in *Twelfth Night*. Shakespeare does not always extend to his blocking figures this kind of generosity, however, and sometimes they do not warrant it. Perhaps one of the most intriguing and out-of-place characters in Shakespeare's comedies is Don John in *Much Ado about Nothing*. This character is inexplicably nasty for a comedy, a figure often talked about as a prototype of Shakespeare's most terrifying vision of evil, Iago in *Othello*. Don John wants to be (and thinks he is) in a tragedy, but it turns out that he is in one of Shakespeare's more perfect comedies. What impact does his mismatched or miscast presence have on the play?

3. **The inconstant or superficial male lover:** In what ways do the men of Shakespeare's comedies so often come up lacking in comparison to their female counterparts?

Plays that provide good material here include *The Two Gentlemen of Verona, A Midsummer Night's Dream, As You Like It,* and *Twelfth Night*. One of Shakespeare's preoccupations in the comedies seems to be inconstancy, the capacity of human beings to change their hearts and minds, often suddenly and dramatically. In his comedies, Shakespeare often subverts traditional stereotypes of the time, which associated fickleness with women, and routinely makes his male characters the canvas on which he illustrates mutability and the ephemeral nature of identity and emotion. Men, it seems here, can fall in and out of love with unnerving ease, and, as might be expected, if male love is understood as so transient, its expressions of love are typically viewed as inauthentic or immature. How does Shakespeare depict such inconstant male lovers? How do their lovers respond? In what ways are these men "corrected" by their partners and by the action of the play?

Philosophy and Ideas

People tend to think of Shakespeare's comedies as intellectually inferior to his tragedies. This observation, however, can be seen as inaccurate or overstated. Though the philosophical power of *Hamlet,* for example, unquestionably trumps that of *The Merry Wives of Windsor,* it is often a case of how implicit the philosophical discourses of a play turn out to be. *King Lear* wears its angst and anguish at the surface, to make us shudder. *The Comedy of Errors,* on the other hand, looks at first glance to be a somewhat silly version of an ancient farce, frenzied and zany. Yet the play is, nonetheless, obsessively philosophical. It offers a lighter experience for those who wish it but rewards those who seek out something more substantial with its often uncomfortable meditations on and conclusions about human identity. Like all great artists, Shakespeare is a philosopher. As a potential essay writer, you should assume that in his comedies Shakespeare is exploring complex, nuanced, and rich ideas, even if the surface looks too light to contain such seeming depths of insight. Moreover, you can also be confident that Shakespeare is likely thinking in a certain way, that he is engaged in a project of destabilization, allowing what appears as concrete and natural to be viewed instead as unstable and constructed.

Sample Topics:

1. **Identity:** What are the implications of Shakespeare's repeated meditations on identity?

   Helpful plays here include *The Two Gentlemen of Verona, The Comedy of Errors, The Taming of the Shrew, A Midsummer Night's Dream, As You Like It,* and *Twelfth Night.* As you can see from the number of plays listed here, Shakespeare consistently uses his comedies as a vehicle for the philosophical exploration of identity. The man who encounters a twin, the woman who is forced to become a tame wife, the lovers in the forest whose affections are disoriented by magic, and the strange and uncontrollable desires that develop around the crossdressed body all become focal points for questions about who we are and how reliable our sense of self, our sense of a knowable and unchanging I, might be. These questions can, of course, be approached at the level of the individual play, but to explore them within the context of two or more plays facilitates essays that begin to grasp the scope of the comedies' philosophical ambitions.

2. **Crossdressing:** In Shakespeare's comedies, what possibilities and what "dangers" emerge from the crossdressed body? Can the energies released by these bodies be contained by a return to orthodoxy at the play's close?

Key plays for this topic include *The Two Gentlemen of Verona, The Merchant of Venice, As You Like It,* and *Twelfth Night.* The philosophical implications of crossdressing in these plays are compounded by early modern English stage practices. Women were not allowed to appear onstage, and so the convention of boys playing female parts forced writers, actors, and audiences (as well as moral critics of the stage) to face the implications of putting a boy in women's clothing. Shakespeare seems to have embraced the comic and philosophical potential of this and amplified it by having his boy actors don women's clothing only to then disguise themselves as men. At what point is a person's gender, or even a person's whole identity, lost in this shuffle? What effects does this multigendered body have on other characters? Consider the most complex example of such a presence, Viola of *Twelfth Night.* She attracts the desire of a man and a woman while in disguise, but does Orsino desire the woman underneath the man's disguise or the masculine disguise itself? Does Olivia feel attraction to the man Viola is pretending to be or to the woman she supposedly really is?

History and Context

Throughout this volume, particular historical concerns are examined in relation to a given play. For example, it may be useful to approach an essay on Shylock in *The Merchant of Venice* with an understanding of the anti-Semitic context of Shakespeare's Europe. An essay on *The Merry Wives of Windsor* can only be strengthened by research into the marriage debate taking place in early modern England or the simultaneous shifts occurring in the class system. In short, heavily historical essays will be tremendously effective for students with an appetite for such research, and these essays can be driven by intensive attempts to understand Shakespeare's world and explore the forces that shaped his imagination. Shakespeare did not write in isolation, after all, and even though popular opinion envisions him as a "timeless" genius, like all human beings he was of his time and place, a product clearly shaped by contemporary events and ideas. Essays that attempt to understand and explain this relationship between Shakespeare's plays and Shakespeare's world will be in good company; such approaches have dominated Shakespeare studies for the last several decades. Even if the central focus of your essay is not historical, some knowledge of vital contexts will be obviously beneficial to you and allow you to write more nimbly and creatively.

Sample Topics:

1. **Homosocial/homosexual relationships:** What is the nature of the apparently amorous relationships between male characters in some of Shakespeare's comedies?

   Useful texts here include *The Two Gentlemen of Verona, The Merchant of Venice,* and *Twelfth Night.* This approach is an example of a topic that simply cannot be legitimately approached without an understanding of the historical context. Sometimes students are quick to embrace or dismiss the idea of a homosexual Antonio in *The Merchant of Venice,* for example, a man in love with a younger man and saddened by the object of his desire's plan to court and win a wife. Michael Radford's film version of the play places a wistful Antonio (Jeremy Irons) on a bed for a conversation with the seductive and scheming Bassanio (Joseph Fiennes), perhaps too clumsily making the suggestion of homosexual desire on the older man's part and an awareness and exploitation of this desire on the younger man's. Though this account of the relationship is by no means unlikely, it largely ignores the historically specific notion of what has been termed by critics as Renaissance homosocial love. Such relationships, intense and profound friendships between men, were prized in the early modern period precisely because, theoretically, they did not involve sexual or romantic relations. These friendships, these platonic loves, were seen as cleaner, purer, and more spiritual than a relationship could be with a woman, the latter coupling inevitably "polluted" by sex.

This intense relationship, for which we really have no conceptual standard equivalent in our time, allows us to find new layers in plays such as *The Two Gentlemen of Verona*, in which the concept perhaps helps explain—though by no means justify—Valentine's despicable treatment of Silvia in favor of his friend Proteus.

2. **Festivity:** How does the festive world of early modern England shape Shakespeare's comedies?

You may wish to look at the following plays as you consider this topic: *A Midsummer Night's Dream* and *Twelfth Night*. Although only two of the plays included in this volume explicitly treat the world of early modern festivity, many of the works include moments of festive ritual, particularly wedding celebrations. Nonetheless, the relationship between the kind of festive rituals that took place in England throughout the calendar year (festivals to celebrate the bounty of summer or mark the end of Christmas revels, for example) and Shakespeare's broader comic output and the idea of comic drama in general is close and undeniable. Theater historians have suggested that theatrical performance grew up in the ancient world around festivals of ritual observance, comedies emerging from the more joyful celebrations and tragedies from more somber rites. Shakespeare takes this historical connection as far as it can go by transforming the spirit of a particular festive moment into the action of a play. We see this, for example, in *A Midsummer Night's Dream* with the riotous rites of May, a celebration characterized by puritan critics of the day as full of wild revelry and sexual liberty, synthesized in the plot of four young lovers fleeing into the woods and haplessly stumbling on a twisting maze of desire and love.

Look for and research these connections where they obviously exist (in the two previously cited plays and, much later in Shakespeare's career, in *The Winter's Tale*), but also be aware of moments of festive ritual in each play. A wedding, for example, typically serves as the ritual conclusion of a comedy; marriage is the goal romantic comedies seek in the early modern period. However, if you look at the wedding scene of Claudio and Hero in *Much Ado about Nothing,* the performance by the rude mechanicals at the aristocratic wedding in *A Midsummer Night's Dream,* or the reported nuptials of Kate and Petruccio in *The Taming of the Shrew,* you can begin to make some significant, historically rooted points about how the festive world of Shakespeare interacts with his comic experimentations on form.

Form and Genre

The plot summaries that began this chapter reveal the extent to which Shakespeare's comedies question and resist the expectations of the comic form. Essays treating the failure of comic resolution can be written about all of Shakespeare's comedies (with the likely exception of *The Merry Wives of Windsor,* which could, on the other hand, be used in an essay on Shakespeare and "pure" comedy). Such papers present strong opportunities because they typically contain a built-in outline for you to follow: Establish the problems introduced in the body of the play and then, through a careful reading of the final scene, assess to what degree the problems have been "solved."

Sample Topic:

1. **Comic form and the success of Shakespeare's comic resolutions:** Can we say that one of the defining characteristics of Shakespeare's comedies is nothing less than the failure of the comic from?

Each of Shakespeare's comedies suffers from some variety of loose ends, a lack of conclusiveness, insufficient answers, excluded characters, or veiled or explicit threats hanging over the comic resolution. This lack of a final, unifying clarity is an element in each of the comedies. Sometimes you will have to work a little harder to suggest that a comic resolution is ambiguous (such as a darker reading of the action of *A Midsummer Night's Dream*), while at other times, such as in *The Merchant of Venice* or *Love's Labour's Lost,* the task is easier though nonetheless important to a better understanding of the play and Shakespeare's comic art in general.

Compare and Contrast

Compare and contrast essays can be seen as "internal" models of the essay, based on and arising from relationships within a single text (comparing or contrasting two characters in a single play, for example, or the high and low plotlines from the same play). Alternatively, the comparisons or contrasts noted can be "external" options based on comparing one play to another or even to a contemporary stage or film production of a play. Such essays can be a strong approach for all writers but especially useful for less confident writers as the tensions and interactions in two or more texts can generate a momentum and sense of direction that may be harder to establish in essays on a single text.

Sample Topics:

1. **Comparing one comedy to another:** How can we use pairs or larger combinations of plays to create conversations and dialogues within Shakespeare's comic canon?

   This chapter has suggested usable groupings and interactions throughout, not just in this particular section. However, some plays form natural pairings that at times will appear inevitable: *As You Like It* and *Twelfth Night,* for example. Such plays can even be termed *companion plays,* as they are so closely related that it seems as if Shakespeare intended for them to be considered alongside each other. At the very least, the plays were somehow aesthetically or structurally aligned in his imagination and may have even germinated from the seed of a single idea. In approaching an essay of this type, look for movement and development, even if the plays do not seem to form an obvious thematic pair. For example, while *As You Like It* and *Twelfth Night* both address the problems of the desires present in a woman disguised as a man, the implications of this seem more playfully handled in the former text and more anxiously so in the latter.

2. **Comparing a comedy and a tragedy:** How integrated are these two genres of Shakespeare's drama?

Remarkable and unexpected combinations can be generated by comparing comedies to tragedies. The consistencies and commonalities witnessed by such essays are striking. The seed of Shakespeare's great villain Iago, for example, potentially first sprouts in the playful comedy *Much Ado about Nothing*. Thematic connections can be adventurously made between seemingly distant plays such as *Macbeth* and *The Taming of the Shrew*, both texts devoted to containing excessive female power and agency. Even the idea of "companion plays," those works that seem to be essentially thematic pairs, can be found intersecting the comedies and tragedies. For example, *A Midsummer Night's Dream* and *Romeo and Juliet* were composed at the same time and, essentially, take the same situation in different directions, one toward tragedy and one toward comedy. As if to reinforce this connection to himself and his audience, Shakespeare even inserts a version of *Romeo and Juliet* (the Pyramus and Thisbe play performed by Bottom and his troupe) into the height of *A Midsummer Night's Dream*'s apparent comic fulfillment. This pairing, and others like it, show us that to imagine a great distance between comedy and tragedy is to escape into fantasy and denial. If Shakespeare's comic art is to speak rightly of human life, then light and dark, wish fulfillment and the frustration of human desire, as Shakespeare reveals to us in his comedies, must share the same stage.

Bibliography for "How to Write about Shakespeare's Comedies"

Barber, C. L. *Shakespeare's Festive Comedy: A Study of Dramatic Form and its Relation to Social Custom.* Princeton, N.J.: Princeton University Press, 1959.

Bloom, Harold, ed. *Shakespeare: Comedies and Romances.* New York: Chelsea House, 1986.

Gay, Penny. *The Cambridge Introduction to Shakespeare's Comedies.* New York: Cambridge University Press, 2008.

Hopkins, Lisa. *The Shakespearean Marriage: Merry Wives and Heavy Husbands.* New York: Palgrave MacMillan, 1998.

Salingar, Leo. *Shakespeare and the Traditions of Comedy.* New York: Cambridge University Press, 1974.

Smith, Emma, ed. *Shakespeare's Comedies.* New York: Blackwell, 2004.

AS YOU LIKE IT

READING TO WRITE

O F ALL the plays covered in this volume, *As You Like It* may say the most about how Shakespeare views comic themes and the comic form itself. In many ways the play, with its pastoral setting and extended contemplation of love, seems traditional, but it does not take much of a leap to see the play as experimental or satirical. The final act of the play can be seen as a parody, a spoof of Renaissance comedy (even a third brother, for example, one we have not met nor particularly want to meet, triumphantly returns to join Orlando and Oliver). In light of this interpretation, the play is a masterpiece of self-awareness, of winking playfully at the audience. As can be expected from any engagement with Shakespeare's drama, however, little is ever clear and certain. Rather than being purely inventive, the play could also be seen as an over-the-top and lovingly affectionate embrace of the comic mood, a jubilant celebration the spirit of comedy.

There is, of course, so much more to the play than just form. *As You Like It* is rich with topics for discussion, complex ideas, and ample room for interpretation. It is one of Shakespeare's most profound engagements with the great human themes of love and time. A representative passage from the play demonstrates how Shakespeare nimbly weaves pleasure and meaning. This is the celebrated response of Rosalind, disguised as Ganymede, to Orlando's claim that he will die if Rosalind does not return his love for her.

The poor world is almost six thousand years old, and in all this time there was not any man died in his own person, videlicet, in a love-cause.

Troilus had his brains dashed out with a Grecian club, yet he did what he could to die before, and he is one of the patterns of love. Leander, he would have lived many a fair year though Hero had turned nun if it had not been for a hot midsummer night, for, good youth, he went but forth to wash him in the Hellespont and, being taken with the cramp, was drowned; and the foolish chroniclers of that age found it was hero of Sestos. But these are all lies. Men have died from time to time, and worms have eaten them, but not for love. (4.1.81–92).

First, you might notice that this quotation looks different from most of the other passages cited in this volume. It continues across the page and does not start each new line with a capital letter. These hallmarks indicate that Shakespeare is writing in prose, not in verse as he often does. This difference matters, and you should note when poetry is used and when prose is used. What is the effect of Ganymede/Rosalind's prose speech here? One function of the passage could be to naturalize Rosalind, to make seem her more real and less theatrical. This significant formal detail opens up at least two possible avenues for the writer.

First, how could Rosalind's rejection of poetic speech be connected with a larger theme? Look always for links between content and form, what is said and how it is said. If Rosalind spoke these lines in poetry, she might be laying herself open to charges of literary hypocrisy. Her whole purpose here, after all, as it is elsewhere in the work, is to dismantle hyperbolic, distorted, and idealized notions of love. Orlando, despite his dramatic protestations, will not die of unrequited love. She attempts to make Orlando aware of a more realistic and true form of love, one more organic than ornate. This attempt is mirrored in the distinction between poetry and prose speech, revealing how a careful reading of Shakespeare's form can illuminate thematic concerns.

Merely the form of this passage, then, might serve the writer as a springboard from which to begin an essay on love. It might also prompt consideration of Rosalind as a character. If the effect of employing prose over poetry here is to connect Rosalind more immediately to an audience, to strip away one important element of theatrical artifice, how does this knowledge help us to better understand her character? From this perspective, we might be encouraged to see in this passage some contradictions. For a start, while the passage argues in both form and content for honest estimations of love, it is spoken by someone in disguise and having some slightly less than honest fun. Moreover, the simpler, more natural prose style—often reserved by Shakespeare for his clowns and peasants—is in direct contrast to the classical allusions that betray Rosalind's uncommon and deep intelligence. Rosalind is a remarkably complex character, and writers should seek this complexity out, looking for the paradoxes and dualities surrounding her. These qualities are made manifest in the mixture of harmony and discord existing between content and form in this passage.

TOPICS AND STRATEGIES

Every essay requires a focus; you cannot write about everything in the play at once. The starting point is nearly always finding an initial focus, making first observations that can then be transformed into a suitable thesis. This discussion of *As You Like It* is geared toward helping you make the most of the budding ideas you will have as you read the play. By no means should you feel limited to these topics, however.

Themes

In the previously cited passage, Rosalind is disguised as a young man, Ganymede. Over the last several decades in particular, this detail has developed into a major thematic concern. Writing on the role of gender in *As You Like It*, critics have discovered many implications beneath the multiple layers of Rosalind's disguise. Certainly, gender will play a role in a number of the essay topics presented in this chapter, so (as with, for example, race in *Othello*) the important thing for the writer is to refine a broad, central theme into a specific statement or argument. Assess how the basic speech and action of the play are changed, subjected to new and "hidden" meanings by Rosalind's male disguise.

Shakespeare enlivens several of his plays with the dramatic, comic, and philosophical potential of crossdressing; always follow carefully the dizzying sleight-of-hand he employs to get his audience thinking about issues of gender. Ask what it means, for example, that Orlando is wooing Rosalind dressed as Ganymede pretending to be Rosalind. Examine the consequences of such distortions not only for Rosalind's representation of gender and sexuality but also for those around her. We recognize that

Phoebe's attraction to Ganymede raises questions about the orientation of her desire (Ganymede is, of course, a woman), but the questions that grow around Orlando are no less pressing (Ganymede *is* a woman, but Orlando does not know this, and he "pretends" to woo the young man with undeniable passion and fervor).

Sample Topics:

1. **Love:** What different models of love are offered in *As You Like It*? How might the play's favored idea of love be described?

This being an example of "new comedy," the most popular comic style of the 1590s, the expectation is that we will watch lovers overcome obstacles in order to marry at the close of the play. However, as a variety of commentators have variously suggested, in *As You Like It*, the chief obstacle to the lovers is not the interference of a spiteful parent or harsh law but the need to clarify what love is before the play can be concluded. There are a number of competing definitions, and a good start to your prewriting process might be to attach to each character a particular model of love. For example, Silvius displays a decidedly pathetic form of love, committing himself to the service of Phoebe even in the act of wooing another man (or what Phoebe thinks is another man) on her behalf. This is an example of a kind of courtly love made commonplace in the Renaissance by sonnet writers, writing in the style of the Italian poet Petrarch. The speaker in these sonnets, just like the lovesick Silvius, often stressed the pain of unrequited love and the highly exaggerated beauty of the beloved—as well as her cruelty. Look at Orlando and consider if his model of Petrarchan love differs from Silvius's. Most importantly, look for moments when these stylized expressions of love are challenged. Examine Phoebe's actions in act 3, scene 5 (3.5) but especially scrutinize Rosalind's rebuffs of Orlando's idealism in 3.5 and 4.1. Think, too, about the problems of attraction. What does the play have to say about love at first sight, for example? Think about Celia's dismissal of it early in the play, but then consider her hasty pairing off with Oliver. Also consider, as discussed in the chapter introduction, the implications of crossdressing for physical attraction, as both Phoebe and Orlando woo the disguised Rosalind.

2. **The forest:** In what ways is the forest of Arden different from the court setting at the beginning of the play? What is life like for the exiled characters in the forest, and what threatens the sense of idealism that at first seems to surround the forest?

Many of Shakespeare's comedies are structurally organized by the contrast between a court setting and a pastoral or idyllic setting, often labeled by critics as the "green world." Along with *A Midsummer Night's Dream, As You Like It* features Shakespeare's most concentrated examination of the power and possibility of the green world space. The play begins with scenes from the court, revealing a number of political and personal troubles that drive the protagonists into the forest of Arden. Look carefully at these opening scenes, identifying the central problems of the court. You may also find that these problems share a common nature, finding a relationship between Oliver's mistreatment of Orlando and Duke Frederick's usurpation of Duke Senior's authority. Think, too, about the political undertones of Frederick's decision to banish Rosalind, but also of the nature of the relationship between Rosalind and Celia that helps to explain why the banishment of the former also necessitates the flight of the latter.

Traditionally, the green world space is a setting from which the rules of the court are absent, and a kind of freedom operates to allow characters a broad liberty to learn and develop. Try to assess the "conditions" of the forest. Look at the banished Duke's idealism in 2.1, but also note the darker tones immediately following in the talk of hunting. You might even want to follow the recurring use of hunting. What effect does it have on our sense of idealism? How does Jaques equate the hunting of deer to the problems of the court? Think, too, about the curious episode of the lioness and the snake, identifying what effect the presence of these creatures has on our perception of Arden. Finally, follow the debates over the merit of court versus country life between Touchstone and the rustic inhabitants of the forest. In your opinion, who has the upper hand in these discussions?

Characters

Rosalind may be the play's central presence, but there is much to say and write about her companions in the forest. While many critics have suggested that Orlando is an amiable but inadequate partner for Rosalind, he is by no means without substance. Think about the gendering of Orlando, for example. Assess the strange juxtaposition of masculine and feminine attributes, such as his wrestling prowess alongside his tender, maternallike care for Adam. Think, too, about Orlando's ideas of love and why these must be overturned by Rosalind. Duke Senior, along with his woodland courtiers, might make a good choice for a character study for those interested in exploring the theme of the green world. Charles the wrestler tells us that the Duke is like Robin Hood of old, but you may be able to come up with a more complex (and accurate) portrait of this man and his followers. With most of the characters in *As You Like It*, however, a good point to keep in mind is that of transformation. The forest changes many of the characters significantly—the immediate transformation of Frederick as he enters the fringes of Arden makes for the most striking example—and that process or concept can usefully underpin a number of character studies.

Sample Topics:

1. **Rosalind:** In what ways can Rosalind be considered Shakespeare's surrogate in *As You Like It*?

It is perhaps proof of Rosalind's vitality and centrality to the play that some critics have talked about her as Shakespeare's representative in *As You Like It*. Exploring this idea gives the writer a good point of focus through which to approach Rosalind's extremely layered character. As your task is to show how Rosalind is not only central to the dramatic action of the play—how she essentially controls and drives the action—you might well begin by broadly assessing her character in the early scenes. Think about her relationship with Celia, along with her head-over-heels attraction to Orlando. She is a figure of intense emotional capacity, characterized most, perhaps, by her ability to love.

In exploring this topic, consider also the apparent contradictions between her intensity of love—be that love for Celia or Orlando—and the challenges she offers to Orlando's expressions of love. Such an essay might even assess any subtle distinctions that exist between Rosalind and Rosalind as Ganymede. After all, Rosalind speaks of realistic and reasonable expectation of love when dressed as Ganymede. Undisguised, however, Rosalind can be more than a little giddy in love herself.

With all this as background, how does Rosalind become the voice and spirit of the play (if you agree she does)? How does she become the narrative engine of the plot? You might find this role most prominently staged in the final act of the play. By this point you may also be ready to question how successful Rosalind has been as the playwright's stand-in, even perhaps asking the difficult question of whether Shakespeare in the end pokes gentle fun at his heroine's capabilities.

2. **Jaques:** What is the function of Jaques? What is his philosophy, and how does that challenge or complement other ideas in *As You Like It?*

Jaques is an example of the malcontent figure, a person on the fringes of the community who uses his removal and alienated status to comment on the behavior within his society. An essay focusing on his role in the play might try to examine Jaques's observations on life in the forest, employing them to formulate a sense of his philosophy. Pay close attention to the way he introduces melancholy or darker tones to the activities of Senior and his followers, noting how the courtiers have imported the problems of the court to the pastoral setting. Again, think especially of his sympathies for the deer killed during hunts. Look at the conversations he has with other characters, which seem to generally take the form of challenges and disagreements. Can you spot a pattern or governing logic to his arguments? What sentiments does he challenge? Notice, too, the role of time in many of his musings. Finally, search out moments when he talks about himself, such as his explanation to Rosalind of his particular breed of humorous melancholy.

History and Context

As You Like It is a play with no clear historical or geographic setting. There are traces of England in his supposedly French scene, and a nostalgic but timeless world of trees and animals resists any fixed temporal location. None of this means that historical interpretations of the play are impossible; the marks of Shakespeare's time and world are etched onto his plays like Orlando's poems on the trunks of Arden's trees. Louis Montrose, for example, has written powerfully about the role of primogeniture in *As You Like It*. This dominant legal and social convention insisted on the passing of inheritance to the firstborn son, a tradition abused by Oliver. Montrose argues that anxieties about potential faults in this system would have made Orlando's plight particularly relevant to many in Shakespeare's audience.

Yet another important cultural issue from Shakespeare's day is uncovered by Rosalind's disguise.

Sample Topic:

1. **Crossdressing in Shakespeare's England:** How does Shakespeare handle this subject, controversial in his day? How does the English theatrical convention of boy actors playing women's roles form an important dimension of this play?

Like in other places and moments throughout history, Elizabethan England was the site of "culture wars." They took the shape, broadly, of contention between puritanical forces bemoaning the collapse of order and progressives who sought to push social boundaries. Clothing was an important focal point for this contest. In early modern Europe clothing acted as a symbol of order, demarking rich from poor, servant from master, and male from female. Sumptuary laws were implemented to ensure that people could not dress above their station, to prevent the blurring of clear social categories. As consumerism developed in the economic markets of Europe, clothing became more available and diverse. As a result, it was increasingly difficult to enforce strict codes of dress. Conservative commentators, aside from the troubling class implications of finer clothes being worn by those aspiring to a more affluent life, were distressed by the effeminacy seen in some of the more popular styles of dress for men. Perhaps an even greater source of concern was the phenomena of women dressing in more masculine attire. In his *Anatomy of Abuses,* Philip Stubbes (a kind of Elizabethan equivalent to today's talk radio hosts) ranted against such acts of crossdressing, labeling women who wore traditionally male clothes or styles as monstrous aberrations of nature.

Stubbes was also a prominent opponent of the theater, and the issues of clothing and playgoing were closely linked for him. It was, he argued, onstage that audiences saw the potentially corrupting sight of males dressed as females, a spectacle that might ignite strange and unusual sexual impulses. For such critics, the tradition of boy actors playing women's roles contributed significantly to the moral depravity they saw in stage plays. For a fuller account of these and more related issues, see Ann Rosalind Jones and Peter Stallybrass's book, *Renaissance Clothing and the Materials of Memory.*

These debates certainly fascinated Shakespeare and are obviously present in *As You Like It.* Think about how Shakespeare plays with the concept of gender, a set of clearly fixed, identifiable and natural categories to people like Stubbes. Suddenly, gender becomes a construction, a fluid marker that to a certain extent can be blurred and distorted. Look for scenes highlighting this notion; for example, the moments when Rosalind as Ganymede is courted by Phoebe and Orlando toy with gender boundaries and stimulate, as Stephen Greenblatt has argued, sexual friction generated through misunderstanding.

Think, too, about the effect of using boy actors to play female parts. How does this intensify the sexual and gendered complexity of the Rosalind/Ganymede figure?

Philosophy and Ideas

Through crossdressing, then, *As You Like It* enters into the philosophical debate of essentialism versus constructivism. When Rosalind/Ganymede offers to cure Orlando by posing as Rosalind, the resulting construction is a boy playing a woman playing a man playing a woman. This multiplicity of identities surely serves as a challenge to the idea that we have one fixed, concrete identity beyond our control. This kind of thinking is not new to a twenty-first-century philosophy prone to questioning absolutes and the possibility of single all-encompassing truths and shows how the history of ideas is not necessarily a story of progress but also one of reinvention. In the Elizabethan era, Shakespeare was by no means alone in working with this theme. Essay writers seeking other treatments of the topic might even consult John Middleton and Thomas Dekker's early seventeenth-century play, *The Roaring Girl*. An essay might examine how that work develops the delicate philosophical playfulness of *As You Like It* into a radical social and moral commentary.

Shakespeare explores the idea of identity in *As You Like It* alongside contemplation of another entity typically perceived as natural and beyond our control.

Sample Topic:

1. **Time:** What does Shakespeare say about time in *As You Like It*? Is Rosalind anything more than just literally correct when she says there are no clocks in the forest? Where are the clocks in this play, and what power do they have over the characters?

The most memorable speech in *As you Like It*—and one of the most recognizable in all of Shakespeare's writing—is Jaques's moving, melancholically beautiful depiction of the Seven Ages of Man. Time is, of course, a philosophical theme that has consistently preoccupied and fascinated people. Yet in Shakespeare's day, time was not merely a phenomenon to meditate on; it was a cultural, social, and economic construct being revised and designed anew. In short, the early modern period witnessed the steady transformation of time from a natural, cyclical sense of existence to the precise, quantifiable, and demanding sense of time most of us perceive it to be today. The title of Ricardo Quinones's book, *The Renaissance Discovery of Time*, states the transformation plainly enough.

So Rosalind's observation that there are no clocks in the forest may be rooted in a collective desire to return to a time less aware of the quick evaporation of our hours, days, and lives. Look for evidence of the play's obsession with time. Be careful to note that there are different models of time on offer. For example, how would you describe Jaques's understanding of time, including his account of Touchstone's anxious fretting about rotting (see, in particular, the entirety of 2.7)? Ask, too, whether time is truly absent from the forest. Again, reflect on the hunt motif as a source of contrast to the Duke's idyllic dream of Arden (after all, to introduce death into the forest is certainly to introduce the most dramatic reminder of time's power over us). Finally, consider the characters of Corin and especially Adam, two men who have experienced the passage of time. How are these characters employed? What contrasts do they offer to events and characters in the play?

Form and Genre

As You Like It is either Shakespeare's most emphatic comedy (containing, as it does, four weddings) or a brilliant satire on the comic form. As you read, consider the evidence for each case.

Sample Topic:

1. **Comic failures in *As You Like It*:** What details can we find in Shakespeare's play to make us question its apparently exuberant comic outcome? How are traditionally comic movements and devices undercut in *As You Like It*? Do these "problems" finally challenge our categorization of the play as a comedy?

An essay on this topic might begin by exploring some of the darker qualities of Arden, the play's apparently idealized pastoral setting. Again, the hunting motif and fascination with time will be of use here. However, the bulk of this essay could focus on the final act. After all, it is in the final scenes that comedies tend to solidify their generic outcome, almost universally through weddings and community feasts uniting characters and resolving earlier difficulties. *As You Like It* appears to offer an ideal comic finale, blessed not just by four weddings but an appearance by Hymen, the god of marriage. What could be more suggestive of pure comedy than romantic bliss offered as its conclusion? First, examine in your essay the quality of the relationships that end in marriage. Of particular concern, perhaps, are the unions of Silvius and Phoebe along with Touchstone and Audrey. Surely, marriages can only be truly comic if they are good matches. Why might we question, then, not only these pairings but even the marriage of Oliver and Celia? Some writers might even extend this line of analysis to include problems with the pairing of Rosalind and Orlando—these tend to focus on uncertainties raised by the text's playfulness with gender and identity. Second, the apparent ease with which everything is resolved appears to almost mock the conventions of comedy—the conversion of Duke Frederick seems the most guilty twist, but Rosalind's conveniently quick solutions to the lovers' problems may appear to be another. Putting all this together, consider whether you find satire or parody in the inclusion of four weddings and the appearance of Hymen. Is this perhaps Shakespeare winking at his audience, gently teasing them for their comic desire to see such spectacle and romantic resolution?

Compare and Contrast

One potentially strong compare and contrast essay might find unexpected similarities between the green world and the court. The theme of love, also, could be explored through compare and contrast format, perhaps usefully shaped by the central division of male visions of love contrasted with female models. Notice that Silvius and Orlando seem to approach love as an idealized and highly aesthetic form of worship, while Phoebe and Rosalind appear to debunk such fanciful notions. There are also Celia's doubts over Rosalind's love at first sight for Orlando, to add another voice of female pragmatism and reason. However, as with any compare and contrast essay, within the overall movement of your main argument—here the division between male and female visions of love— look to add some intriguing complications. Is there a clear difference in the play between male visions of love, which seem to be governed by poetic ideals, and the more pragmatic, realistic model envisioned by the female characters? Or does a more careful investigation of the play reveal that there is no such distinction, that instead the play offers a model of love as a shifting and inconstant phenomenon? What would be the evidence for such a counterclaim? You might, for a start, want to consider Touchstone's far from admirable or idealistic reasons for marrying Audrey. Perhaps more significantly, you should think about the way in which each of the female characters actually succumbs to or espouses a more starry-eyed vision of love, despite their protestations against such a definition of love.

As previously noted in this chapter, a good comparison text for *As You Like It* might be *The Roaring Girl*, but students wishing to stay within Shakespeare's canon might find an obvious candidate for comparison in *Twelfth Night*. While both plays have a number of similarities, complex differences can be found both in the tone or mood of the plays and in the way crossdressing is employed to create confusion in the gendering and identities of characters. In many ways, *Twelfth Night* takes these ideas further than *As You Like It*, arguably intensifying the philosophical impact of the crossdressing motif. An essay considering the bodies of Rosalind and Viola as ambiguous spaces transcending gender could generate rich discussion. *Twelfth Night*, however, is by no means the only Shakespeare play that might offer an interesting point of comparison.

Sample Topics:

1. **A comparison of Rosalind to Portia from *The Merchant of Venice:*** Traditionally labeled as two of Shakespeare's greatest heroines, are Rosalind and Portia actually more different than alike?

With an essay such as this, you could adopt and support either position, but the most potentially promising path might lie in arguing for difference rather than similarity. Certainly, though, the similarities are striking, at least on the surface: Two highly intelligent women who crossdress in order to carry out a plot that will set up an apparently comic resolution to their respective plays. However, the differences are meaningful. You might talk, for example, about the different ways the crossdressing motif is used in each play. Portia primarily uses her crossdressing as a disguise that grants the legal and social status of a man, while later she uses her disguise to gain moral authority over her husband, Bassanio. Consider how this compares to Rosalind's use of crossdressing. The kind of power or authority she seeks and gains through crossdressing appears quite different. Such an essay might consider how each of these strong heroines uses her authority within the play, what outcomes they engineer, and what motivates them to these actions.

2. **Comparing the play text with Kenneth Branagh's film version,** *As You Like It* **(2007):** How does Branagh's movie handle the comic closure of the play?

The movie transfers the play's action to nineteenth-century Japan, a place of cultural change and transformation. It may, indeed, be the only Shakespeare movie to date to feature a ninja attack squad in the first few minutes. Here, the trick to writing a good essay on a film adapted from a Shakespeare play is to move beyond a "shopping list" of similarities and differences between text and film (see a more detailed discussion of writing about "Shakespeare films" in the "How to Write About Shakespeare" chapter at the beginning of this volume). Equally, it is useful to reach beyond qualitative judgments ("the film wasn't as good as the book," for example). Instead, focus your comparison with a clear thesis, just as you would if writing an essay solely on the Shakespeare text. You can do this in many ways. You might characterize the tone of the film against the play (see the discussion of Michael Radford's explicitly tragic version of *The Merchant of Venice* in the section on that play). Alternatively, work in detail with one component or part of the adaptation. In this case, how does Branagh handle the resolution of the film? Like Shakespeare's play, the final scenes of Branagh's film can be read as jubilant comedy or elaborate parody. The prolonged frolicking and dancing that close the film, for example, seem to suggest that Branagh, like Shakespeare also, is using the conventions of his medium (in this case, comic cinema) to encourage questions about the gap between form and meaning, what happens and how those events should be interpreted.

Bibliography for *As You Like It*

Gay, Penny. *As She Likes It: Shakespeare's Unruly Women.* London: Routledge, 1994.

Greenblatt, Stephen. "Fiction and Friction." *Shakespearean Negotiations.* Berkeley: University of California Press, 1988.

Hunt, Maurice. *Shakespeare's* As You Like It*: Late Elizabethan Culture and Literary Representation.* Basingstoke, UK: Palgrave, 2008.

Jones, Ann Rosalind, and Peter Stallybrass. *Renaissance Clothing and the Materials of Memory.* Cambridge: Cambridge University Press, 2000.

Quinones, Ricardo J. *The Renaissance Discovery of Time.* Cambridge, MA: Harvard University Press, 1972.

Shapiro, Michael. *Gender in Play on the Shakespearean Stage.* Ann Arbor: University of Michigan Press, 1996.

Stubbes, Phillip. *The Anatomie of Abuses.* Ed. Margaret Jane Kidnie. Tempe, AZ: Arizona Center for Medieval and Renaissance Studies, 2002.

THE COMEDY
OF ERRORS

READING TO WRITE

*T*HE COMEDY *of Errors* is fun, fast, and rich with philosophical implications; it is an ideal text to write about. Importantly, the writer should be aware that just because the text is breezier than most of Shakespeare's plays, this does not mean that the task of writing about it is necessarily any "easier" as a result. You must approach the text looking for difficulty and complexity, just as you would with an apparently denser work.

The play is one of Shakespeare's earliest, but it feels more successful than *The Two Gentlemen of Verona*, even perhaps equal to the better known *The Taming of the Shrew*. Add to this grouping the play often described as Shakespeare's first masterpiece, *A Midsummer Night's Dream*, and we can see *The Comedy of Errors* as part of a collection of early works interconnecting in provocative and productive ways. These plays lend themselves well to a compare or contrast essay, but some of the issues that can be explored and developed in that format, key ideas in Shakespeare's comedies—such as identity, gender, dream and illusion, as well as performance and theater itself—are central to the intellectual substance of *The Comedy of Errors* (as well as to its sensational entertainment value, of course) as a stand-alone subject for writers.

The following passage from the play demonstrates how a number of these core themes intermingle. Here Luciana, Adriana's sister, confronts Antipholus of Syracuse (though she thinks it is Adriana's husband, Antipholus of Ephesus, she is talking to) about his poor treatment of Adriana:

And may it be that you have quite forgot
A husband's office? Shall, Antipholus.
Even in the spring of love, thy love-springs rot?
Shall love, in building, grow so ruinous?
If you did wed my sister for her wealth,
Then for her wealth's sake use her with more kindness:
Or if you like elsewhere, do it by stealth;
Muffle your false love with some show of blindness:
Let not my sister read it in your eye;
Be not thy tongue thy own shame's orator;
Look sweet, be fair, become disloyalty;
Apparel vice like virtue's harbinger;
Bear a fair presence, though your heart be tainted;
Teach sin the carriage of a holy saint;
Be secret-false: what need she be acquainted?
What simple thief brags of his own attaint?
'Tis double wrong, to truant with your bed
And let her read it in thy looks at board:
Shame hath a bastard fame, well managed;
Ill deeds are doubled with an evil word.
Alas, poor women! make us but believe,
Being compact of credit, that you love us;
Though others have the arm, show us the sleeve;
We in your motion turn and you may move us.
Then, gentle brother, get you in again;
Comfort my sister, cheer her, call her wife:
'Tis holy sport to be a little vain,
When the sweet breath of flattery conquers strife.

(3.2.1–28)

The first thing to note, perhaps, is that for all of the passage's careful argumentation and eloquence, it is absolute gibberish—at least to Antipholus, anyway, who can understand nothing of the speech because he lacks the context, is the wrong pair of ears for Luciana's fine speech. It is an example, then, of linguistic failure, of words that can suddenly mean nothing and hold no sense depending on who speaks them and who hears them; context, in other words, is everything. Just as identities break down, language and communication fail jarringly in the play as well. Unlike Antipholus, though, for us, the passage is understandable and, in particular, addresses two of the most prominent and resonant themes of the play. First, the passage could clearly be used in an essay addressing identity and disguise or deception in *The Comedy of Errors.* The play focuses on involuntary disruptions of the self, the way in which the fragmentation of one's identity happens uncontrollably. Here, however, we see an interesting parallel to this unwilling dissolution of identity as Luciana tells Antipholus of Syracuse that he should "Be secret-false," should pretend to be something and someone other than he is. He should, she suggests, put on the disguise of a faithful husband and "Bear a fair presence, though your heart be tainted." The result of this conscious deception, however, would be, of course, the creation of yet another duplicitous identity, that of Adriana as the loved and revered wife of a good husband. As you write about *The Comedy of Errors,* always be aware of the fact that the confusion and uncertainty are multidirectional, never contained simply in one character. The consequences of the twins' instability are felt deeply by everyone; a collective sense of dislocation from "reality" is woven through all the characters.

Another thematic essay that could utilize this passage is one addressing gender concerns in the play. As will be discussed in greater depth in the Themes section, this topic makes for an interesting and rich discussion. After all, the play foregrounds a debate about the proper balance of power within a marriage and, more broadly still, about a woman's political identity and potential claims to authority. This approach naturally references the notion of identity as well, closely related to the broader philosophical inquiry the play conducts, but gender provides a specific sociological and political context for the debate. More importantly, as was Shakespeare's custom throughout his career, he approaches this theme in what might be seen as a debate format, giving certain contrasting opinions to different voices, rarely making one point of view more compelling or convincing than another. Luciana can be broadly characterized as submissive in her gender politics, while Adriana might be seen as more forceful and dynamic. The advice Luciana gives in this passage is in keeping with such a sketch of the two women, essentially empowering the man to create himself and simultaneously disenfranchise the female partner in the marriage.

By Shakespeare's standards, the play is unusually plot driven, events twisting and turning at breakneck pace once the device of mistaken identity is introduced; less emphasis is placed on linguistic beauty and complexity than we are accustomed to in his work. There are few if any particularly complex soliloquies in *The Comedy of Errors,* though there are some shorter speeches offering interesting images or conceits. The comparative lack of "major" speeches in the play means an essay writer will likely engage in relatively little sustained close reading of densely packed passages. Students have sometimes remarked that the soliloquies (along with other major speeches in a given play) are an important way of navigating Shakespeare's text and preparing material for use in the essay. There are few examples of such material in *The Comedy of Errors,* so as you read you will be looking to note individual lines or groups of lines for use as evidence in your essay. You will have to read with this in mind, never failing to miss the few complex linguistic moments Shakespeare introduces, such as Antipholus of Syracuse's often-cited but briefly stated "drop of water" metaphor (1.2.35), while also picking up on the enormous philosophical resonance of lines such as "I know you not" or "known unto these, and to myself disguised!" (2.2.214). These lines may have a direct, more straightforward quality to them on first reading, but you will need to examine them to explore their resonance and implication in the text. For example, from the three-word phrase "unto myself disguised," you could generate comments on the penetrating confusion experienced by the Antipholi, the way in which the confusion others experience in encountering them is mirrored internally by their own self-doubt or self-alienation. The implications of being disguised to oneself, then, include a fragmentation of the self into at least two parts, a kind of "true" self that is authentic enough to recognize and understand the strangeness of its experiences, and the "other" within, a component of the self foreign enough to be unrecognizable to the authentic self. This observation can give rise to more nuanced claims. Once such a fracturing of identity has occurred, on what authority might one component of the self claim authenticity, claim to be "genuine," over any other? The implications of these three words, then, are significant, and you should not shy away from generating many paragraphs and pages of analysis out of a few words of text.

TOPICS AND STRATEGIES

Every essay requires a focus; you cannot write about everything in the play at once. As a specified focus evolves into a thesis, so observations develop into arguments. The starting point, nonetheless, always comes from a direct engagement of the text. The topic suggestions included here are geared toward helping you make the most of the budding ideas you will have as you read *The Comedy of Errors*. By no means should you feel limited to these topics, however.

Themes

The most prominent and obvious theme of the play, Shakespeare's investigation of the porous nature of human identity, will be treated in the Philosophy and Ideas section. In this section, two alternative themes vital to the play's discourses, gender and language, are broached.

Sample Topic:

1. **Gender:** Does the play finally advocate for a particular version of marriage, a specific domestic power dynamic?

Obviously, you may want to answer this question with a carefully nuanced *yes,* followed by ample supporting evidence to clarify the case, but you can also suggest that while the play's level of interest in the issue is deep, it finally avoids embracing one model of female behavior over another. This may sound like deliberate avoidance of taking a definitive position on the matter, but it is actually a statement that shows great awareness of Shakespeare's particular penchant for self-effacing evenhandedness.

The essay will pay close attention to the three female characters in the play. A careful evaluation of the debate between Adriana and Lucian in 2.1 would be a fine place to begin, perhaps looking at the forcefulness of the points made by each figure. Adriana's short speech in 2.1.86, for example, has particular rhetorical and logical power. The same can be said of Adriana's speech at 2.2.110, though it is additionally important to note here that Adriana is actually addressing the man she thinks is her husband rather than conversing with her sister. What do you make of Adriana's claims in these lines about the relationship between marriage and personal identity? Another scene to look at with special care is 5.1. Here, we meet the Abbess, a somewhat paradoxical figure who seems to represent both the arguments of the more submissive positioning of Luciana and the more forceful one of Adriana. See the Characters section for a related discussion of these topics and issues.

Language

What is the relationship between linguistic instability and personal instability in *The Comedy of Errors*? Language is fundamentally important to how we imagine and represent ourselves. As a poet and playwright, naturally, Shakespeare is deeply invested in understanding and exploring the role of language in our interior and exterior lives.

Sample Topic:

1. **Linguistic failure and disconnection:** How is language used to alienate, distort, and misrepresent in the play? What are instances of the failure or breakdown of language and what is the importance of such a lapse in communication?

Beyond a general fascination with the intricacies of language, Shakespeare seems intrigued by the subject of linguistic failure and explores this phenomena explicitly in both *The Comedy of Errors* and *Love's Labour's Lost,* two early comedies that form a strong comparative pair. In these plays, we are frequently given utterances that fragment and splinter into failed and distorted communications. Language becomes a faulty and unreliable bridge between interlocutors, and in *The Comedy of Errors,* this failure contributes meaningfully to the deep-seated confusion plaguing the characters. Look for moments in which linguistic disconnection in the play is sharpest and most painful, then attempt to show how these moments of words gone wrong are integral to the issues of individual identity at the heart of the text.

Characters

Like other early Shakespearean comedies, *The Comedy of Errors* hardly seems to prize the creation of deep, multifaceted characters. Far from a fault, however, this seems to be consistent with Shakespeare's philosophical ends. In plays like this one, *The Two Gentlemen of Verona,* or *Love's Labour's Lost,* the essential subject matter is the shifting nature of the self, the unreliable foundations on which each of us treads or bases our identities. Solid, consistent, and coherent characters would be at odds with this line of inquiry, perhaps. It seems fitting even to displace discussion of the Antipholi to another section of topic suggestions, such as Philosophy and Ideas, so little can they be said to resemble well-defined characters. Perhaps only Adriana resembles a carefully crafted character, the apparently longsuffering wife who readies herself to take a stand, though even she can be said to represent her situation rather than be judged a fully-formed creation. Reflective of this, if attempting a character study of Adriana, you may essentially follow a modified version of the suggestions for the thematic essay focusing on gender.

Being a character in *The Comedy of Errors*, then, largely means being the physical body through which ideas are tested and explored, and the writer should never lose sight of the fact that character analysis in a play such as this is essentially the same thing as thematic analysis. The hapless Egeon, a man who essentially represents the misfortunate, the man who turns up by chance in the wrong place at the wrong time, is a good character to examine more closely. His backstory—the backstory of the play—could be analyzed nicely as foreshadowing the central themes of the play as a whole, but by the time he reemerges in act 5, scene 1, ready for death, he has acquired additional symbolic meaning, now signifying a man disconnected even from his children and fearful of the passage of time to the point where he imagines a handful of years have left him unrecognizable to his closest kin.

Sample Topics:

1. The Dromios: Why does Shakespeare add the two servants to his play?

In the source text for *The Comedy of Errors*, Shakespeare found only one set of twins. He adds a second set—why? Many have suggested the move is one of basic amplification; the zaniness is doubled and the philosophical issues multiplied by adding more identical bodies to the stage. These issues could certainly be developed in an essay, but it seems the role of the servants may be even more extensive than merely adding confusion and additional instances of manic misidentification comedy.

Think, for example, of the relationship between servitude and the theme of fate, or, additionally, the connection between the servant and the wife as it involves issues of submissiveness, power, and gender.

2. **The Abbess:** If the gender dialogue of the play is articulated through the conflicting voices of Adriana and Luciana, how does this third figure of the Abbess contribute to the debate?

Focusing on an apparently minor character can, as has been suggested throughout this volume, be an effective writing strategy and a useful way to distinguish your work. Some might feel that there might not be enough to say about a character appearing in just one scene, but a strongly constructed and argued essay can prove otherwise. If you have a slightly longer essay to write, there is no harm in spending a page or two assessing the other female characters in the play, Adriana and Luciana. If you tell the reader this is necessary in order to fully understand how the figure of the Abbess works in *The Comedy of Errors,* then you have likely justified your decision and deflected any potential criticism. The most important strategy in such essays, however, is often a move in the second half of the paper, signaled already in the thesis, into the relationship between the minor character and the wider themes of the work. So, in this case, a careful reading of 5.1 would pose questions, for example, about the apparent contradictions in the Abbess's words to Adriana. In addition, the Abbess and her priory seem to represent a safe haven for Antipholus and Dromio of Syracuse. To what extent does the hoped-for stability of the priory and the Abbess's protection turn out to be real or illusory, though? Note, for example, how even in the end the Abbess does not exactly know who she herself is (wife and mother to those present on or just offstage) through most of her scene. Both the analysis of her speech and her function within the text would naturally lead to an opportunity to make points about the play that are much bigger than the character of the Abbess, either in regard to gender discourses or issues of identity.

Philosophy and Ideas

The Comedy of Errors, despite its slapstick exterior, is a meditation on the stability of human identity and, less prominently but no less meaningfully, on questions of fate and happenstance. The material and topic strands discussed here could be effectively incorporated into many if not most essays on the play, irrespective of the specific point of departure and approach.

Sample Topics:

1. **Fragmentation of the self:** In *The Comedy of Errors,* what forces and pressures work to destabilize the characters' sense of self?

The first challenge of working with this topic is sifting through the text and selecting lines, passages, and episodes to use; there is an abundance of relevant material in regard to identity in the text, and it is important to select the more important and useful moments. One potentially strong place to start is with the often-quoted "drop of water" speech from Antipholus of Syracuse (1.133–42., allowing the essay writer to engage in detail with the images and philosophical implications of the passage. One approach would be to unpack the image of Antipholus as a drop in the ocean, "Unseen, inquisitive, confound[ing] himself." You may also want to ponder the fact that this loss of self is articulated *before* (though, tellingly, only seconds before) the mistaken identity antics begin.

Adriana's speech to Antipholus of Syracuse, asking and riffing on the key question "O how comes It / That thou art then estranged from thyself?" (2.2.120), as well as his aside after she leaves the stage ("What, was I married to her in my dream?" 2.2.183), also expose the fantastical and bewildering nature of the problems at hand. Look for lines such as these that cut to the heart of the dilemma, reaching for tentative glimpses of understanding rather than simply stating confusion. Another example can be seen in Antipholus of Syracuse's retort to the pleading Luciana: "Would you create me new?" (3.2.39). Is it that easy to tear someone down and build something else in his or her place? Perhaps the implication of the play is that it is far easier than we would wish to believe. For the effect of this knowledge on the characters involved, you can do little better than reflect on the barely contained panic inherent in the exchange between Antipholus of Syracuse and his servant Dromio beginning at 3.2.72. Finally, of course, a detailed reading of 5.1 is likely to be an important part of this essay, offering, as it does, the chance to reflect on whether the play appears to believe that these problems might be containable by the comic resolution of the play.

2. **Fate:** How does the play mix questions of who we are with questions of how things happen to us?

Philosophically speaking, questions of why things happen to us are going to be tightly bound with questions of who we are. After all, the threats to identity experienced by the Antipholi began when their boat was separated by ocean rocks many decades before the action of the play and are intensified all the more in the chance encounter of the two in Ephesus. You may want to ask why and to what degree Shakespeare integrates these two themes. A close reading of 1.1 may likely reveal that Shakespeare foregrounds the theme of fate from the beginning and that Egeon's play on the words *happy* meaning "happy" and *hap* indicating "fortune," prompts us to think about these questions. Are we finally servants to fate in the way that the Dromios are servants to the Antipholi, taking more than occasional beatings at the most unexpected moments?

3. **Magic, madness, and miracle:** In what ways do these three concepts function in *The Comedy of Errors* as a way of understanding psychological phenomena? How effective are they intended to be?

This essay calls for writers to utilize the efforts characters make to explain and understand the bewildering events of the play. You may wish to explore how these three discourses (magic, madness, and miracle) provide the characters with a language and framework through which to comprehend the incomprehensible. How effective is this for them? How effective do you think the play intends these discourses to be? Moments and lines such as 1.2.95 and 5.1.188 demonstrate how, lacking a system of terminology adequate to the task of providing insight into the most unfathomable elements of the human self, the characters slip easily into talk of witches, demons, and possession. Magic and madness belong to this particular category, while miracle seems to occupy a different philosophical space in the play. Perhaps an exploration of the function of miracle in the play could be aligned more closely to the preceding discussion of fate or perhaps to the discussion on the comic form of the play in the Form and Genre section. However you choose to incorporate it, it is fascinating to reflect on how the benign force of a fate so positive (a reunion of long-separated family members) that it can only be called miracle is at odds with the frightening and profoundly unsettling implications of a self prone to disintegration.

Form and Genre

There are a variety of strong essay options that could arise from the play's formal concerns. A strong inquiry could be made, for example, into the nature of the farcical comedy employed by Shakespeare in the play. Alternately, essay writers could attempt a comparison of the play to its ancient source text, Plautus's *The Menaechmi*; yet another direction is suggested by an appraisal of the spirit and sincerity of Shakespeare's comic resolution in the work.

Sample Topic:

1. **Comedy:** For all of the chaotic confusions of the play's central action, does the close of the play offer a return to order and stability? If it does, is this return convincing?

Look for sources of stability in 5.1, but also be on the search for words or actions that may undermine the push to order and unity. You may consider, for example, the priory as a place of stability, but what do you make of the Abbess's oddly contradictory speech or the fact that outside the sanctuary of this place another confused Antipholus and bewildered Dromio run amuck? Moreover, reflect on the fact that the Abbess may rightly claim that "one day's error" has seemingly resolved so much, but that this is juxtaposed by her painful image of a prolonged and pregnant sadness: "Thirty-three years have I gone but in travail / Of you, my sons, and till this hour/ My heavy burden ne'er delivered" (5.1.402–04). Finally, amid the celebration of the concluding lines look for moments of tension and anxiety that suggest the seemingly crystallized identities of the four men may still be vulnerable. Think, for example, about the brief but telling confusion at line 5.1.413 or the safety precautions agreed on by the two Dromios in the final lines of the play.

Compare and Contrast

The play lends itself naturally to compare and contrast essays, papers studying character pairings in particular. After all, there are two Antipholi, two Dromios, and two sisters. Moreover, the philosophical movement of the play is, of course, toward division and the breakdown of wholes, so the idea of treating multiple subjects is encouraged by the work. Indeed, as we have seen, even the analysis of a single character in the play has the potential to be recast in the compare and contrast mode, thus taking on more than a single subject.

The play also fits in nicely with other Shakespeare plays and offers rich interactions with both earlier and later plays. *The Comedy of Errors* could be productively read alongside the late play *The Winter's Tale.* Both of these texts turn on similar devices and culminate in a miracle, the power of which is overwhelmingly hopeful and yet clouded by the significant passage of time lost between separation and restoration. Then there are opportunities to view *The Comedy of Errors* through the lens of gender studies alongside other early play such as *The Taming of the Shrew, The Two Gentlemen of Verona*, or *A Midsummer Night's Dream.* An interesting and promising angle when incorporating one or more of these works may be to address the possibility in which *The Comedy of Errors* appears more explicitly sympathetic to its female lead and arguably more receptive to her complaints. For example, *The Taming of the Shrew* and *The Comedy of Errors* both reflect on the struggles of a married woman to assert her influence on a troublesome husband. An essay could effectively look at the characters and struggles of Kate and Adriana side by side.

Sample Topics:

1. ***The Comedy of Errors* compared to *A Midsummer Night's Dream:*** In what ways does Bottom from *A Midsummer Night's Dream* resemble the hapless Antipholi?

This essay connects a group of characters that might not, at first glance, belong together. For the *MND* component of the play, focus on Bottom's transformation into an ass, his disorientation and confusion (both during and after his romantic encounter with Titania), and even his obsession with stagecraft and acting, yet another example of the way identity and the division between the self and the other can be conflated in Shakespeare's drama. Alternatively, the theme of gender could be used to connect the plays. In this case, Titania or Helena would take center stage alongside Adriana.

2. **Comparing *The Comedy of Errors* and *The Two Gentlemen of Verona:*** What differences distinguish these two studies of self-dissolution?

Begin by asking whether the two texts at first glance look more alike than different. As these two plays are early comedies obsessed with philosophical questions about the unstable nature of human identity, it seems a good bet to claim that similarities are more apparent than differences. With this starting point, then, the best direction to take the essay would be the pursuit of differences, showing how these similar plays can actually be characterized by their important differences. For example, while both texts give us characters who face bewildering change and transformation and the loss of control over the self, could we argue that in *The Two Gentlemen of Verona* the catalysts for self loss are internal while in *The Comedy of Errors* they are external? If this observation can be effectively argued, then you could make larger claims for viewing these plays as a dialogue on the same subject rather than statements of repetition.

Bibliography for *The Comedy of Errors*

Brooks, Harold. "Themes and Structure in *The Comedy of Errors*." *Early Shakespeare*. John Russell Brown and Bernard Harris, eds. New York: Schocken, 1966: 55–71.

Cartwright, Kent. "Language, Magic, the Dromios, and *The Comedy of Errors*." *SEL: Studies in English Literature 1500–1900*, 47, 2007: 331–54.

Freedman, Barbara. "Egeon's Debt: Self-Division and Self-Redemption in *The Comedy of Errors*." *English Literary Renaissance*, 10, 1980: 360–83.

Schalkwyk, David. *Shakespeare, Love and Service*. Cambridge, England: Cambridge UP, 2008.

Taylor, Gary. "Textual and Sexual Criticism: A Crux in *The Comedy of Errors*." *Renaissance Drama*, 19, 1988: 195–225.

Van Elk, Martine. "'This sympathized One Day's Error': Genre, Representation and Subjectivity in *The Comedy of Errors*." *Shakespeare Quarterly*, 60, 2009: 47–72.

LOVE'S LABOUR'S LOST

READING TO WRITE

*L*OVE'S *LABOUR'S Lost* is an extraordinarily strange work that can pose its own distinctive challenges and rewards to the student writer. First, there is no plot to speak of, the characters are largely mouthpieces for different varieties of linguistic display, and the whole thing is capped off by Shakespeare's most disruptive and out-of-tune ending. More than any other play represented in this volume, *Love's Labour's Lost* tests an essay writer's ability to form an argument and pursue that argument cogently. All of Shakespeare's plays are, to a greater or lesser degree, puzzles, and *Love's Labour's Lost* can potentially be seen as a puzzle that does not really want to be solved, one that ostentatiously flaunts its own cleverness and wit until we are frustrated and exhausted. Still, the play contains its own critique, bemoans its own dizzying wit, and, finally, seems to thoroughly and soberly undercut itself, even deconstruct itself from the inside out. In short, Shakespeare provides his readers with a lot to work with.

In developing and pursuing your thesis and essay, make use of the complications and implications you encounter in the text, even though it may seem easier to ignore them. The pre-writing stage, carefully outlining what you are going to say and when you are going to say it, including a clear sense of which parts of the text you will use and what you will make them say in your essay, will be essential in providing an essay with the unity and cohesion needed. As an example of the play's sinuous linguistic paths, consider the letter penned by Armado for Jaquenetta:

'By heaven, that thou art fair, is most infallible;
true, that thou art beauteous; truth itself, that

thou art lovely. More fairer than fair, beautiful
than beauteous, truer than truth itself, have
commiseration on thy heroical vassal! The
magnanimous and most illustrate king Cophetua set
eye upon the pernicious and indubitate beggar
Zenelophon; and he it was that might rightly say,
Veni, vidi, vici; which to annothanize in the
vulgar,—O base and obscure vulgar!—videlicet, He
came, saw, and overcame: he came, one; saw two;
overcame, three. Who came? the king: why did he
come? to see: why did he see? to overcome: to
whom came he? to the beggar: what saw he? the
beggar: who overcame he? the beggar. The
conclusion is victory: on whose side? the king's.
The captive is enriched: on whose side? the
beggar's. The catastrophe is a nuptial: on whose
side? the king's: no, on both in one, or one in
both. I am the king; for so stands the comparison:
thou the beggar; for so witnesseth thy lowliness.
Shall I command thy love? I may: shall I enforce
thy love? I could: shall I entreat thy love? I
will. What shalt thou exchange for rags? robes;
for tittles? titles; for thyself? me. Thus,
expecting thy reply, I profane my lips on thy foot,
my eyes on thy picture. and my heart on thy every
part. Thine, in the dearest design of industry,
DON ADRIANO DE ARMADO.'

(4.1)

Obviously, *Love's Labour's Lost* is a play obsessed with language, how it
works and does not work. The text offers countless examples of failed
language, splintered and fragmented words, and fluid meanings, and
it revels in the infinite complexity of language. Thus, you should think
about the clear failures of the letter (the text) before moving on to how
that text becomes fragmented and fluid (because of the context). The
quoted passage is, of course, composed of a love letter, but the joke
is that it is a terrible love letter, one written in the wrong language.

Courtly love language of the day was linguistically rich and sophisticated. We see the four male lovers speaking in this style (and employing it in sonnets of love) throughout the play. But it is fundamentally different from the style adopted by Armado. Typical of Renaissance love rhetoric is the idea of suffering; for example, how the male lover/speaker aches and pines for the affections of an unresponsive beloved. Hyperbolic praise of the beloved's beauty is another typical element, in poetry often appearing as a blazon (a list of the beloved's features figured metaphorically, often outlandishly). We can see that Armado employs none of these standard devices (though the first few lines serve, perhaps, as a botched attempt at emulating this heightened and particularized mode of expression). Instead, he employs a dry and scholastic style, pedantic not romantic. He structures the letter as a debate to be won, advancing, he hopes, through the rhetorical strategy of question and answer. The comedy, of course, comes from the incongruity of speaking of love yet using the language of exaggerated early modern scholarship.

To complicate matters, although the letter is clearly written in the wrong language, it nonetheless resembles Renaissance "lovespeak" in several key ways. First, just as with standard love poetics of the day, Armado's letter speaks in a superior male voice that controls and dominates the female object. Although Renaissance male sonneteers may superficially claim to be writing about their beloved, complete with chivalric declarations of obedience, even enslavement to the woman, they are almost always understood as being about the male poet himself. The woman appears finally as an idealized shadow of a human being, usually silent and powerless. Here, Armado brings this will to power out into the open, does not hide the fact that he is asserting his authority over a woman. Moreover, and perhaps the key point to make, the letter is highly stylized, self-conscious of the language it uses, a performance rather than a natural utterance. Shakespeare seems to lampoon such hyperbolic displays of language in *Love's Labour's Lost* and elsewhere in his plays as well. This fact alone could make for a good short essay, finding and analyzing moments in which Shakespeare satirizes exaggerated and hollow linguistic displays.

Having looked at the text and one aspect of its context (a failed love letter), turn to the context of the letter's delivery in the play. First, the letter is written by Armado but read aloud by Boyet. The letter was written for Jaquenetta but is read to the Princess, her ladies, and Costard. The letter has acquired a speaker and audience distinct from its identity as a love letter from Armado to Jaquenetta; it has a life of its own. Armado's act of communicating his love to a specific woman was bungled in the first place by his own linguistic ineptitude, but now that failure of expression is infinitely amplified by the misdirection of the letter and the new eyes and ears that take possession of the misbegotten words. The result is the total failure of language to fulfill Armado's original purpose, an example of how all language can fail and every speaker can lose control of his or her utterances for a variety of reasons. Finally, someone might add that Armado is not really the author of the letter anyway: Shakespeare is. This reality adds yet another layer of complexity to the linguistic fabric of the words that collectively make up the play. A number of critics note how the play's emphatic use of linguistic artifice and performance draws attention to the play's existence as a piece of artifice and linguistic creativity, something clearly staged rather than lived. This is yet another aspect of the mazelike function of language in *Love's Labour's Lost*.

TOPICS AND STRATEGIES

Every essay requires a focus; you cannot write about everything in the play at once. As a specified focus evolves into a thesis, so observations develop into arguments. The starting point, nonetheless, always comes from a direct engagement of the text. The topic suggestions included here are geared toward helping you make the most of the developing ideas you will have as you read *Love's Labour's Lost*. By no means should you feel limited to these topics, however.

Themes

Like the theme of race in *Othello*, for example, language in *Love's Labour's Lost* appears to loom large over the play and demand the essay writer's attention. Typically, when considering the topic for an essay, it can be useful to reach for subjects you feel will not be employed by your class colleagues. But when a theme so dominates a play and is so complex and multifaceted, you can certainly head off in the same direction as the pack but, with a sharp eye and independent mind, still find a fresh approach.

The main challenge you may encounter, though, is conceptualizing an essay based on such a broad, densely packed theme. Here there is a particular danger that a writer may produce an unfocused and poorly argued essay that basically announces, "In this essay I will be studying the role of language in *Love's Labour's Lost*." An essay pursuing such a thesis would almost inevitably become a list of points and observations that, while perhaps individually noteworthy, do not form a unified and cohesive whole.

To avoid an overly simplistic reading of the theme you choose, create a clear argument that still allows you to discuss much of the material the play offers. Suggesting the play is about the actual failures of language and communication opens up some potentially strong avenues to pursue. Alternately, you may wish to refine your use of the theme to follow one particular strand. In this case, "writing" or "written texts" is one possibility (it has been pointed out by critics that numerous kinds of texts recorded on paper circulate throughout the play), while the rhetoric of love employed or the romantic utterances offered might be another. Such a targeted approach will help you structure your essay and find suitable evidence from the text before you write. The clarity and distinctiveness that should be gained by the narrowing of focus will be evident in the essay.

As another approach, possibly tie or relate the theme of language to another theme in the play, always a potentially effective move for a writer to make. We find an example of this linkage of various themes in Katherine Eisaman Maus's analysis of language and gender in "Transfer of Title in *Love's Labour's Lost*: Language, Individualism, Gender" (see Ivo Kamps's *Shakespeare Left and Right*, 1991). Like Maus, an essay writer can show that another, often lesser theme is intricately tied up with a more prominent theme, so that they inform each other or "speak" about and to each other. The strength of this approach is that a statement emerges that could never have been reached by looking at each theme in isolation.

Finally, do not restrict your inquiry to the way language functions in the play, as *Love's Labour's Lost* offers alternative options and approaches that do not center on language. Gender could arguably be one such theme. After all, the play comes from a particular moment in Shakespeare's trajectory when the dramatist is clearly interested in and attracted to the comic and philosophical possibilities of gender and romantic relations. After all, the men do not just receive a playful drubbing from their female counterparts; it can be reasonably argued the men look profoundly silly and small alongside the women of the play.

Language

In what ways does language fail in *Love's Labour's Lost*? The key moments in the play foreground its importance. Collectively, these moments help to show how language in the play is obscured and dispersed by "the sweet smoke of rhetoric" (3.1.55). Look, for example, at the miscommunication rooted in the malapropisms (the wrong choice of words) of Dull and Costard in 1.1. Linguistic incompetence such as this, however, can be studied alongside the equally confusing and distracting eloquence and verbosity of the other, socially elevated characters. A scene that juxtaposes both kinds of linguistic failure is the almost unreadable 3.1, which tests our patience and tolerance for wordplay up to the point when Armando retorts "We will talk no more of the matter" (3.1.107). The promise of relief, however, is not kept, and after Armado's exit from the scene, Biron enters to continue the wordplay with Costard. You may want to consider these kinds of linguistic failure—in which the words themselves and the linguistic talents of the speaker are at fault—alongside the many moments when words are disrupted because of a distorted relationship between speaker and listener. We saw Armado's letter being wrongly delivered, and another similar instance may be found in 4.2. The purely spoken equivalent to such moments, perhaps, might be found in the central eavesdropping scene of 4.3 and in Boyet's account of his own eavesdropping (5.2.89). In the former scene, there is a comic crescendo of utterances out of the speakers' control, something that warrants treatment alongside the important episodes of miscommunication, disguise, and distortion witnessed in 5.2. Finally, perhaps, what do you do with Biron's rejection of stylized linguistic wit (5.2.315–35; 5.2.394)? Can these be incorporated as part of an argument about the play's philosophy of language, for example?

Sample Topic:

1. **Learning and knowledge:** Does the play offer an ideal mode of learning or form of knowledge?

> The ridiculous discourses of the pseudoeducated are among the most amusing and contemptible linguistic excesses in *Love's Labour's Lost.* However, behind this comedy is a reflection on the distinctions between false and true learning. If you focus on this particular thread of the play's unreliable

discourses, you will be asking epistemological (concerning knowledge and how we acquire knowledge) questions that may help, in part, to explain the peculiarities of the ending and some of the play's dogged obsession with language. You may wish to begin with an analysis of the King's vision of a scholarly life in the first lines of the play. What are the merits of this life as he presents them? What are Biron's objections? What is the function of Holofernes and the kind of faux or false intellectualism on display in 4.2 and 5.1, or the purpose of the burlesque of classical learning witnessed in the laughable Nine (but in actuality three) Worthies in 5.2? Of course look for additional voices of dissent or contrary positions, too, such as the Princess's. Most importantly, however, examine the contrast between the acquisition of knowledge envisioned at the beginning of the play by the King and then as outlined at the end by the Princess. In what ways do the tasks set for the men form a sharp critique and undercutting of the King's earlier ambitions for learning?

Characters

Character studies are a major component of student literary criticism, of course, and an exploration of a character's development and growth from beginning to end is often the framework for an excellent essay. With this comedy, however, aside from two or possibly three characters that are sketched with more detail, the characters seem frequently to be little more than the bodies that are required for language to exist. This is an especially intriguing and bizarre development because, as has been noted and addressed by a number of critics, Shakespeare gives his characters the names of real historical persons. Seemingly, these characters have little if anything to do with their factual namesakes, however. While a critic like Gillian Woods can make strong and convincing claims about the religious undertones of the specific names used and the possible resonance of such for early modern audiences (see Woods's essay in *How to Do Things With Shakespeare*, 2008), for the more casual reader the dissonance between historic names and the play's characters simply offers another example of linguistic slippage in which the names and what they are supposed to signify disconnect. One response to this particular challenge would be to pursue a theme that treats language and character in combination, paying special and careful attention not just to what is said but who says it. In this way, patterns of linguistic identity may emerge and be assigned carefully and precisely to the individual characters. You could also think about the general nature of identity in the play, something that seems to be interrogated not just by the recurring moments of miscommunication and misunderstanding that blur our ability to establish a concrete identity through language, but moments of literal disguise and confusion over identity such as are witnessed in 5.2.

Sample Topics:

1. **The Princess:** Can it be argued that the Princess is the voice of "reason" in the play? Is she the character who articulates the play's ideology and world-view?

In *As You Like It,* the brilliant Rosalind acts as a kind of surrogate for Shakespeare, the agent of the playwright working hard to bring about the unlikely comic conclusion and voicing what appears to be Shakespeare's frustration with and disdain of an elaborately stylized language of courtship. It is Rosalind's task to correct the naïve Orlando's misguided and impossible ideals of love before the pair starts their life together. In this way, she may be said to be the voice of the play's conscience (though this is a claim that could be contested). Is it true to say that the Princess occupies a similar role in *Love's Labour's Lost?* If not, how might we characterize her? She stands out from the crowd and only Biron matches her presence in the play. Look at moments such as her dismissal of linguistic ornament (2.1.13) or her fascinating display of confidence when verbally tussling with the King later in the same scene. Pay close attention, of course, to her role in the conclusion of the play. How would you characterize her authority at the close of the final scene? Thinking about her, too, as the agent of the playwright, how would you characterize the conclusion she engineers, and what does this resolution say about her character and purpose in the text?

2. **Biron (alternatively named Berowne):** How does Biron provide a counterweight to the excesses of the King?

The key to this essay will be engaging details, to say as much as possible and to complicate issues that appear somewhat straightforward. A good place to start may be in carefully outlining the King's vision of scholastic retreat as represented at the beginning of the play, followed, of course, by an equally detailed account and analysis of Biron's skepticism in the first scene. His soliloquy at the close of act 3 should also provide good material. Strong additional quotes might also be found in several descriptions of Biron given by the women in 2.1. Of course, you should consider fully Biron's rejection of highly stylized and inauthentic language at the close of the play (see the Themes section for more on this aspect).

Form and Genre

It is often said that Shakespeare's later comedies, those produced toward the end of his career, are so strange that they warrant the special label *problem plays.* The term was coined late in the nineteenth century by the critic F. S. Boas and has been widely used ever since. The term is a useful one, routinely applied to *All's Well That Ends Well, Measure for Measure,* and a handful of other late plays. However, the term is also problematic, and the notion of limiting it to several later works is even more problematic. Shakespeare's comedies invariably refuse an easy ending and simplistic comic resolution. In a sense, all of Shakespeare's comedies are "problem comedies." Think, for example, of *Twelfth Night* and the list of loose ends and shadows that linger among the apparent happiness of the resolution. There is the exclusion of Antonio, Sir Andrew, and Malvolio from the feast, of course, not to mention the heinous treatment of the latter by Sir Toby and his accomplices. Then there are the difficulties raised by the confusion of gender and sexuality so openly treated throughout the play. Can these problems really be imagined to vanish because of Sebastian's fortuitous and improbable arrival on the scene just in time to avoid romantic catastrophe and pronounce that everything is basically back to normal? Still, despite this catalogue of anticomic threats cluttering up the close of the play—most loudly articulated by Malvolio's angry and bitter desire to be "revenged" on the whole happy "pack" of romantic winners at the end—*Twelfth Night* is not commonly classified as a problem play. So if this list of troubles is not enough to earn the distinction, what is? One of the archetypal problem plays, *All's Well That Ends Well*, shows us that the chief ingredient is most likely the heavy use of irony and satire more than the presence of ambiguity and a lack of resolution alone. While that work appears to end happily, the central couple uniting after negotiating numerous hurdles, the fact remains that one of the pair does not love the other and has, frankly, gone to great lengths to never see his partner again. The form of comedy is present and correct, but the expected content or spirit is wholly absent.

When it comes to *Love's Labour's Lost,* the ending is even more unexpected and deflating than that of *All's Well That Ends Well.* Unlike this latter work, *Love's Labour's Lost* makes no superficial claims to a happy ending; rather, like *Twelfth Night,* it openly speaks of sadness where we had expected only nuptials, joy, and wish fulfillment. In addition, the play makes sadness and uncertainty not simply a dark strain in the overall comic resolution but the only shade visible at all. It is not an ironic or tempered comic resolution; rather, it is not a comic resolution at all. Such a singular and strange use of comedy thus presents one of the most promising opportunities to the writer, something that opens up much of the play for discussion though maintains a sharp focus on the task of characterizing the generic makeup of the play.

Sample Topic:

1. **Comedy:** Can *Love's Labour's Lost* be accurately referred to as a comedy at all?

A majority of an essay on this topic is likely to provide a close reading of the end of the play and offer analysis of the strange events that unfold therein. However, it is probable that, to whatever degree you see fit, you will make use of the whole play. You may wish to open the essay by talking about its unorthodox use of language, its relatively underdeveloped plot and characters and offer commentary on what this means for the play's generic intentions. How, for example, do the dominant themes of miscommunication and confusion foreshadow the oddity of the play's ending—the final and biggest moment of failed communication in the play? It is a comedy that finally cannot speak the language of comedy. Of course, everything after the entrance of the messenger at 5.2.698—and the intrusion of death into comedy he brings with him—should be given careful attention. The characters' struggle to come to terms with the unexpectedness of events, the sudden shift in direction and tone, and their efforts are worth tracking. What do you make of the Princess's proposals and the likely outcomes for all involved? Finally, what is the significance of the two songs by Winter and Spring that conclude the play?

Bibliography for *Love's Labour's Lost*

Maus, Katherine Eisaman. "Transfer of Title in *Love's Labour's Lost*: Language, Individualism, Gender." *Shakespeare Left and Right.* Ivo Kamps, ed. New York: Routledge, 1991: 206–23.

Mazzio, Carla. *The Inarticulate Renaissance: Language Trouble in an Age of Eloquence.* Philadelphia, PA: University of Pennsylvania Press, 2009.

Montrose, Louis Adrian. *"Curious-Knotted Garden": The Forms, Themes and Contexts of Shakespeare's* Love's Labour's Lost. Salzburg: Institute fur Englische Sprache und Literatur, 1977.

Woods, Gillian. "Catholicism and Conversion in *Love's Labour's Lost*." Laurie Maguire, ed. *How to Do Things with Shakespeare: New Approaches, New Essays.* Malden, MA: Blackwell, 2008: 101–30.

THE MERCHANT
OF VENICE

READING TO WRITE

THOUGH *THE Merchant of Venice* is dominated by the figure of Shylock, and the tragedy of the Holocaust and continuing discord in the Middle East make the play's discussion of Judaism especially resonant to modern audiences, the play offers many different approaches for the writer. The work has a large cast of characters whose actions and motives are intriguing; the play also functions as a snapshot of changing economic realities in early modern Europe. Moreover, it has significant formal and generic consequences for Shakespeare's future career, especially his comedies.

The play also contains one of the dramatist's finest set pieces. You could write an essay entirely about the trial scene of act 4, scene 1, analyzing the virtuoso display of dramatic action and characterization on display. It is fascinating to see Shylock push ahead with his claim on Antonio's flesh, while the entire judicial and political authority of Venice presses back against him. Although Shylock trusts in nothing more than the letter of the law, you could develop a strong essay by observing the ways in which the accumulated machinery of the state works consciously and deliberately against him. Particularly worth noting and incorporating into your essay are any shifts in sympathy you sense as the scene progresses: While we might begin the scene resenting Shylock for his unrelenting malice, by its end, a modern audience might find it difficult to take any pleasure in the thwarting of Shylock and the punishment meted out to him. The scene concentrates the play's action, skillfully condensing so many of the work's core themes and concerns. As a result, a close reading of it will allow you to synthesize many broader elements of the play. What might such an essay consider? Here is perhaps the most memorable and often quoted passage from the scene. Portia, disguised as a learned doctor called to adjudicate the dispute between Shylock and Antonio, lectures Shylock on the need to be compassionate and release Antonio from the bond:

> The quality of mercy is not strained.
> It droppeth as the gentle rain from heaven
> Upon the place beneath. It is twice blest:
> It blesseth him that gives, and him that takes.
> . . . It is an attribute to God himself,
> And earthly power doth then show likest to God's
> When mercy seasons justice. Therefore, Jew,
> Though justice be thy plea, consider this:
> That in the course of justice none of us
> Should see salvation. We do pray for mercy,
> And that same prayer doth teach us all to render
> The deeds of mercy. I have spoke thus much
> To mitigate the justice of thy plea,
> Which if thou follow, this strict court of Venice
> Must needs give sentence 'gainst the merchant there
>
> (4.1.179–200)

One of the things that is immediately noticeable about the passage is that the speaker, Portia, is a remarkably intelligent, eloquent, and assertive woman. As these are probably Portia's most recognizable lines of the play, a close reading of them would be a strong starting point for character analysis. In addition to displaying rhetorical skill, consider what these words say about their speaker. Traditionally, Portia was viewed as one of Shakespeare's most admirable heroines, but her popular appeal dipped in the late twentieth century. Why? Compare this speech to Portia's treatment of Shylock moments later. What does it say about the socially constructed limits of Portia's authority that she must speak these words disguised as a young man?

The opening lines of the speech praise the value of mercy, implicitly contrasting this attribute with Shylock's remorseless determination to execute Antonio. But as Portia gives her argument a religious turn, she sets up another contrast that directly reflects the core of the play's action. Comparing representations of Christian and Jew in Shakespeare's Venice might make for a very strong essay. In her speech, Portia proposes a Christian model of mercy, acknowledging that no person can be saved without the ultimate mercy of God, thus urging compassion among humans in their worldly affairs. If this sentiment is supposed to represent the Christian species of forgiveness, what is implied (or assumed) about the Jewish model? Commentators have traditionally viewed this as a conflict between two interpretations of law: the Christian one focusing on the spirit of the law and the Jewish one bound to the letter of the law. The writer might look for evidence of this dualism throughout the play. However, it might be wise for the writer to ask if this really is the full extent of what Shakespeare has in mind. After all, such a theological statement would be little more than an eloquent voicing of stereotypes. A student looking for more than this in the play should contextualize Portia's speech, locating it within the scene and play as a whole. The most important thing for the writer to seek out in this play might be irony, ways in which spoken words are undercut by a character's actions. Look for moments in which the Christian characters of the play say one thing and do another; they are often guilty of the same sins they hate and condemn Shylock for practicing. Portia's speech is followed almost immediately by an extremely harsh and merciless punishment of Shylock, one that not only denies him his bond but strips him of his identity and dignity. From this perspective, Portia's famous speech on mercy is a fake, a cruel trick no less disguised than its speaker.

Finally, Portia's speech raises an important point about Shakespeare's authorial presence and intention. It is, of course, impossible for us to know what the dramatist wanted to say, what he thought and felt. Nonetheless, for centuries critics and scholars have made great efforts at attempting to do just that. *The Merchant of Venice* provides the writer with an ideal opportunity to participate in this time-honored tradition: To what extent are the previously quoted lines—and others like them throughout the play—intended by Shakespeare to be ironic, or to what degree do we as modern readers and writers insert or project that irony because we wish to find it present? In other words, what balance should we as writers discussing *The Merchant of Venice* strike between what we hope is the spirit and what we can see is the letter of the play?

TOPICS AND STRATEGIES

Every essay requires a focus; you cannot write about everything in the play at once. As a specified focus evolves into a thesis, so observations develop into arguments. The starting point, nonetheless, always comes from a direct engagement of the text. The topic suggestions included here are geared toward helping you make the most of the budding ideas you will have as you read *The Merchant of Venice.* By no means should you feel limited to these topics, however.

Themes

When approaching some of the themes in the play, it may help the writer, first, to see if Shakespeare appears to make the theme you are considering a point of contrast between Shylock and the Christians of Venice. Next, you might ask whether any simple dichotomy (Christian mercy versus Jewish cruelty, for example) is undermined by the actions of Bassanio, Portia, and the other Christian characters.

Other themes, of course, will not necessarily invite that exact approach. For example, think about the theme of love in *The Merchant of Venice.* On the surface, the play appears to celebrate love and make use of it to shape the comic movement. But look closely at each of the couplings in the play, and you may find that the relationships in each case have question marks lingering over them. You might also want to extend your essay to cover different forms of love, such as the relationship between Shylock and Jessica (a potential source of sympathy for Shylock) or Antonio's "love" for and devotion to his friend Bassanio. Are there any idealized forms of love present in the play? Or, once you have scraped at the surface with a pointed reading of the text, can you see this as a text governed by cynicism and irony rather than romance and love? It might even be possible for the writer to turn the answer to this question into a thesis statement. An essay assessing the role of irony as a theme might provide the writer with a focused way of discussing *The Merchant of Venice* as a whole, while still allowing wide discussion of the play's characters and themes.

Sample Topics:

1. **Money and wealth:** Does money mean different things to the Venetian Christians than it does to Shylock? How much of the play's action is motivated by money?

For many critics, money is what propels the world of Shakespeare's Venice. It seems to motivate many of the choices made by characters, from Bassanio's quest for Portia to Lancelot Gobo's desire for a better livery. Look for ways in which money and wealth structure other characters and their actions. Assess, too, whether there are differences in how money is valued and treated between Belmont and Venice. What does money mean to Shylock? Look for examples in the text that hint at other factors motivating him, even while money continues to play a central role in his character formation. What does the play seem to say about usury, the act of charging interest on a loan? Compare Shylock's zeal for money to the Christians' financial dealings. Also, you might try to connect the theme of wealth and money to another recurring motif, that of "hazarding" or gambling. These two closely related themes overlap in parts of the text, especially the casket scenes in which Portia tests her suitors. Love and business perhaps become connected by the notion of gambling and risking all, just as Antonio does, first with his ships and then with his dangerous bond to Shylock on Bassanio's behalf.

2. **Fidelity:** This is a play that seems obsessed with bonds of different kinds, as well as the consequences of not honoring those bonds. What does the play have to say about faithfulness? How might this theme be influential in evaluating other thematic areas of the play?

Such an essay might establish a connection between the action surrounding Shylock's bond, and the subplot of Portia's ring in act 5. While the final act can seem at first glance unnecessary, a strong case could be made that it is integral to the play. Look for interconnecting issues raised by the two trials, that of Shylock in court and Bassanio in Belmont. With this essay, you might want to let the unexpected connection between the two plot lines suffice as your thesis, allowing room in your essay to show and explain similarities and meaningful points of difference. For example, obviously the marriage bond represented by Portia's ring is one that should be kept, while Shylock's bond is one that the play wants to see broken. Perhaps you might expand your essay to include other signs and symbols of faithfulness, from Jessica's sale of Shylock's engagement ring to the statements of religious devotion that reappear throughout the text—a writer might certainly extend her discussion to the infidelity of the Venetian Christians to their much professed and flaunted moral values. Finally, try to cement your discussion by asserting what faithfulness or fidelity finally means in the play. Are there any faithful characters? What are they faithful to? Does the play value fidelity?

Characters

All of the main characters in this play deserve and can support their own essays. While not drawn with the psychological complexity of Macbeth or Hamlet, for example, the characters in *The Merchant of Venice* are nonetheless fascinating, in part because of the gap that exists between so many of their statements and actions. Take Bassanio, for example. An essay on this character might turn on the question of his motives: Why does he pursue Portia? Should we see him as a gold-digging playboy or a romantic hero in the traditional vein? Begin by outlining what we learn of Bassanio's past in the opening acts. Assess his relationship with Antonio, and closely examine his reasons for seeking Portia (look, for example, at his ordering of Portia's qualities in act 1, scene 2, lines 161–76). Look for irony, too, in Bassanio's victory in the casket scene. What is the relationship between the moral of the lead casket and what we know of Bassanio's history and character?

An equally rich essay could be written about Shylock's daughter, Jessica. Like Bassanio, she is a character we seem asked to admire but might not be able to. Such an essay would begin by establishing the relationship between father and daughter, noting Jessica's various complaints but also carefully observing Shylock's treatment of and feeling for his daughter. Then ask yourself what motivates Jessica to elope with Lorenzo, sifting through her "escape" scene to assess once again the role of money and wealth. You might then proceed to look at how Jessica's flight influences our sympathies for Shylock as he discovers her loss (and the loss of his stolen money).

Sample Topics:

1. **Shylock:** How are we to view Shylock's character? What are his redeeming features, and how might we assess his function and meaning in Shakespeare's play?

There is so much to say about Shylock that one could write an entire book about him. John Gross has done just that with his readable and impeccably researched *Shylock: A Legend and Its Legacy.* The first challenge of dealing with Shylock, then, is in focusing your essay on a specific aspect of him, such as his redeeming characteristics, showing how a man who is clearly the antagonist of the play is also a victim. Once you have established this sympathetic position, next you might show how Shakespeare situates Shylock into his complex system of meaning. Both of these steps might involve pinpointing Shylock's position within the culture and society of Venice.

What picture of Shylock emerges in the opening scenes? Look for any evidence of how he is treated and viewed by Venetians, including Antonio. Equally, assess how Shylock views the citizens of Venice. Try to piece together Shylock's philosophy of money and wealth, looking in particular at any justifications he offers for his usury. Look, too, at his domestic life with Jessica. Locate details that might endear us to Shylock, especially in his response to Jessica's flight. Why does he pursue his revenge against Antonio? How do we feel about him once he has been defeated in the court, stripped of his money and religion?

This final question urges us to reflect on Shylock's function within the play's production of meaning. Try to think why Shakespeare creates such an ambiguous and rounded figure where other lesser artists might have settled for a stereotypically presented Jewish man to vilify. This approach, then, puts Shylock at the heart of the play's moral compass, again encouraging us to question the differences between Jew and Christian in Venice.

2. Antonio: Why is Antonio marginalized by the play, left out of the comic resolution? What is the cause of his unexplained melancholy voiced in the play's opening line?

Antonio is a somewhat obscure figure who has received considerable critical attention in recent years. Much of that interest has centered on his relationship with Bassanio, with critics commenting on the homosocial nature of his love for the young man. This affection, and the despondency caused by Bassanio's quest for a profitable marriage, is suggested as the root of Antonio's notable sadness. If you wished to pursue this aspect of Antonio's character, you might marshal other entries from Shakespeare's canon to your side. You can find Shakespeare treating the importance of male friendship in his early play *The Two Gentlemen of Verona,* but more readily available and interestingly rendered in his sonnets and the (coincidently named?) figure of Antonio in *Twelfth Night* (for a fuller discussion of what this latter essay might look like, see the Compare and Contrast section of the chapter on *Twelfth Night*). Bruce R. Smith and Valerie Traub are two critics who have led the way in considering these issues in Renaissance drama, and their work would be of help to students looking to bolster their writing with reference to outside sources.

More traditional approaches to Antonio focus on his financial dealings and what some critics refer to as his martyrdom. Compare Antonio's handling of money to Shylock's. Equally, however, you might find that Antonio can be contrasted to many of the play's characters in other ways, not least by way of his faithfulness to Bassanio. If you can arrive at a distinction or difference that separates Antonio from the other characters, see if you can use this to help explain why Shakespeare leaves Antonio noticeably out in the cold as the comic feast of resolution closes the play.

3. Portia: While Portia is an admirably strong and intelligent woman, how does she employ these virtues in controversial ways?

One starting point for an essay on this topic could be a consideration of the function of Belmont, Portia's home to which she is symbolically linked. Shakespeare's comedies typically feature a "green world," a setting in which characters escape the rules and logic of the court in order to find themselves and resolve problems that are rooted back in "the real world" of the city. While Belmont is the green world of this play, assess whether it serves the typical function of such a setting. How similar or different is Belmont from Venice? Again, it is the role of money and wealth that may be your starting point here.

Finally, look critically at the ring plot that occupies the fifth act. While Portia's trick with the ring and barely veiled threats of infidelity are bawdily funny, how do they further threaten the already compromised comic ending and connect back to themes of trial and fidelity established earlier in the play?

History and Context

We have already seen how a character study of Antonio might take our writing down a distinctly historical route. If we are to understand the implications of a homosocial love between Antonio and Bassanio, we must cite more than our twenty-first-century notions of sexuality. An essay treating this aspect of Antonio, or this theme in Shakespeare generally, must attempt to understand the historical context. Although historians disagree as to how the Renaissance perceived intimate, even sexual relationships between men, it is certain they did understand and view them differently than we do today. Many argue that the category of homosexual did not even exist in the Renaissance, and it appears it was common for some men to speak of a male friendship as idealized, "better" than a relationship with a woman precisely because it lacked the complicated and potentially ruinous sexual dimension. This theme was of enormous interest to Shakespeare and appears frequently throughout his work, so it is clear that a reading of Antonio might benefit from historical research.

If a character study of Antonio could be redirected by relevant historical research, the theme of money and wealth is unquestionably another essay topic that could likewise benefit. Historians talk of the early modern period as witnessing the birth of what we call capitalism. The way wealth and status were generated changed during Shakespeare's lifetime. Medieval economic practices such as the feudal system receded and were gradually replaced by what we might think of as early free markets. New attitudes to private property and consumerism radically changed the meaning of wealth, and some critics have suggested that in *The Merchant of Venice* Shakespeare breathes a sigh of disappointment and disapproval with the emerging ethos of capitalism. To explore this contention, find ways in which Shakespeare's play seems to speak out against a culture preoccupied with mercantilism and profit, then, from these observations, develop a reading of Shakespeare's play as satire or social commentary. Lisa Jardine's book on consumption and business in Renaissance Europe, *Worldly Goods: A New History of the Renaissance,* is a good place to begin research in this area. However, there might be one strand of social commentary in the play more apparent to many readers that the emergence of capitalism: the representation and treatment of Jews in Elizabethan England.

Sample Topic:

1. **Judaism in Renaissance Europe:** Does Shakespeare use *The Merchant of Venice* to condemn anti-Semitism or at least to challenge some of its harsher commonplaces?

   Such an essay attempts to see Shakespeare's text as social commentary, a document in which the dramatist contemplates the figure of the Jew in his time. Obviously, the important thing here is to recognize that you are no longer treating Shylock as a self-contained character in a self-contained play but as a creation pieced together out of cultural tradition and a particular historic moment. Asking what Shakespeare does with that mix, how he processes the ideas, beliefs, and images of his age, is the key to this essay. James Shapiro's *Shakespeare and the Jews,* a seminal work in this particular aspect of Shakespeare studies, would make an excellent point of departure for the researching writer.

   It will be helpful if the writer is aware of the literary tradition forming the backdrop to Shakespeare's play. In early modern Europe and even earlier, anti-Semitism was rooted in biblical accounts of the death of Christ. It was this perceived "blame" for Christ's death that spawned popular resentment of Jews and a virile tradition of folk belief and literature peopled by countless variations of the murderous Jew. This culture of hatred can be found even in the works of Chaucer, whose "Prioress's Tale" (one of *The Canterbury Tales*) tells the quintessential story of a young Christian boy killed by envious Jews. As is discussed in the Compare and Contrast section, this tradition was present in Shakespeare's day, most visibly in Christopher Marlowe's play *The Jew of Malta* (a work most certainly at the forefront of Shakespeare's mind as he wrote *The Merchant of Venice*).

Though Shakespeare was surrounded by stock literary representations of Jews, he probably never encountered an actual Jewish person. The number of Jews in Shakespeare's England is difficult to estimate but probably numbered only in the low hundreds. Jews had been expelled from English soil in 1290, and the remaining small number was made up mostly of immigrants from southern Europe who did not openly practice their faith. It might seem, then, as though Judaism was hardly a topical matter for Shakespeare to address, but Marlowe's play and the arrest and execution of a man named Roderigo Lopez gave the subject contemporary resonance. Lopez was a Jewish doctor accused of plotting to kill Queen Elizabeth, and his traitor's death—hung, drawn, and quartered—in 1594 would have stoked anti-Jewish sentiment enough to make Shakespeare's play very much of the moment.

The writer might wish to investigate this cultural and historic context further, assessing Shakespeare's response to it. The essay could be structured around the posing of a provocatively simple question: Is this an anti-Semitic play? Of course, you should answer this as you wish, but a safe path to steer might be the predictably qualified answer of "yes and no." As many commentators have reminded us, it would have been impossible for Shakespeare to entirely discard the intellectual baggage of his time; look for ways in which Shylock retains some of the elements of the stock Jew and how Shakespeare's play employs them to bring paying customers into his theater. Equally, seek ways in which Shakespeare, even if he does not reject the anti-Semitic tradition of his culture, at least reconsiders and revises it. Your task as writer here is to catalog your evidence on either side, then assess the balance that Shakespeare strikes.

Form and Structure

The Merchant of Venice is, of course, a comedy, but an essay exploring the problems of this definition could prove rewarding. Most critics do not label the work as one of the problem plays or problem comedies, a small group of later works that explicitly and innovatively challenge the meaning of comic drama. In many ways, however, *The Merchant of Venice* anticipates the challenges to comic form offered by later plays such as *All's Well That Ends Well* and *Measure for Measure*. When Shakespeare challenges the comedy as a dramatic form, the approach he seemed to favor most, he typically included all the saccharine elements of traditional comedy present, shifting and transforming them just enough to produce a final and lingering bitter flavor. One of Shakespeare's problem comedies may well end in marriage, as a comedy typically does, and avoid death as it must, yet its resolutions appear intentionally incomplete, its air tainted by the breath of tragedy.

Sample Topic:

1. **The limits of comedy in *The Merchant of Venice*:** Despite the comic closure of the play, does *The Merchant* function successfully as a comedy? What elements of the play question or hinder its comic movement, even after the union of lovers in marriage?

Such an essay might start by looking at the end of the play, the moment in which a comedy should offer resolution and hope. Irrespective of the appearance of unity, look for sources of discord and dissent in the final acts. The most obvious character to start with might be Shylock, but note also how Antonio, despite the return of his ships, seems excluded from the festivities at the close of the play. How are these two figures marginalized? Consider the impact of the ring plot on the comic movement, also. While it is funny, its consequences are far from comic in the formal sense of that word. Think about how Portia's threats of infidelity undercut the reconciling comic power of marriage. The thing to consider as you write this essay is effect; how does this play, despite its seeming comic promise, finally manage to spread a little of Antonio's enigmatic sadness to its audience?

Compare and Contrast

One of the most prominent approaches to this play, the weighing of Shylock against the Venetian Christians, inherently takes the form of compare and contrast. If adopting this approach, be aware of the way Shakespeare draws parallels where audiences would have only expected distinctions. An essay comparing Belmont to Venice might also encourage the writer to find unexpected similarities. Look for ways in which the magical, carefree Belmont is as focused on money and superficiality as Venice, the city that embodied luxurious excess and wealth for the early moderns. Approaching a compare and contrast essay from a character perspective, writers might look for yet more unanticipated common ground between Shylock and Antonio. While the play hinges on Shylock's antipathy for Antonio, what do they have in common? Look for ways in which they are both cogs in the wheel of Venetian capitalism, perhaps to explain how both characters seem to lead marginal lives despite their wealth. Yet another approach might be to look elsewhere in Shakespeare's canon for related works. *The Tempest* and *Othello* are major plays that also treat "otherness," exploring the confrontation between white Europeans and people of different religions or races. Such an essay might turn on a comparison of Shylock with Othello or Caliban, arguing as you see fit for similarities or differences in Shakespeare's level of sympathy for these characters. However, perhaps the most resonant compare and contrast opportunity that links *The Merchant of Venice* to another text requires the discovery of another great playwright of the English Renaissance.

Sample Topics:

1. **Comparing Shylock to Christopher Marlowe's Barabas in** ***The Jew of Malta:*** While both Shakespeare and Marlowe base plays around a Jewish antagonist, how much do Shylock and Barabas have in common? Despite their essential differences, how might Shakespeare and Marlowe finally be using these central characters from *The Merchant of Venice* and *The Jew of Malta* to create related effects and social commentary?

Marlowe's play came first, so a good approach might be to assess how Shakespeare builds on *The Jew of Malta* to create his work and his representation of Shylock. You might first consider the differences between Barabas and Shylock, some of which should be quite clear. Marlowe seems to be relying far more on the stereotypical figure of the villainous Jew, much like that found in Chaucer's "Prioress's Tale" and countless vulgar ballads and stories. Is he doing so ironically? Find examples of this tradition in Marlowe's portrait, looking at moments such as the slave market scene in which Barabas boasts of his astonishingly prolific evil. Contrast this to Shylock's altogether subtler villainy. However, you may find a few ways in which Barabas is less stereotypical. For example, critics have observed that, while Shylock earns his money through usury, Barabas has earned his great wealth primarily through long-distance business ventures like Antonio's. Other distinctions can be found, for example, in the relationships Barabas and Shylock have with their daughters, Abigail and Jessica.

Having found similarities or differences as you wish, such an essay might turn to a consideration of what effect each dramatist seeks through his central Jewish figure. Look especially at how both Marlowe and Shakespeare set up divisions between Jewish and Christian communities that essentially become engines for satire and comparison. Although vastly different, what might connect, for example, Ferneze in Marlowe's play to Bassanio in Shakespeare's?

2. **Contrasting Shakespeare's play to Michael Radford's film adaptation of *The Merchant of Venice* (2004):** What strategies does Radford use in adapting Shakespeare's play? What are the most significant interpretative moves made by the film, and what are the effects of these choices?

Radford's film adaptation of the play, a lavish production with a star cast, will surely feature regularly in classroom discussions of *The Merchant* for many years to come. While it is faithful to the play to a great extent, it does offer some interpretations beyond the text, primarily through visual additions to the original text. One aspect of cinematic adaptation to consider is the shot that, without adding a word to the dialogue that was not in Shakespeare's play, can radically alter the play. Pay close attention to such moves made by Radford. For a start, what is the effect of staging Antonio's spitting on Shylock, an act that is only mentioned but not portrayed in the play? Why does Radford invent and show us a number of early scenes in which Christians victimize Jews? Such an essay might reflect, too, on the visibly eroticized relationship between Antonio and Bassanio. Most importantly, however, think about the effect and meaning of the final montage. Consider the effect of shots showing Shylock and Antonio alone as the play closes, but especially think about what might be Radford's most daring visual invention: a closing shot of Jessica and the ring she was rumored to have sold for a monkey. What are the implications of Jessica not selling the ring, both for her character and, in a sense, for Shylock? As your thesis, attempt to characterize early in your essay the governing logic or pattern of Radford's interpretative choices in *The Merchant of Venice*.

Bibliography for *The Merchant of Venice*

Gross, John. *Shylock: A Legend and Its Legacy.* New York: Touchstone, 1992.

Edelman, Charles. "Which is the Jew That Shakespeare Knew? Shylock on the Elizabethan Stage" *Shakespeare Survey: An Annual Survey of Shakespeare Studies and Production 52, (1999).*

Jardine, Lisa. *Worldly Goods: A New History of the Renaissance.* New York: W. W. Norton, 1998.

Levin, Carole. *Shakespeare's Foreign Worlds: National and Transnational Identities in the Elizabethan Age.* Ithaca, NY: Cornell University Press, 2009.

Orgel, Stephen. "Shylock's Tribe." *Shakespeare and the Mediterranean.* Tom Clayton, et al, eds. Newark, DE: University of Delaware Press, 2004.

Shapiro, James. *Shakespeare and the Jews.* New York: Columbia University Press, 1996.

Sinfield, Alan. "How to Read The Merchant of Venice without Being Heterosexist." *Shakespeare, Feminism and Gender.* Kate Chedgzoy, ed. Basingstoke, England: Palgrave, 2001.

THE MERRY WIVES OF WINDSOR

READING TO WRITE

*T*HE *MERRY Wives of Windsor* is in many ways different from the rest of Shakespeare's comic output. First, and most importantly, it is genuinely comic. It is the only extant Shakespeare play that can make claims to pure comedy, to being truly and unambiguously joyful. To support this claim, though, we have to see the punishments meted out to Falstaff as humorous and justified (and the case has been made by critics that the latter, especially in the case of the braggart knight's final humiliation at the hands of the vindictive fairy children, is actually *not* justifiable). Moreover, we have to undermine the happiness of Shakespeare's apparently joyous mature comedy, *As You Like It,* a work that may challenge any notion of *The Merry Wives of Windsor*'s relative uniqueness. However, the over-the-top resolution of that play invites us to actively question the comic forces at work. Thus, it seems that *The Merry Wives of Windsor* is alone among Shakespeare's comedies for its wholehearted and unironic embrace of the comic spirit and mode.

The play emerges as different from the rest of Shakespeare's canon not only in style but in tone. Perhaps the only other Shakespeare play that resembles this one is *The Comedy of Errors,* another slapstick farce that gets its kicks from violent beatings and mistaken identities. *The Comedy of Errors,* however, is an unmistakably sad and anxious play despite its frenzied plot and outlandish premise. The play, after all, begins with a man being sentenced to death and his nervous meditations throughout on the instability of human identity. While *The Comedy of Errors* is primarily philosophical, *The Merry Wives of Windsor* is principally socio-logical, interested not in the abstract so much as the everyday lives of ordinary people. While *The Comedy of Errors* ends somewhat ambigu-ously, the confusion over identities persisting after the apparent final resolution, *The Merry Wives of Windsor* resolves happily with even Fal-staff rehabilitated and forgiven for his lecherous scheming. Moreover, the play ends without *As You Like It*'s recourse to magic and miracle, the comic resolution brought about by nothing more fantastic than the wit of its titular characters.

To get a sense of the play's comic meanderings, take a look at a short and often cited passage from the play. The famous lines come as Mis-tresses Ford and Page get ready to dress Falstaff as "the witch of Brent-ford," a move they rightly expect will lead to the lewd knight's beating at the hands of Ford's husband:

> Hang him, dishonest varlet! We cannot misuse him enough.
> We'll leave a proof by that which we will do,
> Wives may be merry, and yet honest, too.
> We do not act that often jest and laugh.
> 'Tis old but true: 'still swine eats all the draff.' (4.2.86–91.)

The first thing to note here is one of the most important critical points made about the play: Mistress Page (the speaker) and Mistress Ford are in charge. Their language confirms this with bold statements and sure claims about what they will do coupled with confident moral certainties about their actions. Many critics have discussed this fruit-fully, but it seems clear that Shakespeare is once again interested in giving women authority in his plays. We see him do this with Rosa-lind, too, in *As You Like It,* but her considerable talents are employed in finally far less subversive ways than the merry wives'. *The Merchant of Venice*'s Portia, with her sharp legal mind that coldly cuts down Shy-lock, perhaps resembles the wives most closely, but she must dress as a man to achieve this authority and seems in the end unnervingly mean-spirited and untrustworthy. The wives emerge as unique, then, among Shakespeare's comic heroines; they are both edgy and in control, sub-versive but never destructive. Somehow Mistresses Ford and Page never let their considerable agency go to their heads in a way that might risk alienating them from the audience, as is the case with Portia, and, more clearly still, with Helena in *All's Well That Ends Well.*

These distinctions, however, raise issues of threat and containment that are important within Shakespeare's comedy as a whole. Mistress Page tells us that wives can be merry and honest, playful and honorable at the same time. As often with Shakespeare, the implications of this range or complexity appear to center on striking a balance between extremes, finding that sacred and cherished middle ground. The wives are contained by the system, the society in which they live, and work only within it, though unquestionably at its edges, but never outside it. They know the extent to which they can challenge gender expectation, and while they may walk the gender line, they never cross it. Thus, if you write on gender in the play, look for ways to illuminate complexity rather than settling for somewhat bland statements about early modern female power.

Finally, with the quoted passage, it is worth noting the folksy axiom at the end. Mistress Page uses this saying, the meaning of which is essentially that the quiet ones are often the most misbehaving, to justify the raucous punishment of Falstaff but also to explain away their deceit of Ford's husband. However, an aspect worth noting is the everyday quality of the phrase, its connection with the real lives of real people. The phrase (not in use now) is clearly well-known to Shakespeare's audience, familiar as both "old and true." It is attuned to a rustic life, one in which the habits of livestock can provide important insights into the behavior of friends and neighbors. The phrase provides a minute example of a broad and deep aspect of the play's identity, namely its desire to represent the adventures of ordinary people, magnified as farcical entertainment must be, of course, but loyal to their world and the details of their lives. Many critics have eloquently and powerfully written on what they have called the "middle class" nature of this play, the way in which it depicts, as they term it, the formation of a new class grouping during the Renaissance. These social concerns offer the opportunity to write politically insightful essays as well as historically sensitive papers informed by accessible research.

TOPICS AND STRATEGIES

Every essay requires a focus; you cannot write about everything in the play at once. As a specified focus evolves into a thesis, so observations develop into arguments. The starting point, nonetheless, always comes from a direct engagement of the text. The topic suggestions included here are geared toward helping you make the most of the budding ideas you will have as you read *The Merry Wives of Windsor*. By no means should you feel limited to these topics, however.

Themes

Writing on themes in *The Merry Wives of Windsor* is ideal for students who prefer to work with sociological or historical material, rather than the kind of abstract and philosophical concerns that dominate the essay writer's landscape when facing a play such as *The Two Gentlemen of Verona* or *The Comedy of Errors*. However, there is a link between these three texts that is worth noting. While *The Two Gentlemen of Verona* and *The Comedy of Errors* are explicitly engaged in a meditation on human identity, and in particular on the unstable and shifting nature of the individual, *The Merry Wives of Windsor* seems much more grounded in the real or everyday world. Still, the subjects of the respective plays are essentially the same, though viewed through different lenses. *The Merry Wives of Windsor* is, after all, also about identity—its instability and transformation—specifically an individual's social identity, as well as the broader societal identity of early modern England. Just as the characters in *The Two Gentlemen of Verona* and *The Comedy of Errors* are faced with their own evolutions and transitions, *The Merry Wives of Windsor* is a snapshot of a society experiencing significant change and transition. The term *early modern* aptly suggests the mix of continuity and change experienced in Shakespeare's time; the world around him was not "modern" (by our standards), was unmistakably a different place from the world we inhabit, a mindset and lifestyle still rooted in the centuries-old ways and traditions of the medieval period. Nonetheless, Shakespeare's age witnessed the beginning of social and political systems we recognize as integral to the fabric of our society—not "modern" to our eyes, but nonetheless we see ourselves hazily in the mirror of their lives: *early* modern. *The Merry Wives of Windsor* vividly represents some of these social transitions and, in doing so, offers rich opportunities to the essay writer.

Sample Topics:

1. **Marriage:** What does the "marriage debate" in *The Merry Wives of Windsor* entail?

During Shakespeare's lifetime, the idea of marriage was hotly contested but not in the sense that people were asking whether or not marriage was a good option or the right thing to do. It was unquestionably still the case that marriage was expected and, for women especially, the failure to be attached could have dire social consequences. Instead, people were asking questions about how a marriage should appear, how it might best be structured and organized. For example, what should the relationship between husband and wife be? It was, of course, taken for granted that a man would be in charge within the domestic sphere, just as the monarch must be in charge in the political sphere; these were viewed as the natural hierarchies of power, and to threaten them, at the state or domestic level, carried severe penalties respectively. Obviously a traitor to the state, someone who threatened the existing order, would face torture and execution. Equally, a woman who asserted too much control over her husband, as well as a husband who let his wife have too much control over his household, could be subjected to a variety of officially sanctioned public humiliations and punishments. The debate, then, was not about whether women should possess or wield domestic power but about issues that seem more fundamental: Should men respect their wives? To what extent should men be able to beat their wives? Although the man is clearly in charge, Shakespeare's age asked, should the domestic sphere resemble something like a democracy or a tyranny, a partnership or the autocratic rule of the husband? Moreover, another fundamental question emerged: Should we marry for love, or should other concerns take priority? Particularly at the upper end of society, marriages were often arranged by two sets of parents long before the husband and wife to be were ready to wed. These strategically planned relationships might be used to consolidate wealth or forge useful political alliances, but traditionally speaking they had not been based on love.

It is easy to see, then, how *The Merry Wives of Windsor* captures aspects of this debate onstage. As a writer, you should obviously seek out the different voices in this debate. What is interesting, however, is that you will likely be able to identify definitively the position the play takes on the issues it raises. The play appears to come to fairly solid conclusions, unlike Shakespeare's dramas in general and certainly his comedies in particular.

How you shape the abundance of material on this subject is up to you, of course, but it is likely you will want to include treatment of Master Ford's jealousy (look closely at passages containing the lines 2.1.60, 2.2.270, and 3.2.30) set in opposition to Master Page's more trusting and easygoing respect of his wife. You should certainly include mention of the issue of balance in this regard too (4.4.5). Then, you may want to explore the implications of the subplot for the marriage debate, as well. Demonstrate how the Pages disagree over Anne's marriage partner and, most importantly, how the play seems to endorse Anne's plotting to outwit her parents and marry Fenton. The passage containing the line 5.5.200 will naturally allow you to make some bold but justifiable claims about the play's marriage politics. Finally, you will most likely also want to assess the role of wife as understood and enacted by Mistresses Page and Ford. The next topic discussion could prove helpful in this regard.

2. **Gender:** Is the play Shakespeare's boldest advocacy of woman's agency? If so, what kind of female power does he appear to be endorsing in *The Merry Wives of Windsor*?

Even at the surface level, the gender politics of *Merry Wives* are fascinating and worth exploring. It is possible to see the wives as unique creations among Shakespeare's women, sympathetic and subversive at the same time. As many critics have observed, the wives take control of their situation and push the plot forward by punishing Falstaff and correcting Master Ford's distrust of his wife. By looking at the passages containing these three lines, 2.1.25, 3.3.165 or 4.2.190, for example, you should be able to illustrate effectively the kind of power you feel these women exert on the men around them and the play itself. Obviously, you may want to include

Anne Page in your analysis of self-confident women (perhaps making something of the irony that her victory comes at the expense of her mother's wishes and own plotting against her husband). Also, as it appears so central to the play's vision of dynamic women, what do you make of the insistence on the connection between being merry and "honest"?

To enhance your discussion of this topic, it may be a good idea to look at how men view women in the play, too, and the punishment or correction meted out to them by the dramatist. Looking at the figures of Ford and Falstaff through such moments as Falstaff's loaded image of conquest (1.3.56–64) or Ford's sometimes vicious expressions of misogyny (4.2.220, for example) will usefully support your material on the women themselves. However you arrange this material, you will most likely want to spend a good amount of time on the fifth act, assessing how the merriment of the wives is maintained and the implications of this for the play's politics.

3. **Society:** In addition to issues surrounding marriage, what other kinds of social flux can be witnessed in the play?

It can be difficult to follow the subtle currents of class consciousness running throughout the play. However, along with historical research into class mobility in the early modern period (one valuable recent work to consult is H. R. French's *The Middle Sort of People in Provincial England: 1600–1750*, Oxford University Press, 2007), this theme could be the foundation for a sophisticated discussion.

First, there is Falstaff's example of a nobleman down on his luck, someone with a title but little else to trade with. You may want to note, for example, as others have effectively done, the class connotations of Falstaff's lines preceding and following 2.2.253. Related to Falstaff in this way is the titled but poor Fenton, someone who openly admits he had originally sought Anne for her money (3.4.10). Together, these two provide examples of a traditional elite being overtaken by social change and a new kind of mercantile class. These and more social nuances can be witnessed in the intrigues of the Pages' marriage negotiations, and you should follow these carefully.

Characters

Characters provide a promising avenue for the student writer. As is evident in other works, sometimes the characters of earlier Shakespearean comedies can be little more than mouthpieces for a particular ideology or bodies through which to explore a particular philosophical concern. So in a play like *The Two Gentlemen of Verona* or *The Comedy of Errors*, character analysis and thematic analysis overlap to the point of becoming all but one. In *The Merry Wives of Windsor*, however, though there will obviously be significant overlap, for example, between an essay on gender and an essay on Mistress Page, the characters here are vivid and individual. Master Ford is far more than simply an emblem of misogynistic bigotry; in his disguise as Brooke, we are witness to some odd, intriguing moments of psychological complexity. The play also contains one of Shakespeare's great characters, the legendary Falstaff. Wherever Falstaff appears in a Shakespeare work, the writer can be sure of ample material.

Sample Topics:

   1. **Falstaff:** Commentators often talk about such things as Falstaff's comic "spirit" or power. With reference to the *Merry Wives of Windsor*, in particular, how is this comic presence defined?

   Falstaff most memorably appears in Shakespeare's *Henry IV, Parts 1* and *2.* In these plays, he is an ambiguous figure attempting to influence the young Prince Hal, who is soon to be crowned Henry V. Falstaff is a creation of comic excess and selfishness in the first of these plays, a sometimes dark presence that is often said to represent the untamable spirit of self-indulgence and even of life itself. However, by the second play, when Hal finally breaks from Falstaff, we see the latter in a more sobering light, an old man on the eve of a death we only learn of in *Henry V.* Falstaff's appearance in *The Merry Wives of Windsor* is partially in keeping with the Falstaff of these two history plays, but in its purely comic milieu the play represents a major relocation of the braggart soldier. This shift is traditionally explained by stage folklore telling us that Elizabeth I requested Shakespeare write a play in which Falstaff was in love. If this is indeed true, Shakespeare did not quite, in a sense, meet the demands made of him. After all, Falstaff's motives seem to have nothing to do with love and everything to do with the flesh and money. We cannot say we see Falstaff in love, then, but we definitely see him in trouble. These troubles, moreover, are both universal and particular to the early modern moment—the desires and limits of the physical body set alongside the particular concerns of a nobleman whose title and estate have come to be of very little value in practice.

You may want to make use of the early sketch of Falstaff provided in and around 1.3.36, as well as his loaded image of conquest about 30 lines later. His fascination with his body is likely to be worth discussing (see 2.2.125, for example, among other moments), as is his sense of social superiority articulated notably in 2.2.246. There is another moment of self-appraisal from Falstaff at 4.5.89–90, and an interesting self-portrait of a body even Hell cannot contain (4.5.31). These are worth exploring and citing in an essay assessing Falstaff's moral identity, but perhaps more unexpected is the move toward reconciliation and shame at the close of the play. Does *The Merry Wives of Windsor* finally tame Falstaff?

2. **Master Ford:** What threat does Ford pose to the comic movement of the play, and how is he reconciled within the comic resolution?

Like Falstaff, Ford presents a threat to the happiness of the women, and their plot to punish Falstaff fortuitously serves as an opportunity to correct the error of Ford's ways too. He is the model of a certain kind of masculinity, and, interestingly, it is he who must yield to a new understanding of marriage politics, not the women (the very opposite, say, of *The*

Taming of The Shrew, in which it is Kate who must learn how to become a more understanding and cooperative spouse by early modern standards).

Ford's gender politics and philosophy of marriage are explicitly articulated at a number of points in the play: 2.1.160 and 2.1.205, for example. You could make very good use of the odd moments of irony on display when Ford is disguised as Brooke (2.2.175, 2.2.270, 3.2.30, 3.5.120) and will almost certainly want to reflect on the general viciousness of Ford's speech at 4.2.16–22 and his violent behavior later in the same scene. All of this is likely to lead you to Ford's epiphany at 4.4.5, part of an exchange worth careful attention, as the reformed Ford is welcomed back into the fold and in on the joke against Falstaff.

Incidentally, an essay on Master Page could be constructed using much of the same material cited above—Ford's articulation of his own philosophy is usually accompanied by an explicit rejection of Page's way of thinking. You will need to sift through these, of course, to find the most appropriate material, but also consider adding discussion of how Page rejects Fenton and of Page's own final acceptance of the lesson *The Merry Wives of Windsor* teaches him.

Form and Genre

The Merry Wives of Windsor can be distinguished from all other comedies Shakespeare wrote by its genuinely comic resolution. Even the punishment of Falstaff, a potential problem if it can be viewed as extreme, disproportionate, or a joke taken too far, seems to be viewed as nothing more than "honest knaveries" (4.4.79). To understand the implications of this further, look at a related plotline from a later comedy, *Twelfth Night*. In that play, Sir Toby and his fellow conspirators play a practical joke on the puritanical Malvolio, which ends with the latter imprisoned, treated like a man gone insane, and roundly mocked and humiliated. Even Sir Toby acknowledges that he would like to be rid of the joke, suggesting that even he, the Falstaffian spirit of comic excess in that play, thinks the joke is no longer funny. Malvolio emerges from confinement at the end of the play as a pained and unforgiving man, storming offstage for the final time as he vows revenge. The contrast between Malvolio and Falstaff's response to their respective predicaments is illustrative of the fundamental differences between the versions of the comic form as presented in each play.

Sample Topic:

1. **Comedy in *The Merry Wives of Windsor*:** Does this play actually have a perfectly happy ending?

If this question were asked of any other comedy by Shakespeare, the answer would be a resounding or qualified but nonetheless confident "no." As Malvolio's vow of vengeance at the end of *Twelfth Night* effectively demonstrates, Shakespeare routinely refuses to end his comedies by fully giving into the force of comic or blissful resolution. Even as the two central pairs of lovers come together amid seemingly miraculous revelations, Malvolio's bitterness, as well as the removal of Sir Andrew and Antonio from the comic feast, cast a conspicuous shadow over the festive conclusion. A similar reading could be offered for every other comedy by Shakespeare, except, that is, *The Merry Wives of Windsor*. Falstaff seems reconciled to the justice of his punishment, and the play hardly seems to be anxious in the face of the social changes the work mirrors.

For an analysis of the upbeat nature of the play's comic closure, you should focus on issues of acceptance and goodwill amply displayed in the fifth act. Consider the numerous ways that people who should have legitimate complaints at the outcome of the action (and this movement actually stretches back to Ford's epiphany in 4.4) are easily reconciled to events at the end of the play. Think, too, about issues of education and improvement, how people are "better" than they were at the beginning of the play.

Compare and Contrast

The Merry Wives of Windsor offers a range of potential compare and contrast topics for the essay writer. There are numerous internal options, pairings generated within the play, as well as "external" combinations, pairings that take elements of the play and consider them alongside one of Shakespeare's other texts. For an example of the former, in addition to the combination of Masters Ford and Page considered in this section, a comparison of Fenton and his fellow suitors would be a strong approach, particularly if infused with the kind of class consciousness the play raises. An obvious choice for an external compare and contrast paper, on the other hand, would be to look at Falstaff's different appearances in Shakespeare's drama.

Sample Topics:

1. **Comparing *The Merry Wives of Windsor* and *The Taming of the Shrew*:** Can we say that gender roles in these two plays are reversed, making Master Ford the "shrew" figure of his play? If so, what is the political impact of this move?

   There are several useful intersections between these two plays. For example, they are both discussions of marriage, though it is ultimately harder to pin down *The Taming of the Shrew*'s politics than it is that of *The Merry Wives of Windsor*. It is possible that both plays make a strong case for the so-called companionate marriage, the idea that a marriage should be a partnership founded on mutual respect and love. Do you see this in *The Taming of the Shrew*? For example, you may want to make something of the much discussed equality of wits between Kate and Petruccio, two outsiders who resemble each other in their disregard for social conventions, possibly suggesting that Kate's transformation is the result of politic calculations on her part as she seeks an agreeable life with her new husband. The case for an endorsement of companionate marriage in *The Merry Wives of Windsor* is, of course, notably clearer. However, this clarity can be also used to support a like-minded reading of *The Taming of the Shrew*—it seems a reasonable deduction that Shakespeare's thinking could not have shifted so radically in the several years separating the plays.

   Another way of approaching a comparison of these two plays would be to observe that, in *The Merry Wives of Windsor*, it is the husband rather than the wife who must be "tamed,"

moderated in order to fit in with the expectations of his partner. An essay exploring Master Ford's position as the play's
Kate then, with the direct implication that the antics of his wife
signal her resemblance to the boisterous and abusive Petruccio, might make for an unexpected variation on a theme.

2. **Comparing Master Ford and Master Page:** Despite their
   obvious differences, in what ways can these two men be said to
   finally resemble each other?

While most readers would anticipate an essay on these two
men to stress obvious differences in the way they treat their
wives, an interesting and unexpected essay might focus on
similarities. While you certainly do not want to dismiss the
important conversation that comes out of the Ford/Page
opposition, it may increase our awareness of the play's gender
dynamics if we can explore how the two husbands nonetheless
can be said to resemble each other. This can primarily be done
through careful analysis of the subplot in which Page also
tries to curtail the choices of the women in his life, his wife
and daughter. In addition, you may wish to discuss how the
play symbolically joins the two husbands through the motif of
epiphany and acceptance, both men being "corrected" despite
the apparent moral advantages of Page over Ford. Perhaps *The
Merry Wives of Windsor* playfully believes that if many a late
Elizabethan man needs to be educated and reformed in his
maintenance of the domestic sphere, there may be no better
instructors than the likes of Mistresses Ford and Page.

Bibliography for *The Merry Wives of Windsor*

Barton, Anne. "Falstaff and the Comic Community." *Shakespeare's "Rough
    Magic": Renaissance Essays in Honor of C. L. Barber.* Peter Erickson and
    Coppelia Kahn, eds. Newark: University of Delaware Press, 1985: 131–48.
Erickson, Peter. "The Order of the Garter, the Cult of Elizabeth, and Class-Gen-
    der Tensions in *The Merry Wives of Windsor*." *Shakespeare Reproduced: The
    Text in History and Ideology.* Jean Howard and Marion F. O'Conner, eds.
    New York: Methuen, 1987: 116–42.

Holland, Peter. "*The Merry Wives of Windsor*: the Performance of Community." *Shakespeare Bulletin*, 23, 2005: 5–18.

Hunt, Maurice. "'Gentleness' and Social Class in *The Merry Wives of Windsor*." *Comparative Drama*, Winter 2008: 409–32.

Parker, Patricia. "*The Merry Wives of Windsor* and Shakespearean Translation." *Modern Language Quarterly*, 42, 1991: 225–61.

Salingar, Leo. "The Englishness of *The Merry Wives of Windsor*." *Cahiers Elisabéthains: Late Medieval and Renaissance Studies*, 59, 2001: 9–25.

A MIDSUMMER NIGHT'S DREAM

READING TO WRITE

THE CHALLENGE of writing about *A Midsummer Night's Dream* lies partly in ordering and structuring the play's purposeful disorder. The reader or spectator of the play has the pleasure of losing herself in its maze of magic and misunderstanding, but the writer must move beyond this delightful confusion toward clarity and a solid argument. *A Midsummer Night's Dream* houses its motifs of confusion, blurring, and distortion in a tightly arranged and scrupulously written play, one filled with parallel movements and consistent thematic patterns, each of which is extremely useful to the essay writer. Another aspect of the work, the presence of the seemingly indistinguishable lovers and the twisting movement of their affections, is actually just another part of the play's well-structured conversation on the theme of love. The interchangeable lovers and their oscillating passions become symbols for that most fickle, illogical, and bewildering of emotions. So for all its playfulness, at the core of *A Midsummer Night's Dream* are serious and complex ideas about human relations, romantic and otherwise. Bringing these ideas to the surface, examining and engaging them, will, of course, also be at the core of many good essays about the play.

Different types of love are on display in the play, not just romantic passion but familial love as well. The following passage comes from act 2, scene 1. As Titania and Oberon argue over the guardianship of the changeling boy, Titania bases her claim on a deep emotional connection to the boy's mother.

His mother was a vot'ress of my order,
And in the spiced Indian air by night
Full often hath she gossiped by my side,
And sat with me on Neptune's yellow sands,
Marking th' embarked traders on the flood,
When we have laughed to see the sails conceive
And grow big-bellied with the wanton wind,
Which she with pretty and with swimming gait
Following, her womb then rich with my young squire,
Would imitate, and sail upon the land
To fetch me trifles, and return again
As from a voyage, rich with merchandise.
But she, being mortal, of that boy did die;
And for her sake do I rear up her boy;
And for her sake I will not part with him. (2.1.122–37)

Perhaps the first things to emerge from a close reading of this passage are the twin notes of the exotic and the erotic. The "spiced Indian air by night," the yellow sands of Neptune, and the sight of trading ships hauling foreign cargos across the ocean all contribute to a lush, exotic, and fanciful pattern of imagery present in much of the play. Closely related are the powerfully erotic connotations of the passage, again striking a tone found throughout the play. While some critics suggest that both Oberon and Titania display an eroticized attraction to the boy himself, Titania's memory of her "vot'ress" seems unambiguously physical, fleshy and sexual. The Fairy Queen's recollection of the two women carefree and sportive on the beach, her devotee's "womb then rich with my young squire," exemplifies two important trends in the play worth the writer's attention. First, of course, this relationship becomes merely one strand in the play's tangled web of sensuous, even sexual relations. Tracing these interwoven strands can reveal to the writer how dizzying, unpredictable, and even unreliable love is intended to be in the play (though, arguably, Titania's devotion to her disciple is the most convincing example of unwavering, honest love in *A Midsummer Night's Dream*. Certainly the final two lines of our passage speak to this with simple but strong eloquence). Second, the passage provides us with one of several moments when the play reflects on the bonds between the female characters. The student writer could certainly develop this motif into an effective essay, studying closely the way in which bonds between women in the play are interrupted or even destroyed by men. Think, for example, about the implications of Theseus stealing his bride from a tribe of Amazon warriors, as well as the more obvious problem of Helena and Hermia's ruined friendship.

Finally, the passage succinctly illustrates the oft-ignored darkness lapping at the play's bright shores. The idyllic, sensual mood of the passage is suddenly, sharply undercut by the intrusion of the line "But she, being mortal, of that boy did die." If the writer searches for it, she will find a great deal that is cynical, even ominous in *A Midsummer Night's Dream*. This kind of "reading against the grain," against the surface detail of the play, can provide much material for the writer. The student would do well to recognize—and help her reader to recognize—that for all its whimsy and pleasure, *A Midsummer Night's Dream* is a play rich with complicated, sometimes even unhappy ideas.

TOPICS AND STRATEGIES

Every essay requires a focus; you cannot write about everything in the play at once. As a specified focus evolves into a thesis, so observations develop into arguments. The starting point, nonetheless, always comes from a direct engagement of the text. The topic suggestions included here are geared toward helping you make the most of the budding ideas you will have as you read *A Midsummer Night's Dream*. By no means should you feel limited to these topics, however.

Themes

A Midsummer Night's Dream is certainly a favorite with both stage and screen audiences. Productions tend to be enormous fun, making great use of sumptuous fairy bowers and Bottom's enormous comic potential. This tradition is well captured in Michael Hoffman's lavish film version of 1999, starring Michelle Pfeiffer and Kevin Kline. Many students will no doubt be familiar with this adaptation, but delightful as the film may be, it might not offer the essay writer much inspiration. Perhaps closer to the mark is Peter Brooks's now famous 1970 stage production, which stripped the play's setting of its traditional extravagance, instead presenting the action on a sparsely furnished, bare white stage. What Brooks and his audiences discovered was that, without the luxuriant exterior, the play's provocative and engaging themes became more apparent and ready for dissection. These themes are both substantial and accessible enough to suggest multiple writing opportunities.

Sample Topics:

1. **Love:** Does the play actually challenge the conventional, fairy tale model of love it appears to champion? If so, what does *A Midsummer Night's Dream* offer in place of that romanticized model?

Such an essay might begin by attempting a definition of love as presented in the play. Unquestionably, there are many types of love present in *A Midsummer Night's Dream*, so it is essential to define the scope of your scrutiny. For example, you might want to argue that in the play love is presented as an illogical, somewhat fickle force. You could decide to make your claim even stronger, suggesting that the work undermines love altogether by repeatedly showing how quickly love can turn to cruelty (or, indeed, in the case of Theseus and Hippolyta, is born of cruelty). The enigmatic moment where Hermia dreams she is attacked by a snake (act 2, scene 2. provides a puzzle for the writer to interpret, a nightmarish vision of cruelty in the increasingly dark dream world of the forest. Certainly, at the very least, the four lovers that we struggle to tell apart are also caught up in the problems of their own identities. We hear it asked again and again, for example, how it is that love is kindled, how one person might encounter two people of equal merit—it often appears as though the lovers are only too ready to acknowledge the homogeneity of their identities—and love one but scorn the other. Look for moments, such as act 2, scene 2, in which the lovers develop such questions into a fully fledged discussion about the role of reason (or its lack of a role) in love. Perhaps, too, include in your essay the most exaggerated example of unreasonable love, that of Titania for Bottom. You might also want to employ in your essay the many moments when love is forced, whether on the part of the lover or the beloved. Magic incorporated into the play becomes a symbol for our lack of control and love merely a spell placed unknowingly on a lover. If however, you disagree with this more cynical reading of the play, you will certainly be able to make a case that a more positive understanding of love is reached by the end of the play. Of course, you would have to acknowledge—and ideally challenge—some of these ideas, but it is entirely reasonable to interpret all of this in a more positive light. In such a view, the play might be seen as arguing that love is not a mindless and random force at all but rather an active one that seeks to rectify and counter the blindness of the lovers. Demetrius, for example, loved Helena before the play's action begins (1.2.242., and so the confusions in the forest might be said to correct romantic mistakes, binding each character to his or her rightful partner. Or, alternatively again, Demetrius is to be pitied when the play's curtain falls as he marries a woman he no longer loves. Of course, it is entirely possible that as you write you will get lost in the woods yourself, and like the lovers will have a change of heart as to what love means and who loves whom in *A Midsummer Night's Dream.*

2. **Gender:** What kind of relationship exists between the sexes in the play? How might we describe the balance of power within those relationships? In what ways do we see these power dynamics repeated throughout the play?

An essay of this kind need look no further than the opening scene for strong material. The control of women by dominant male characters seems to be stressed so robustly in act 1, scene 1 that the reader can be left in little doubt that this will emerge as a major theme in the play. Pay close attention to the details of Theseus's forceful wooing of Hippolyta as well as the cruel, controlling demands of Egeus on his daughter Hermia. Explore how Theseus responds to the complaints of Egeus, developing a sense of how the laws of Athens enforce a patriarchy. Think, too, about the significance of making Theseus's wife a captured Amazon, a domesticated member of a tribe of women warriors known for their independence from (and aggression toward) men.

If you make a case for the existence of a (really quite severe, perhaps) patriarchal presence in the play, you will want to establish that this is in evidence not only in the court of Theseus but in the woods outside Athens too. This is vital because we might have reason to expect that in the magical, somewhat chaotic world of the forest the harsh laws of Athens would disappear or even be reversed. Look for ways in which patriarchy is maintained in the woods no less strictly and troublingly than it is in Athens. Most obviously, perhaps, assess the treatment of Titania at the hands of Oberon. Less apparent but no less worrisome is the way in which female friendship and communities in the play are consistently disrupted by men. One passage particularly rich in the pathos of ruptured female friendships can be found in Helena's complaint in act 3, scene 2 (l.193–220). Given all of this, you may also wish to suggest a connection between the themes of love and gender, perhaps exploring the idea that the failures of love in *A Midsummer Night's Dream* are frequently caused by the abusive control of women by men.

Characters

Writing about individual characters in the work is a slightly more difficult prospect than it is in other Shakespeare plays. The four young lovers are not well rounded, multidimensional characters (though this fact itself could prove to be fertile ground for the writer). Moreover, the pairings of Oberon/Titania and Theseus/Hippolyta are so thoroughly interconnected or parallel that individual treatments of the characters might ultimately be less fruitful than a careful study of one or both couples.

Sample Topics:

1. **Bottom:** What function does Bottom serve in the intellectual fabric of *A Midsummer Night's Dream*? Does the play merely mock him, or is its treatment of him more generous?

As much or more than any other of Shakespeare's comic creations, Bottom can still elicit swells of laughter from contemporary audiences. His two most memorable scenes, the ass's head sequence with Titania and his bravado performance at court, are the humorous highlights of the play and, if done well, among the funniest in Shakespeare. But are we laughing at or with him? Certainly you can take either side here, but it may be easier to explain how Bottom is victimized by the aristocrats of the play. Students interested more broadly in the theme of oppression might choose to connect the mistreatment of Bottom by his social superiors (primarily Theseus and King Oberon) with the abuse of the female characters by the same male, aristocratic characters. There is certainly more to Bottom than meets the eye. After all, there is always reason to pause and take stock whenever Shakespeare represents any kind of theatricality or aspects of performance in one of his plays. Bottom is, in this sense at least, the representative of Shakespeare, a writer and actor seeking to please his audience and gain stature through success. Louis Montrose has written memorably about social fantasies sublimated deep inside the play, and much of his hypothesis rests on Bottom as a hapless social climber who is loved by a queen and rewarded by the state. For all his social aspirations, however, Bottom also has profound artistic ambitions. Consider whether Shakespeare is an established member of the stage elite making fun of a theatrical novice or a self-reflexive artist having a laugh at his own expense. Either way, Bottom might also be used by the writer as a gateway to an essay on the role of art in the play. Certainly Theseus, in his famous speech at the beginning of act 5, scene 1 suggests a link between the artist and the lover (and the lunatic) that makes the symbolic connections between Bottom and the four young lovers more firmly established. An essay evaluating this link between art and the "reality" of the play—with all its love potions and spells—might discover a fascinating way into the text. Look for characters who control the action of the drama, similar to how a playwright or overmastering aesthetic or authorial presence would. Puck, Peter Quince and his troupe, Oberon, and Theseus all exert some influence on the action of a play, controlling other characters and directing action toward a conclusion.

2. **Oberon and Titania:** Is the resolution between Oberon and Titania powerful enough to undo the couple's earlier divisions?

Such an essay could begin with the sources of discord between the pair early in the play, move on to Oberon's strategies to "defeat" Titania, and finally address the quality of their restoration at the play's close. This essay will inevitably overlap with considerations of gender in the play, but it is definitely possible to have broad gender concerns form the backdrop of an essay that deals in detail with Oberon and Titania specifically. A close reading of act 2, scene 1, for example, will offer an opportunity to carefully work with the complicated root causes of the rift. At the center of the argument is the disputed Indian boy, but evaluating the volatile mix of anger, jealousy, attraction, desire, and aggression on display is no simple matter. Pay special attention to the darker components of what can be presented onstage as a lighthearted spat. For example, what do you make of the consequences of this conflagration for the mortals of Athens (2.1.81–118)? Consider, too, that while Titania's infatuation with Bottom may provoke laughter from audiences, the mirth is at the expense of both these unlikely lovers; Oberon's significant cruelty (not to mention the joy he seems to take in that cruelty in act 2, scene 2 and act 3, scene 2. is a source of serious concern for many careful readers. Finally, try to evaluate the means by which the dispute is ended. Do you feel that the resolution is actually nothing more than the total defeat and humiliation of Titania?

Form and Genre

Much of what is intriguing about the work challenges the notion that *A Midsummer Night's Dream* is a purely joyous, happy comedy. Philosophical and social struggles cast long shadows over the beginning, middle, and end of the play. As with other Shakespearean comedies, the thematic tensions of the work have significant implications for the form and genre of the play. However, in this regard, *A Midsummer Night's Dream* is unlike many other plays in Shakespeare's canon. Unlike his later comedies, as well as his earlier *The Merchant of Venice, A Midsummer Night's Dream* takes its comic pretensions seriously. In these other plays, the darker notes sound unmistakably and uncomfortably— the tension at the end of *The Merchant of Venice* or *All's Well That Ends Well,* for example, is amplified and evident and prevents comic satisfaction from being derived from the obviously hollow "happy ending." In many of Shakespeare's earlier comedies, on the other hand, such as *The Comedy of Errors, The Two Gentlemen of Verona,* or *The Taming of the Shrew,* threats to the comic resolution are either faint or the product of anachronistic thinking. *A Midsummer Night's Dream* seems to occupy a middle ground between these two approaches to Shakespearean comedy. Its dark subject matter is not so obvious that it can be found without specifically looking for it, but at the same time the search for shadows and dark nuances in this play does not require much hunting. Therefore, writers might relish the challenge of appraising this compelling, hybrid species of genre.

Sample Topics:

1. **Comedy:** What structural, thematic, and tonal elements undermine the comic movement of *A Midsummer Night's Dream*?

Much of the material already presented as potential topics could find a home in this essay. It would be difficult to imagine an essay dealing with the play's darker tones that did not mention some of the gender issues present (though the risk here is always that we, as twenty-first-century readers, are seeing problems that Elizabethan audiences would not have). Moreover, the play's representation of love as an illogical bewitchment hardly leads us to embrace the comic conclusion wholeheartedly; the coming together of the lovers was only obtained by the shiftiest of methods. In the face of these viewpoints, the writer might choose to linger on oddly, inappropriately chilling moments that occur in the midst of festivity.

Think for example about Hermia's frightening dream or Puck's peculiar evocation of lions, corpses, and screeching owls in the final scene. In addition, while Puck's memorable quip that every Jack may have his Jill seems to be the unambiguous embodiment of the comic spirit, all of this is placed alongside another play, the rude mechanicals' *Pyramus and Thisbe*, which depicts both its Jack and Jill, much like Romeo and Juliet, suffering the tragic fates of separation and death.

2. **Festivity:** What is the relationship between *A Midsummer Night's Dream* and the festive or holiday world evoked in its title?

It has long been believed that in the ancient world dramatic plays grew out of ritual activities. The genres of drama, in fact, originated in different types of ritual activity found in ancient Greek society; tragedy was born of somber ceremonies, while comedy emerged from celebratory festivities. This contention oversimplifies the development of these complex dramatic forms, but the fundamental connection between theatrical and ritual practice is certain. With this in mind, a number of critics during the twentieth century and beyond studied the connection between Shakespeare's works and the festive world in which he lived. The sixteenth and seventeenth centuries enjoyed and participated in holiday festivals and celebration with a frequency and fervor entirely lost to us. Perhaps the most popular text in this scholarly tradition is C. L. Barber's *Shakespeare's Festive Comedy*. *A Midsummer Night's Dream* has a particularly strong link with festivity because it is an occasional drama—written for a wedding, it seems—but also because its title and its action evoke the summer celebrations of the Rites of May, a familiar observance to Shakespeare's audience. These celebrations (which actually could be held at any point through the summer) were characterized, as many holiday and festive occasions were, by the suspension of normal order. The flight of young people into the woods for a night of revels was a notorious component of these celebrations. Predictably enough, then, during Shakespeare's lifetime conservative forces mounted a sustained attack on such festivals, and the result was a slow but palpable decline in festive celebrations of holidays. Because *A Midsummer Night's Dream* reveals Shakespeare's clear interest in the subject of festival, an essay that explores its role in the play and the conditions of ritual activity that existed when Shakespeare wrote it would be rewarding. The topic has consequences for the play's form and genre because of the connection between comedy and the specific types of ritual evoked by the play. There is also an important element of historical research implied as well, as a writer considers what exactly the Rites of May were like in Shakespeare's time. It seems clear that such research might be compared to the events and setting of the play (Francois Laroque's book on Elizabethan festivity, the details of which are listed in the bibliography, is the standard work to consult here). Finally, the writer might want to explore the connection between the Renaissance playwright and the world of festivity in which he lived. Both were under attack by similar critics for similar reasons, and it is not unreasonable to suggest that Shakespeare and his contemporary dramatists would have felt a keen kinship with festivity, and a sharp sadness for its steady decline. The writer might do well to reflect on how Shakespeare might be using his play as a platform to comment on the holiday world.

Compare and Contrast

Again, *A Midsummer Night's Dream* is structured symmetrically enough to present many compare and contrast opportunities. An essay treating the characters of Titania and Oberon can be rich in its own right, but it is a natural extension of that idea to compare this pair to Theseus and Hippolyta, the fairy royals' mirror image in the human court. Equally, the play is topped and tailed by scenes from the court of Athens inviting comparison with the forest world of the middle scenes. As in many of Shakespeare's comedies, the movement sees its heroes fleeing a strict and harsh society to a place of freedom dubbed by many critics as the green world. Within the green world, characters have the social and emotional freedom to discover themselves and solve problems and tensions rooted in their former court lives. Typically, the comic movement drives toward a reconciliation of characters in the reformed court setting. So the essay topic that presents itself in this case would at first glance appear to be a contrast between the conservatism of the court and the liberality of the green world setting. However, it can often be interesting, having established the basic expectations of the green world/court divide, to explore the more unexpected similarities between the two spaces. In the case of *A Midsummer Night's Dream*, this is a particularly promising approach. Begin by brainstorming as many similarities and connections as you can, ranging from the parallelisms of Oberon/Titania and Theseus/Hippolyta to the questionable green world's "quick fix" that unsatisfactorily reconciles the lovers' problems before they return to court.

Sample Topic:

1. **Contrasting the play within a play to the rest of *A Midsummer Night's Dream*:** In what way does the play staged by Bottom and his fellow actors help us to better understand the overarching work that contains it?

Whenever Shakespeare introduces the staging of a play within a play, it is always worth asking why. This popular device was a winking in-joke for regular theatergoers to savor. It was also a philosophical conceit, one that asked audiences to consider the laws of representation and, ultimately, of the divide (or lack of it) between reality and artifice. Furthermore, the playwright employing such a technique is often asking us to make connections between the larger and smaller plays. An essay that explores these links has an implied structure and relatively contained focal point (a close reading of the play within a play) but will still require a strong knowledge of the larger play as you link the comparative points you have identified as connecting the two texts. First, you may want to approach *Pyramus and Thisbe*, the play the amateurs stage for the nuptial celebrations of Theseus and Hippolyta in act 5, scene 1, as many students, critics, and scholars have approached Shakespeare's plays: by identifying themes and characters. You will find, of course, that both the play within a play and *A Midsummer Night's Dream* as a whole take love as their theme. The challenge for an essay writer tackling this topic is to see the two plays in conversation with each other. Your thesis might be based on a key similarity or difference or, even better, address what effect *Pyramus and Thisbe* has on *A Midsummer Night's Dream*. Think, for example, about the issue of genre. Bottom and his friends stage a tragedy at the moment of comic resolution; a bloody tragedy at a wedding banquet seems a jarring moment of incongruity. Does this undermine the comic conclusion of *A Midsummer Night's Dream*, even though everyone—not least of all Theseus—is trying to turn *Pyramus and Thisbe* into a comedy? As some critics have noted, the workers' drama resembles *Romeo and Juliet*, a play almost exactly contemporaneous with *A Midsummer Night's Dream*. Why combine a tragic vision of love with a comic vision of love? What might be the intended "moral" or meaning behind this juxtaposition? Think about what separates the ill-fated Pyramus and Thisbe from the ostensibly "happy ever after" pairings of Athenian lovers. Pay close attention to their fates, but also make note of how they arrived there, what helped them (or not) through their obstacles. Again, having contemplated this, reflect on whether this difference undercuts the comic resolution of *A Midsummer Night's Dream* even further. Finally, if you are interested in the theatricality of staging a play within a play, you might want to further speculate on another matter of staging. Many critics believe that *A Midsummer Night's Dream* was written to be staged at an English aristocratic wedding, though there is no record of whose wedding it was. What, then, do you make of a wedding party watching a wedding party watching a play about two lovers who die tragically?

Bibliography and Online Resources for *A Midsummer Night's Dream*

Barber, C. L. *Shakespeare's Festive Comedy: A Study of Dramatic Form and its Relation to Social Custom*. Princeton, N. J.: Princeton University Press, 1959.

Laroque, Francois. *Shakespeare's Festive World: Elizabethan Seasonal Entertainment and the Professional Stage*. Tr. Janet Lloyd. Cambridge: Cambridge University Press, 1991.

Legatt, Alexander. *"Midsummer Night's Dream." Shakespeare's Comedy of Love.* London: Methuen, 1974.

"Midsummer Night's Dream: Directors' concepts." http://www.lib.washington. edu/subject/Drama/msndconcepts.html

Montrose, Louis. *The Purpose of Playing.* Chicago: University of Chicago Press, 1996.

Nelson Garner, Shirley. *"A Midsummer Night's Dream*: 'Jack Shall Have Jill; / Nought Shall Go Ill.'" *A Midsummer Night's Dream: Critical Essays.* Ed. Dorothea Kehler. New York: Routledge, 1998: 127–45.

Taylor, Michael. "The Darker Purpose of *A Midsummer Night's Dream." Studies in English literature 1500–1900,* (9, 1969): 259–73.

MUCH ADO
ABOUT NOTHING

READING TO WRITE

A T THE close of Kenneth Branagh's 1993 adaptation of *Much Ado about Nothing*, the music soars joyously, and the cast begins a merry dance of celebration. The camera lifts into an all-embracing crane shot and takes in more and more revelers as if to signal the completeness of the comic ending. The young Claudio, the film's ending suggests, has grown up, learned his lesson, and been united with Hero. Branagh's Benedick and Emma Thompson's Beatrice remain feisty and quick witted but nonetheless enter into what the audience is asked to imagine as a perfect marriage of two independent minds.

With such a triumphant depiction of the play's resolution, the casual viewer might be forgiven for imagining that *Much Ado about Nothing* is Shakespearean comedy as its most festive and heartening. The careful reader of the play text, however, will have some questions. Certainly, finding and attempting to provide some answers to these questions will be the key to producing a strong essay on a play that, as many modern critics have observed, is deceptively simple.

The work's complexity is evident in a close reading of the often-cited passage in which Benedick apparently transforms from a cynic into a lover. He has just overheard the staged conversation between Don Pedro and Claudio in which they dupe him into believing that Beatrice is madly in love with him:

> This can be no trick: the
> conference was sadly borne. They have the truth of

155

> this from Hero. They seem to pity the lady: it
> seems her affections have their full bent. Love me!
> why, it must be requited. I hear how I am censured:
> they say I will bear myself proudly, if I perceive
> the love come from her; they say too that she will
> rather die than give any sign of affection. I did
> never think to marry: I must not seem proud: happy
> are they that hear their detractions and can put
> them to mending. They say the lady is fair; 'tis a
> truth, I can bear them witness; and virtuous; 'tis
> so, I cannot reprove it; and wise, but for loving
> me; by my troth, it is no addition to her wit, nor
> no great argument of her folly, for I will be
> horribly in love with her. I may chance have some
> odd quirks and remnants of wit broken on me,
> because I have railed so long against marriage: but
> doth not the appetite alter? a man loves the meat
> in his youth that he cannot endure in his age.
> Shall quips and sentences and these paper bullets of
> the brain awe a man from the career of his humour?
> No, the world must be peopled. When I said I would
> die a bachelor, I did not think I should live till I
> were married. Here comes Beatrice. By this day!
> she's a fair lady: I do spy some marks of love in
> her.   (2.3.220–46)

This passage would be, obviously, vital to an essay on Benedick but also useful in a variety of other essays, such as one addressing the theme of love in the play. We can consider both issues more or less simultaneously here, and both essays would, of course, contain significant overlap. Benedick's ideas here are wittily peculiar; though they seem to be familiarly romantic at first glance, they are in fact highly unusual. Consider what motivates Benedick to "requite" Beatrice's supposed love. How do the first eight lines of the passage present a mix of several motivating emotions, not necessarily at odds with one another but not exactly in harmony either? The line "I did never think to marry" takes the passage in a new, self-reflective direction. What many commentators have remarked on over the years and found so attractive in both Benedick and Beatrice is honesty. There is something incongruous about the highly rational way Benedick is discussing love here—to be seen again in *As you Like It*'s Rosalind—and the reflections on love (a topic that can elicit speech or dialogue of the most ornate and artificial kind) seem remarkably self-aware and frank. He glosses his sudden and total shift in romantic perspective as simply "mending" "detractions." What follows is a pragmatic account of Beatrice's virtues, to be contrasted sharply with the standard Renaissance poetical device of the blazon, a hyperbolic and implausible reckoning of a woman's idealized beauty. This favorable account of Beatrice on Benedick's part is less about praising his beloved than rationalizing his transformation. This line of thinking takes Benedick back to what he imagines will appear as hypocrisy on his part. Again, another thin, even dismissive remark is offered to account for the change of heart: "but doth not the appetite alter? A man loves the meat in his youth that he cannot endure in his age." This is all the more remarkable because moments earlier, at the beginning of the scene, speaking of Claudio's infatuation with Helena, Benedick remarks:

> I do much wonder that one man, seeing how
> another man is a fool when he dedicates his
> behaviors to love, will, after he hath laughed at
> such shallow follies in others, become the argument
> of his own scorn by failing in love. . .

More surprising still, Benedick's earlier speech contained the glimmers of self-awareness and acknowledgement of personal change that makes possible the coming character transformation:

> May I be so converted and see with
> these eyes? I cannot tell; I think not: I will not
> be sworn, but love may transform me to an oyster; but
> I'll take my oath on it, till he have made an oyster
> of me, he shall never make me such a fool.

As you prepare to write, then, you are forced to address a vital question: How is this transformation to be read? Should it be seen as psychologically realistic? Perhaps, as many have suggested, it is not a transformation at all but rather a confession of what has long been true: Benedick loves Beatrice.

Another possibility emerges too. Should we read this as consciously unrealistic on the dramatist's part? We have seen the fickle and mercurial ways of the heart dramatized in *A Midsummer Night's Dream*. People, especially in matters of desire and passion, Shakespeare seems to argue in that play, are singularly prone to sudden, apparently unaccountable transformations. Is Benedick's own metamorphosis (along with Beatrice's) another example of Shakespeare's thoughts on the matter? Moreover, how does Benedick's famous claim that "the world must be peopled" conclude the passage? As you write, look for the unorthodox elements in the passage, the unexpected rhetorical turns that Benedick produces to help him (and us) understand his own dramatic change in character.

TOPICS AND STRATEGIES

Every essay requires a focus; you cannot write about everything in the play at once. As a specified focus evolves into a thesis, so observations develop into arguments. The starting point, nonetheless, always comes from a direct engagement of the text. The topic suggestions included here are geared toward helping you make the most of the budding ideas you will have as you read *Much Ado about Nothing*. By no means should you feel limited to these topics, however.

Characters

Although, as has often been observed, the personalities of Beatrice and Benedick usually steal the show, in terms of narrative and dramatic structure, all of the major characters are intriguing, a little ambiguous, and deserving of essay treatment. Let us take Claudio, for example. Remember that workable formula for a character essay: "character X is ___ at the beginning of the work but by the end is ___." This ready made thesis statement provides a nice focused argument and a reliable structure for your essay. Sometimes the process of transformation is subtle and quite difficult to interpret (this will be the case with Beatrice and Benedick), as a result deserving ample essay space, while other times the transformation is less extreme or the focus of the paper simply naturally leans toward the pre- or post-transformation stage of the character. This is likely the case with Claudio, and the focus may well rest a little more on discussing exactly what kind of character Claudio is in the first acts of the play. After all, he has traditionally received a rough ride, painted as something of a foolish young man who is gullible, too quick to act, and, frankly, callous. Evaluate Claudio's response to the claim that Don Pedro is wooing Hero for himself, and then the second and more substantial plot involving Margaret at Hero's window. The wedding scene (4.1. presents the culmination of this movement and is certainly worth careful reading in your paper. The Branagh version has Claudio physically throw Hero over and then angrily toss chairs in front of an amazed wedding party. As an interpretive move, this works very well, reinforcing for us the erratic and immature mind of the young Claudio. But is this what you see in the scene? Finally, as the essay moves on, do you discern any significant shift in Claudio at the end? Behind his remorse and penitence, what can be found? A young man painfully forced to see his own foolishness, growing as a result? If you look to complicate this a little, you may want to distinguish between the period in which Claudio is aware that he has caused Hero's death and the period in which he believes Hero to be dead *and* knows she was innocent.

If Claudio has his youth and inexperience to excuse him, the older Don Pedro can make no such appeals. An essay exploring Don Pedro's motivations and purpose in the play could be very interesting. He seems to imagine himself as some kind of human Cupid, a "true love god," as he puts it, one of the authors of the dramatic action. How does he go about this role? How should we judge his success or failures? However, he is in direct competition with his brother, Don John, who also seeks to write the action of the play, though his vision is one of tragedy not comedy.

Sample Topics:

1. **Don John:** What is the effect of having Don John, a character clearly belonging to the genre of tragedy, in a romantic comedy?

   Many critics have seen in Don John a prototype of Shakespeare's most chilling villain, *Othello*'s Iago. It seems remarkable, then, that the seed of such a character is planted in a play that has often been cited as among Shakespeare's most merry comedies. How do you account for this choice on Shakespeare's part? Look at what sets Don John immediately apart from the others in 1.1 (think, for example, about language, such an important aspect of the play). Obviously, pay close attention to the account Don John makes of himself in 1.3, again looking at how he distinguishes himself from the other characters of the play. You may find it useful, especially if the paper needs be a little longer, to incorporate an understanding of Don John through comparison and contrast with Don Pedro (2.1 will offer you some good Don John material with which to begin this work). You may wish, too, to think about connections between Don John and Benedick, both men who foreswear love early in the play. Other than the obvious answer of "a story," what is accomplished by inserting Don John into the play? How might Shakespeare be using Don John not just as a narrative device, a catalyst to make things happen, but as a philosophical or thematic device, part of larger debates in the play about such things as love and stagecraft?

2. **Beatrice:** How can we account for Beatrice's transformation from a woman who claims "I had rather hear my dog bark at a crow than a man swear he loves me" (1.1.108) to one who announces Benedick can tame her "wild heart" with his "loving hand" (3.1.115)?

Attempting to answer this question takes your essay right to the heart of the play. The wit of Beatrice, the quality of her dialogue, and the indeterminate nature of her transformation all guarantee ample material for a strong essay. Now, in selecting this topic, though, the student must make some calculations. Because Benedick and Beatrice are such magnets in the play for our attention and interest, you can be sure that many students will opt to write on these characters. I normally advise students to reach for originality in their essays, to look for arguments and topics that others in the class are not likely to choose. This does not mean, of course, that you should not write essays on popular topics, just that you have to distinguish your essay by the way you treat and explore the material. If one word had to be used to describe how this is done, it would probably be "depth." Others may map out the character's progress and perhaps offer a single idea to account for the transformation, but by lingering on the text, close reading the details of what Beatrice says, what she thinks, and who she is, along with the acknowledgement perhaps of multiple interpretations or possibilities behind the transformation, you will likely still stand out from the pack even though your essay treats familiar material. The golden piece of advice for literary criticism essay writing is nearly always "say more!" This thought, expressed in one way or another, probably accounts for the bulk of comments an instructor will make on a first draft essay, so anticipate it and look for ways to spend more time with each idea and point you make.

So which areas of the text are likely to provide you with this material? Of course, the early sparring between Beatrice and Benedick in 1.1 and Beatrice's rejection of love in 2.1 will be a natural starting point. You may wish to, as some critics have done, reflect on the implications of the history between the couple alluded to by Beatrice (2.1.240). Hero's description of Beatrice (3.1.47–56) may also be useful, as well as Beatrice's response at the end of that scene to the conversation she has heard. The complicated exchange between Beatrice and Benedick at the end of the wedding scene (4.1. deserves to be carefully unpacked as well. And, of course, the oddly ambiguous final lines between the couple at the close of the play may certainly aid you in assessing the nature of the transformation. Remember, in literary criticism it is not necessarily your task to *solve* the problem at hand, but rather to help the reader understand the complexity of the problem. Sometimes, paradoxically, this can actually involve creating new problems and finding complexity where others will look for simplicity and easy answers. This is likely to be the best path for an essay on Beatrice.

3. **Benedick:** How should we read the final lines between Beatrice and Benedick that appear to partially undercut the comic union of the couple? Do they have a happy ending?

It would be very possible to write the essay on character "transformation," the one outlined for Beatrice above, with an emphasis on Benedick, of course. Many of the same scenes would be applicable, with the addition of material treating Benedick's "conversion" scene in 2.3 (see "Reading to Write" section above). The consideration of a "happy ending" is also really just a reformation of this basic movement, shifting the emphasis from how and why the "transformation" takes place to the effect it has on the audience. How does the play seem to want us to respond to the pairing at the close? What, for example, are we to make of both lovers ambiguously claiming they love the other "no more than reason" (5.4.74)? What of the fact that Benedick's second to last speech recalls the anxiety over female sexuality and fidelity so prominent throughout the play? You will certainly be able to devote some of the essay to tracing how and why the lovers come to this point at the close of the play, legitimately opening up much of the first four acts for your use, but some concentrated meditation on the play's final arrangement, so to speak, is vital. You may feel sorry for Benedick and Beatrice, that they have been somewhat bullied and tricked into conformity, or you may feel, conversely, that they in fact represent the image of ideal lovers in the play, perhaps the most ideal lovers anywhere in Shakespeare.

Philosophy and Ideas

One of the key changes to how this play is viewed, as many critics have been eager to point out in more recent times, is that it is a play loaded with serious ideas and complex questions. As these critics point out, this is in contrast with the older view of the play as particularly light and, despite its dalliances with danger and sadness, somehow monotone in its comic vision. *Much Ado* seems eager to play intellectually and linguistically, in fact, and there are many patterns of words and ideas that would make for effective essay topics. For example, one of the play's reoccurring images often pointed to is "Fashioning." Some variation of the word "fashion" appears frequently and deliberately enough throughout the play to give a nice, fairly easy to find structure to your paper. After cataloguing the appearances of the word in your prewriting notes and brainstorming, start to look for both distinctions and similarities in the way the concept of "fashion" is used. For example, of course, you may want to be begin with a useful division between occurrences and references to "fashion" (social trends and preferences; see the conversation between Conrad and Borachio in 3.3 for a particularly interesting appearance of the word in this sense) and "to fashion" (to make or design something). A good thesis statement may attempt to draw these apparently very distinct uses of the word "fashion" together, arguing for a cumulative meaning, a third sense of "fashion," if you will, that emerges by combining these two uses together. You may want to think, for example, about the implications of associating Don Pedro's obsessive need to fashion, and what exactly it is that he is fashioning (conventional marriage between two unconventional people), with the idea of faddish and socially manufactured desires. Look for moments where people make big decisions with one eye on how they are viewed by society. A number of critics have gotten very good mileage out of such connections.

Language

Why does the play so self-consciously draw attention to language itself as a theme not just a medium? Literary art is by definition self-conscious of language (even if that awareness is in the form of consciously minimizing and naturalizing the visibility of the language used in the text), and Shakespeare is justly and famously celebrated for his linguistic and rhetorical gifts, of course. But language seems to be much more than a vehicle for poetry and wit in *Much Ado*. In turns it is both part of the dramatic structure of the play, used to define differences and connections between characters, and a philosophical theme in itself, an integral part of the play's fascination with "fashioning." So an essay on the *function* of language in *Much Ado*, what it does more than what it says in the play, would make for a strong and distinct paper.

You might begin by asking how a character is represented through their use of language. The sparring of Beatrice and Benedick is an obvious place to begin, but think about Don John and Dogberry, too, among others. In the case of the former, his lack of language sets him apart from the other infinitely more verbal characters, while the malapropisms and other linguistic errors of Dogberry provide both comic momentum and vivid examples of blocked and confused meanings, misunderstandings that linguistically mirror the many misunderstandings structuring the plot. Making points bigger than individual observations here will be central, as always. Try to find things to say about the way the play uses language as a whole rather than offering a sequence of observations on how individual characters speak. If language itself does become a theme in the play, what does the play finally "want to say" about that theme?

Form and Genre

Critics have widely debated the generic quality of the play, what proportions it contains of comedy and tragedy, and where it should be placed in the trajectory of Shakespeare's comic development. Should it be thought of stylistically alongside the earlier comedies, at least in part because of a kind of "lightness" that some have seen in *Much Ado*? Should it, instead, be put alongside the comedies of the middle years (which is, in fact, chronologically speaking, where it belongs), rich, ripe with multifaceted emotions and possibilities? (Even here, though, critics discussing this issue have rightfully drawn distinctions between the spirit of *As You Like It* and *Twelfth Night*, the latter being closely related to the former but laced with much darker stuff.) Or, does the play belong in the company of *The Merchant of Venice* and, eventually, the problem comedies such as *All's Well That Ends Well*? Or, finally, does it straddle all of these different subsets of Shakespearean comedy, mixing, say, the early "battle of the sexes" theme seen most vividly in *Taming of the Shrew* and the potential for tragedy witnessed in *The Merchant of Venice* with the neutralizing benign force of an *As You Like It*? All of these are perfectly credible options—though the flexibility of the last option probably makes it the most attractive. So what we have in *Much Ado About Nothing*, then, in a sense, is a microcosm of all Shakespearean comedy, and, as a result, gold for the essay writer interested in exploring generic elements.

Sample Topic:

1. **Tragic threats:** To what extent does the malign presence of Don John destabilize the comic force of the play? What other (if any) elements further threaten the comic outcome?

   First you have to decide how you view the characters. Do you see connections between, say, Don John and Don Pedro that complicate an easy and reassuring opposition between the two? Some have seen Don Pedro in a more negative light than is common, and if we do so, imagining him as schemer and meddler rather than his self proclaimed title of "love god," the pair move closer into alignment. There are potential connections to be forged between Don John and Benedick as well, and we will explore all of this further in the compare and contrast section below. For now, however, it is enough to say that if you are writing about the blend of comedy and tragedy in the play, do note that it might be an effective strategy to view Don John as both outsider and insider, someone at odds with the other characters but also someone who reflects obliquely many of their own thoughts and practices.

Nonetheless, for all of this careful joining of dots between the various characters, it remains clear that Don John is intended to be a clearly anti-comic force in the play, a villain whose motives are not in any way justifiable or explicable, and one that will not be—by nature cannot be—reabsorbed into the comic society and feast of resolution at the end of the play. This marks him out as fundamentally different from the other characters and also marks the play out as fundamentally problematic. Put simply, Don John doesn't *belong* in an early modern comedy. His very spirit is at odds with the genre and his presence reminds us of the artifice of the comic form and ruptures the escapist fantasies of the play. He is, in fact, as many have pointed out, nothing less than a prototype of Shakespeare's great vision of evil, Iago. But whereas Iago, with his unquenchable thirst for mayhem and death, belongs in *Othello*, belongs in tragedy as a depiction of the very darkest of human thoughts and actions, he does not, surely, even in prototypical form, belong in a comedy about love. So why is he there? Exploring the incongruity of Don John will ease you into some important reflections on the shape and spirit of the play as well as, if you wish, broader thoughts on the nature of comedy itself.

It would be possible to write a shorter essay on the comic form of the play by just unpacking the function of Don John, but for longer essays, or simply more varied one, you can expand your treatment of the play to cover a number of episodes and their effect on the totality of the play's structure. For example, 4.1, the wedding scene, is key both thematically and structurally. A wedding is, indeed, the definitive episode of early modern comic resolution, the coming together of lovers, the celebration of their defeating the various obstacles that blocked their path to union, and the celebration of the community brought together in joyous reconciliation. Such is the quintessential conclusion of a comedy, even if such an event is used ironically (as may be the case in *As You Like It*) or downright cynically (as we see in the later *All's Well That Ends Well*). Here, however, as many have noted, the wedding occurs in the wrong place and, in the event, is foiled and becomes a destructive moment of temporary separation rather than unison. The scene is filled with interesting lines and actions worth reading closely. Think for example about the actions of Claudio and Leonto, their motivations and their justifications (or lack of). Think, too, about the roles of Benedick and Beatrice. Moreover, what do you make of the fact that the "wedding scene" actually ends with death (albeit a feigned death), the hallmark of tragic catharsis not comic resolution? Similarly, 5.3, the mourning of Claudio and Don Pedro for the "dead" Hero, is a tragic rather than comic ingredient and can be included effectively in your essay. And, of course, the final scene—as with the final scene of any Shakespearean comedy in an essay on comic form—deserves prominent attention. As ever, assess the dueling elements of comic and anti-comic energy and, essentially, keep score and show your reader the tensions between the two, perhaps even stake a position on the winner. For example, what do you make of the final return of Don John through report of the messenger and the tortures that await him? What of the decidedly ambiguous exchange between Beatrice and Benedick? What of the reunion of Claudio and Hero? Do you find this latter spark of comedy unsatisfying or undeserved, or perhaps even unpromising? Do you sense that Claudio, in other words, has matured enough to deserve Hero after his exceptionally dubious conduct up to this point? To put all of this together, when Benedick offers the play's last line, a call for pipers to strike up, is this finally a reflection of the play's ultimate tone, a celebration of the comic spirit's victory over the darker hues of the play, or a flimsy attempt to cover up the lingering problems unresolved by the play?

Compare and Contrast

As discussed above, *Much Ado* mirrors a number of Shakespeare's comedies in interesting ways. Particularly tight interactions can be developed with *The Taming of the Shrew, A Midsummer Night's Dream, The Merchant of Venice* and *The Winter's Tale.* Less obvious, but still interesting comparisons can be noted with plays such as *As You Like It* and *All's Well That Ends Well. Shrew* and *MND* both depict the idea of the "battle of the sexes" revisited by *Much Ado* several years later. A strong essay could be crafted around the struggle between Petruccio and Kate in *Shrew* and Beatrice and Benedick in *Much Ado.* Though both plays begin with vigorous linguistic tussles between central pairings, it appears as though the plays diverge significantly when Petruccio's "rough wooing" takes a particularly unpleasant turn during the country house scenes. Benedick and Beatrice appear gentile and amicable by comparison. And yet the overarching dynamics of both relationships remain closely connected. In both pairs the lovers struggle with each other in a bid to assert and maintain some sense of individual agency, while, perhaps more importantly, both couples negotiate social expectations and arrive at some sense of harmony that appears to (and perhaps does) resolve the tension between what society expects of them and what they themselves need. (See the *Shrew* chapter in this volume for many more leads that might help with this compare and contrast essay.)

Thinking about *MND* alongside *Much Ado* presents an opportunity to reflect on changes of heart. Both plays draw on the theme of emotional metamorphosis and transformation, the idea that love can be unreasonably found and lost almost in the moment, a fluid tide setting us adrift and washing us back to safety once more. An entirely different train of thought, meanwhile, can be pursued by following *The Merchant of Venice* with *Much Ado.* Here we find Shylock to be a cousin, though perhaps a distant one, of Don John. How do these obstacles to comic resolution resemble or differ from each other? And finally, just as Hermione is believed dead and restored to life and love at the end of *The Winter's Tale,* so too does Hero's "resurrection" return her to the arms of someone whose foolishness and baseless jealousy cost him dear. Though Claudio's suffering is, of course, infinitely lighter than Leontes's 16 years of bitter guilt and lament, the same device sits behind both sets of dramatic action and could be explored productively in a comparative essay. However, surprisingly, the most striking opportunity for compare and contrast in *Much Ado* takes us not to one of Shakespeare's comedies for a partner text, but to the tragedy *Othello.*

Sample Topics:

1. **Comparing Don John to Iago from** *Othello:* To what degree can these two characters be said to resemble each other? Less obviously, are there any important differences between the two? What are the implications of these similarities and differences for the comic framework of *Much Ado*?

The romantic poet Samuel Taylor Coleridge famously remarked that Iago exhibited "motiveless malignity," that the play *Othello* provided too little in the way of explanation to account for the character's ferocious evil. Interestingly, though, Iago seems to have *more* motivation than Don John, or at least Iago takes the trouble to create some half-convincing cover stories for his hatred. Whereas Iago is the consummate deceiver, appearing to be "honest Iago" and fully integrated into the affairs of Othello and the state (see Kenneth Branagh's terrifying switches from amiable to evil, captured in devilish conversations directly with the camera and audience, in Oliver Parker's 1995 film adaptation of the play), Don John eschews all pretenses of civility and (importantly) "fashion." So you might make much of this distinction in your essay, perhaps, but it may be that at the core of each character you find similar stuff: "I had rather be a canker in the hedge than a rose in [Don Pedro's] grace. . ." (1.3.21). Both characters are indeed "cankers" in their respective play worlds, insidiously existing, it seems, only to take away the happiness of others. And both end their plays facing painful extraction from the world, the threat of tortures looming large at the end of each text. But then consider also the effects each character has on others. In *Much Ado*, it is the malice of Don John that seems to bring Beatrice and Benedick together in sympathy for Hero (many critics have pointed out the tenderness between the two in the final movement of 4.1., as well as, arguably, allowing Hero and Claudio to enjoy a stronger and more mature relationship after the too-gullible Claudio has been painfully tested. This may, then, be a difference worth exploring in your work as well, and perhaps a key distinction between a certain kind of comedy, the kind that recognizes the existence of sadness and pain, and the world of tragedy. In the comic universe evil becomes visible just in time to avert disaster, while in the tragic universe it smiles and charms long enough to bring about the ruin of the innocent and naïve.

Finally, too, connections between Don John and Don Pedro as well as Don John and Bendeick were alluded to in the "Character" section above. These, of course, structured even between each character, would make for two great compare and contrast choices also.

2. **Comparing the play text to Kenneth Branagh's film:** What vision or interpretation of the play lies behind Kenneth Branagh's film adaptation of *Much Ado about Nothing*?

Samuel Crowl, a leading Shakespeare-on-film scholar and dedicated ambassador of Branagh's films and legacy (there are certainly plenty of scholars who do not, in general, like Branagh's Shakespearean films), makes some big—and apparently quite justifiable—claims for this film. He argues that it was this film, along with Branagh's earlier film version of *Henry V,* which paved the way for a decade and more of Shakespearean cinema by breaking down the barriers between Shakespeare and a popular audience. A good place to begin your essay, then, might be to study the film for evidence of how Branagh achieves this groundbreaking popularity. Think, for example, about casting decisions, the "look" of the film, really getting down into the contents of individual shots and sequences, and Branagh's careful selection and arrangement of the play text into the screenplay. Crowl argues (without belittling the choice at all) that Branagh aims straight for the younger movie-going demographic, those who might traditionally not venture into a Shakespeare film at the multiplex (and certainly not at the art house theater, the traditional domain of Shakespearean films up to the time of *Much Ado*'s release). What evidence do you see to support this claim? What is gained or lost by Branagh's doing so? Obviously watch the whole film carefully, more than once, but particularly useful and illustrative scenes to watch include the opening sequence, the scene in which Don Pedro and Claudio attempt to gull Benedick (the equivalent of the play's 2.3), the "wedding" scene in which Claudio erupts quite violently against Hero, and, of course, the final sequence of the film. Adding all this together, your thesis could usefully offer a definition of how the film re-imagines the play. You are likely to be working with the idea of "light" when it comes to the film's tone, and this appears very reasonable, but do not ignore the film's many splashes of dark, even if this is just to emphasize how resilient the film's comic glow really is.

Bibliography for *Much Ado about Nothing*

Collington, Phillip. "'Stuffed With All Honorable Virtues': *Much Ado About Nothing* and *the Book of the Courtier.*" *Studies in Philology.* Summer, 2006, 103: 281–312.

Crowl, Samuel. *The Films of Kenneth Branagh.* Westport, CT: Praeger, 2006.

Daalder, Joost. "The 'Pre-History' of Beatrice and Benedick in *Much Ado about Nothing.*" *English Studies: A Journal of English Language and Literature,* 2004 Dec; 85 (6): 520–27.

Gay, Penny. "*Much Ado About Nothing:* A King of Merry War." *As She Likes It: Shakespeare's Unruly Women.* London: Routledge, 1994: 143–77.

Lewalski, Barbara K. "Love, Appearance and Reality: Much Ado About Something." *Studies in English Literature 8,* 1968: 235–51.

Reiff, Raychel Haugrud. "The Unsung 'Hero' in *Much Ado about Nothing.*" *Journal of the Wooden O Symposium,* 2004; 4: 139–49.

Wynne-Davies, Marion, ed. *Much Ado About Nothing and The Taming of the Shrew.* Basingstoke, England: Palgrave, 2001.

THE TAMING OF THE SHREW

READING TO WRITE

*T*HE TAMING *of the Shrew* is an early work by Shakespeare and is one of the most widely read and studied of the comedies in classrooms today. While *Shrew* lacks the depth and sophistication associated with later work, it nonetheless serves as a brilliant introduction to Shakespeare's art. We see in this early piece the playwright's desire to puzzle, to tease the audience or reader with action and speech yielding a multiplicity of possible meanings and interpretations. The play, quite reasonably, can be read as a shocking or revolting story of domestic abuse or as something of a protofeminist fable of Kate's final triumph. Each of these opposing viewpoints, as well as countless points in between, exists, (or can be argued exist) in the text, and the reader must avoid impulsive conclusions about the play's content, morality, and ultimate value. This can be difficult. After all, the reading of *Shrew* that bullies and bustles its way to the forefront is marked by torture and suppression, by Petruccio starving and intimidating Kate into submission. Other interpretations assert more benign and uplifting assessments of the play, making a compelling case for Kate's "victory," not matter how slim, prevailing at the work's conclusion. Which view of the play do you adopt?

Let us start with the most debated and contentious passage of the play, a microcosm of the critical issues contained in the work as a whole: Kate's final speech. The passage appears to show that Kate is beaten, transformed from strong to servile, from free to tamed. She upbraids Bianca and the Widow for disobeying their husbands, launching into an elaborate speech that apparently tells women their highest purpose is to "serve, love and obey."

> ... Thy husband is thy lord, thy life, thy keeper,
> Thy head, thy sovereign; one that cares for thee,
> And for thy maintenance commits his body
> To painful labour both by sea and land,
> To watch the night in storms, the day in cold,
> Whilst thou liest warm at home, secure and safe;
> And craves no other tribute at thy hands
> But love, fair looks and true obedience;
> Too little payment for so great a debt.
> Such duty as the subject owes the prince
> Even such a woman oweth to her husband;
> And when she is froward, peevish, sullen, sour,
> And not obedient to his honest will,
> What is she but a foul contending rebel
> And graceless traitor to her loving lord?
> I am ashamed that women are so simple
> To offer war where they should kneel for peace;
> Or seek for rule, supremacy and sway,
> When they are bound to serve, love and obey.
> Why are our bodies soft and weak and smooth,
> Unapt to toil and trouble in the world,
> But that our soft conditions and our hearts
> Should well agree with our external parts?
> Come, come, you froward and unable worms!
> My mind hath been as big as one of yours,
> My heart as great, my reason haply more,
> To bandy word for word and frown for frown;
> But now I see our lances are but straws,
> Our strength as weak, our weakness past compare,
> That seeming to be most which we indeed least are.
> Then vail your stomachs, for it is no boot,
> And place your hands below your husband's foot:

In token of which duty, if he please,
My hand is ready; may it do him ease.

(5.2.146–79)

This speech could feature in many essays you could write on *The Taming of the Shrew*. It can be used in character studies of Kate and Petruccio, an analysis of the "battle of the sexes" thematic approach to the play, or a study of the philosophical themes of identity and disguise. Some have looked to solve the puzzle of Kate through this passage because of its prominent position at the close of the work. Many actresses, directors, and critics maintained that Kate did not mean what she said, that she spoke the words with a wink, a joke at the expense of Petruccio and the other men. However, it is important to contextualize the speech, reading it not in relative isolation but as part of a subtle and careful shifting of Kate's character in 4.6 and 5.1. Ultimately, do not let this speech steal your attention away from other vital parts of the text in which Kate's words must be studied with equal care.

Nonetheless, look at Kate's final speech and explore the possibilities it presents for the writer. The potential split here is between what Kate says and what she (and the play) actually communicate through the effect and action of her speech; Kate's words may mask a radically different intention both on her part and the play's. Begin with the words themselves. The passage starts by outlining a woman's indebtedness to her husband then progresses to the popular early modern connection between domestic order (where the husband is "king" of the family) and the governance of the state, systems that mirror each other's fixed and orderly hierarchies. The disobedient wife becomes akin to the disloyal subject, a "rebel" and "traitor" whose actions threaten and destabilize the natural and essential order of things. The passage then turns to a concentrated meditation on the weakness of women, in body and spirit. Finally, this weakness of frame and condition is embodied in the radically submissive gesture of offering a hand for Petruccio to stand on. The text does not tell us whether Petruccio accepts this offer—it is usually assumed he does not, but a production of the play wishing to stress Kate's tragedy could indeed stage the action without contradicting the text.

With these considerations in mind, what is the overall intention of the speech? It is perfectly acceptable for you to say that it ends here, so to speak. You can reasonably argue that the words are, in fact, perfectly in line with the intention or effect of the speech, namely, to provide an early modern audience, accustomed to the idea of male dominance over women, with a "happy ending" showing Kate's unacceptable behavior corrected by Petruccio's harsh but ultimately necessary measures. You may wish to provide some historical context for this assessment (see the History and Context section), showing how such a reading is in line with the worldview of Shakespeare's time.

Equally, of course, those who wish to argue that the play does not finally celebrate the defeat of Kate and the triumph of Petruccio must also be ready to defend their position. Those who disagree will be armed, as we have seen, with historical evidence and the letter of Shakespeare's text. In response, you must settle on a viable alternative to reading Kate's speech and, by necessity, the whole play as proof of the title's literal truth: The shrew has been tamed.

As writers, what potential paths are opened up for us by this speech? Some critics have found in the speech a middle ground, a way of saying that Kate is in an important and real sense defeated, but that her "nature" remains largely unchanged. What evidence do you see for this in the speech? You will need to find your own way of conceiving and expressing this kind of argument and, of course, provide your own evidence from the play. In the end, this balanced approach, one in which Kate emerges as something of a "noble victim" who keeps fighting rather than someone who finally yields completely, will show you have both historical sensitivity to the ethical world of Shakespeare's time and the kind of creative reading skills that can complicate (for the better) an apparently simple picture.

Others still have found in the speech evidence to support their case that Kate enjoys a kind of triumph at the end, not only maintaining dignity but manipulating a bad situation into an acceptable outcome. These writers tend to use the tone and form of the speech to help them. In what ways do you think this might be done? For example, compare the length of Kate's speech to other speeches in the play, or look at Kate's degree of prominence in this concluding scene. In what way does the form (the physical presence of the speech) challenge the content (the words it contains)? This reading is difficult to perform without the foundation provided by careful analysis of 4.6 and 5.1. Do you see anything in these scenes that can be read as ingenious and effective resistance on Kate's part (4.6) or as evidence of a peculiar harmony emerging between Kate and Petruccio (5.1)? How would the pretense of submission at the close of the play be helpful to Kate?

TOPICS AND STRATEGIES

Every essay requires a focus; you cannot write about everything in the play at once. As a specified focus evolves into a thesis, so observations develop into arguments. The starting point, nonetheless, always comes from a direct engagement of the text. The topic suggestions included here are geared toward helping you make the most of the budding ideas you will have as you read *The Taming of the Shrew*. By no means should you feel limited to these topics, however.

Themes

Many readers are drawn to the play's signature theme: "the battle of the sexes." This is, after all, to popular culture and popular audiences alike, what the play is about. The theme can be divided in numerous ways and approached from different angles (feminist criticism, historical readings, and psychoanalytic character studies, to name a few), but the same set of basic questions usually animates all such approaches: Why is Kate viewed as a shrew at the beginning of the play? Why does she behave this way? How does she respond to Petruccio's abuses and why? What degree of agency or power over herself is she left with at the end of the play? You may note that all of these questions are framed around Kate's character rather than around both combatants in this so-called battle. This is not to say that Petruccio is not an interesting character or that there is nothing to say about him. As gender critics rightly observe, masculinity is a set of codes and conventions no less constructed than femininity, but the play seems to center its gender scrutiny firmly on Kate. Her responses to the conditions she faces—first as a free-spirited woman in a stifling patriarchy, then as a hostage to Petruccio's calculated madness—are sites of the play's most engaging complexities. Any one of the questions previously posed, then, when answered forcefully and turned into a thesis statement, would give you access to a focused essay on this theme and still allow you to draw widely from the play (This is perhaps the best kind of thesis for a beginning writer, one that combines precision and focus with something of an open invitation to many different parts of the play.

It is worth spending time at the start of the writing process to strike this balance. For example, the question about Kate's responses, if turned into a thesis—something like "Kate responds to Petruccio's abuses with pragmatic resilience, yielding enough to receive her basic needs for food and sleep but not so much as to lose her most vital need for intellectual and spiritual independence"—is both nuanced and precise enough to function well as a thesis while also inviting discussion of almost the entire play).

For this theme, you will find much material in the Reading to Write section (again, 5.2 will be indispensable here), but also in the section exploring character-related topics. You can look, too, if you want, for signs of compatibility between the two, evidence for the frequently touted idea that Kate and Petruccio are well matched and, in a sense, make a good couple. The vigorous and vital wordplay in 2.1, for example, potentially supports this view, and evidence of a strange but real harmony between the two in 5.1 and 5.2 has been widely sought.

Yet there are other themes in the play that deserve attention. If one of the ideal goals of a student writer is for her work to stand out from the pack of other essays being submitted, considering other themes and topical approaches may provide a useful way to do just that.

Sample Topics:

1. **Market forces:** How is the play's treatment of love and marriage tainted by the presence of money?

Talk of money jingles and rattles throughout the play, enough to suggest a deliberate and conscious cynicism on Shakespeare's part. We see this repeated a little later in his career with *The Merchant of Venice,* another play in which marriage and financial success and stability are one and the same. Even more so than *The Merchant of Venice*'s Bassanio, Petruccio does not conceal his desire to marry into money. In this way, his misogynistic diminishment of Kate to an object of possession has a market parallel—she is a thing but a thing of economic value. How does Hortensio's marriage to the Widow at the end of the play provide more evidence of this theme's importance? What should be made of the fact that the final scene of resolution is centered on a bet? With this in mind,

Baptista (see the Characters section) may be the most important figure in this essay, a man who appears coldly driven by market forces rather than paternal affections. Explore the worldview of the play, then, in which Kate and Bianca are reduced to the level of crude financial investments bartered and traded among merchants.

2. **Identity and reality:** How does the play challenge the idea of fixed identities or even of a stable reality?

This essay offers a change of pace and tone, inviting philosophical and abstract reflections on a diverse but connected range of episodes from the play. This is another Shakespearean obsession, it seems, the idea that something as apparently concrete and natural as a person's identity is, in fact, vulnerable and unstable. The comedies seem to find this idea inescapable, a fantasy of equal anxiety and desire that will not let go of the dramatist's imagination. We see the notion recur in plays such as *The Comedy of Errors, A Midsummer Night's Dream, As You Like It* and *Twelfth Night,* but arguably it is *The Taming of the Shrew* that treats this theme most poignantly and hauntingly. The play begins by introducing us to one of Shakespeare's most hapless characters, the enigmatic and disturbingly transient Christopher Sly. Sly's absence from the end of the play is likely a product of the inconsistent way in which early modern dramas were recorded and written down rather than a deliberate experiment on Shakespeare's part, but the result is the same nonetheless: Sly simply vanishes from his already make-believe world. The induction scenes similarly deserve and can provide for an essay unto themselves (see the Form and Genre section) but make an essential starting point for an essay on insecure identities in the play. You may wish to work also with Lucentio and Tranio's exchanging of identities, as well as the unsuspecting Pedant transformed in 4.2. All of this talk of transformation and shifting identity, of course, urges you to make a connection between this theme and the play's central transformation of Kate. How does the first inform the second? Do you believe it makes her transformation more concrete and plausible or, as some critics have suggested, does it suggest that Kate's new "identity" as submissive wife is as vulnerable and liable to change as her old character was?

Characters

Baptista is central to any essay dealing with the role of economics and market forces in the play, yet this theme could also be transformed in Baptista's case to a character study. Studies of minor characters can be rewarding because they are frequently more original and fresh than familiar accounts of major characters (though less familiar accounts of major characters are, of course, equally rewarding). The risk is that you will struggle for material, but when a character embodies a theme—as Baptista does here—it allows you to mix ample thematic consideration into your character study. In this case, Baptista's disquieting mercantilism acts as evidence of the wider social forces subjugating Kate from the start. You will want to look carefully at Baptista's motivations in act 1 and 2.1, as well as the telling indifference he displays to Kate's suffering at the end of 3.3. His role in 5.2 is also worth inclusion, of course.

Most writers, however, will be drawn to analyzing the play's central characters, Kate and Petruccio. As we have seen, especially with Kate, the challenge is to formulate a thesis that is either sharply focused on one aspect of her character or one portion of the play—which you can follow with a rather narrow and precise essay treating this specialized detail or claim—or to formulate a thesis that allows for a general exploration of Kate's character through a well-focused lens. Remember this as you outline some of the broad strokes of Kate's character and role in the play.

Sample Topics:

1. **Kate:** Is Baptista correct when he says Kate is "changed as she never had been" (5.2.19)?

   An essay on the play should never make the mistake of underestimating Kate, of labeling her easily as the men of Padua do at the beginning of the play. Do not see her as one dimensional, looking rather for psychological complexity and, above all, a distinct change in response to her conditions. Your job is to keep up with Kate as she thinks on her toes and adopts different strategies to preserve her body and sanity under extreme tension. Select elements of the character and the text to work with; there will likely be too much to handle satisfactorily in any one essay. Obviously select materials that help you address most directly the thesis exactly as you have formulated it—do not fall into the trap of composing a general survey of her character.

Depending on your approach, you may or may not want to address in detail her early violent presence, the threats of 1.1 and the puzzling scene with Bianca (2.1). You may want to look for places of great uncertainty, such as the much-debated silence accompanying her removal from stage in 2.1. More analysis might be occasioned by her apparent early efforts at resistance, particularly in 4.3. What of her final strategy? A close reading of 4.6 is vital. Do you see Kate's words here, and the tactics they represent, as admirable and clever or cowering and disappointing? The results of 4.6, whatever they are, materialize first in 5.1 and then, of course, in 5.2. As Kate is the axis on which the play turns, you should read this chapter as a whole to find other moments in the text and additional critical questions that could fuel your interpretation of Kate's character.

2. **Petruccio:** Readers spend much time looking for Kate's "transformation" and assessing it, but does Petruccio undergo any transformations of his own?

There is a fascinating and entertaining episode of the iconic 1980s television series *Moonlighting* called "Atomic Shakespeare" (1986). The episode stages a version of *The Taming of the Shrew* but ends with the Petruccio character (played by Bruce Willis) confessing that *he* has been tamed by Kate and renouncing the deal he had earlier struck with Baptista. He has fallen for Kate, loves her, and does not want to change her or profit by her. The change is a blatant one, perhaps even a little weak as it dodges the central problems of the play. Nonetheless, it raises a question that is legitimate: In a play so interested in disguise, how much is Petruccio simply playing a role? Moreover, is he really, in the end, actually the right partner for Kate?

Certainly you will want to establish his early motivations and the tactics he proposes in the opening scenes (1.2 and 2.1). You may also wish to contemplate who this man is. What do you make, for example, of the glimpses into his violent past (1.2.195)? He appears, frankly, deranged in 3.2 and 3.3, humiliating and embarrassing everyone around him at the wedding. As has been observed by some critics, though, much of the worst behavior is kept offstage and conveyed to the audience through reports. Could Shakespeare, this line of reasoning continues, be trying to insulate Petruccio a little, to allow him to be potentially redeemable? How does the play want us to view this man? Do you think the play wants us to be frightened of him or attracted to him? (Again, we need to remember that 400 years separate us from the original Petruccio and his author.) The country house scenes are also key, particularly the alarming flashes of physical violence toward his servants and the abuses of Kate theorized in the often quoted speech starting at 4.1.168. Just as the final version of Kate crystallizes in 4.6, 5.1, and 5.2, so, too, must we say that Petruccio and their relationship are also "finalized" in these scenes. The same questions exist in reverse. Instead of Kate being tamed we ask if Petruccio has been duped, fobbed off with an inspired act of survival and intellectual resistance by Kate. Yet perhaps the most interesting question to ask of Petruccio at this point is "Does he know what Kate is up to"? If so, in not making it known that he perceives the nature of her compromise, he is making a key compromise that nudges us toward a relative sense of harmony and equality between the two at the close of the play.

History and Context

The last few decades of Shakespeare criticism have been dominated by a school of theory called New Historicism, and many critics have sought to explore how Shakespeare's work (and the literary texts of his contemporaries) are both influenced by their historical context and, in return, how these texts help to shape that context. Recently there has been something of a backlash to this with some Shakespeare critics embracing an idea called presentism, the exploration of how Shakespeare exists for us today in *our* world (this includes areas such as performance studies in which modern film and stage productions are studied as the best way to access the "living" Shakespeare). Rather than seeing these approaches as yielding contradictory insights, it is vital to see them each as necessary and illuminating strategies. A play like *The Taming of the Shrew* shows exactly how both these tactics are vital as we seek to better understand and appreciate the text. *The Taming of the Shrew* has been changed through the centuries through forceful intervention, as performances and readings reinvent the play for their own time. Equally, the play is an important historical document, a vivid snapshot of a lost world, Shakespeare's world. This, of course, can be said about every play, but some are more tangibly rooted and anchored in the Elizabethan or Stuart world than others, and *The Taming of the Shrew* is certainly one of them. While there must be attempts to understand the challenges Kate and Petruccio offer a modern audience, *The Taming of the Shrew* demands that we wrestle with its origins too; after all, the play exists today as a product of its own (as well as our) cultural evolution, and the story begins in the early 1590s.

Sample Topic:

1. **Elizabethan marriage:** How is marriage portrayed in the play?

> You may want to begin an essay on this topic with an overview, rich in quotation from the text, of the play's taming story. This then establishes the central problem of the essay: interpreting the dramatic action that as a citizen of the twenty-first century you are not equipped to easily understand. Historical research will thus be necessary to illuminate the cultural and social origins of the play. You are likely not making moral arguments here—"domestic abuse was a common aspect of marital relations of the time *then* and that is how *they* were" —but simply providing information that will be of interest to the thoughtful reader of the play. Your thesis could simply be a statement of this information's importance, as appears at the start of this section. With this in place, the emphasis may switch from argument to research in the body of the essay. As you write, it

will be helpful to keep returning to the text, placing historical research alongside moments of the play that seem to be keenly informed by that particular historical detail. Never lose sight of the play or the idea that the historical research should be driven not by its own intrinsic value but by the desire to better understand the text.

So what kind of information will you likely be treating here? As you begin your research, you will discover that the conditions of marriage are being widely debated as Shakespeare writes his play. The basic ideas that marriage is desirable and that the husband is master of the household are not being challenged, but within this core social framework there is still a degree of fluidity and change being introduced. There are debates about the so-called "companionate marriage," for example, the idea that, while not an equal partnership exactly, there should ideally be loving harmony and cooperation in marriage.

Subjects such as the desirability of divorce or the degree of physical force a husband should exercise over his wife also engendered debate with numerous writers weighing in on these various marital debates. All of this is set within a well-chronicled context of communal oversight. Communities enforced correct domestic order by publicly punishing and humiliating women who apparently controlled their husbands (editions of *The Taming of the Shrew* commonly include woodcut images of such devices as the cucking stool, a harsh and degrading punishment for women who met with their community's displeasure). The importance of order, moreover, can be seen in that men, too, could be punished if they allowed themselves to be controlled by their wives. It is not surprising that such practices and provisions were in place in the early modern period when a firm, symbolic relationship between the domestic sphere of the household and the public sphere of state government had been envisioned. Just as the state had its monarch, so, too, did the house have its husband. The same sense of natural order guided both the domestic and governmental realms; accordingly, threats to that order in the domestic sphere were interpreted as attacks on the broader structures of power and rule.

There is a vast amount of material addressing these issues. For students who want to do extensive research on marriage codes and practices in the play, consult David Cressy's *Birth, Marriage and Death: Ritual Religion and the Life Cycle in Tudor and Stuart England* (Oxford University Press, 1999). For students who want a quicker passage into the material, Paul Thomas's *Authority and Disorder in Tudor Times: 1461–1603* (Cambridge University Press, 1999) contains good, accessible, and concise sections on marriage and related topics.

Form and Genre

In many of the formal and genre concerns related to Shakespeare's comedies, questions about the limits of resolution typically arise. That has included unresolved problems, for example, or characters left out of the concluding feast. The problems in *The Taming of the Shrew,* by and large, are of a slightly different nature. The play proves how ideas of a "happy ending" or acceptable resolution can shift over time: What may have been a celebration of order restored in the early modern period is, in our time, an unpalatable disappointment in need of revision by readers, critics, actors, directors, and audiences. Whether or not Shakespeare deliberately undercuts the taming of Kate—and, as we have seen, there is ample evidence to suggest he does—the play ultimately offers its audience a resolution, the expected "happy ending" in the emotional and physical defeat of a woman through torture and abuse. In light of this conflation of comedy and happy resolution with marital violence, essays about the comic form of the play, then, become indistinguishable from historical questions about the context of the play's composition. However, strong essays could be written exploring how modern filmmakers have confronted this difficulty of a popular and entertaining play tainted or compromised by a conclusion at odds with the prevailing views of twentieth- and twenty-first-century people. Both the teen comedy adaptation of the play, called *Ten Things I Hate About You* (1999), as well as the Franco Zeffirelli film addressed in the Compare and Contrast section could certainly be used in this way. Perhaps surprisingly, the 1929 film version by Sam Taylor, starring Mary Pickford as Kate, can rival more recent film productions for its feminist revisionism of the play. In that version, Petruccio enters the final scene with his head in bandages, his own violence backfiring, and Kate delivers her final speech with a wink that melts the surface of the words and confirms who is in charge at the close of the play. Finally, another fascinating formal component of *The Taming of the Shrew* deserving of attention is the strange and wonderful induction sequence.

Sample Topic:

1. **The induction:** In what ways does the induction anticipate the central themes of the play?

   Because it concentrates on a small section of the play, an essay focusing on the induction sequence alone requires scrutinizing in detail limited amounts of text. (Another approach to discussing the induction sequence is presented in the Compare and Contrast section in an essay that gives equal space to the induction and the play overall.) Two important themes to look at here are, not surprisingly, the two central themes of the play: identity and gender. With this topic, however, the latter, gender, is a secondary concern to identity and is seen mostly in the conversations between Sly and his "wife" Bartholomew and in the brief appearance of the Hostess in the opening lines. Look at how Sly is in subtle and not so subtle forms of conflict with these characters, but note, too, who seems to win these little battles. Do you feel these small incidents invite us to view the action of the main play differently?

   However, it will likely be the questions of identity and reality that most occupy your essay. Alongside the nature of the cruel trick itself—which surely must demand a comparison to Kate's situation in the play—look for the many references to dream and to acting, representations of reality that fade and vanish as Sly himself will do. Again, how does this inform your reading of the play overall? It may also be helpful to look for small hints of continuity, of teasing suggestions of permanence. This can be done, for example, by carefully reading the induction sequence (2.66–73) or by considering Sly's appearance in a related text called *The Taming of a Shrew* (this play may or may not have been an early version of the play written by Shakespeare himself) in which Sly returns at the end. The Norton Anthology helpfully prints the final lines from this other play as an appendix to Shakespeare's *The Taming of the Shrew*, a variant conclusion you may wish to work into your essay as well.

Compare and Contrast

All of Shakespeare's comedies and romances treat the issue of marriage in some way, and those works that create especially strong juxtapositions to *The Taming of the Shrew* are *A Midsummer Night's Dream* and *All's Well That Ends Well*. *A Midsummer Night's Dream* is a particularly strong candidate, because it was written soon after *The Taming of the Shrew* and seems to possibly undercut the misogynistic thrust of the earlier play. Consider how *A Midsummer Night's Dream* dramatizes relationships that echo Kate and Petruccio's situation (Theseus captures his wife and subdues her into marriage, while Oberon restores order in his marriage to Titania by cruelly tricking and humiliating her). Alternatively, look for potential differences in the way the two plays allocate sympathy. If (and, as we have seen, it is quite a considerable if) *The Taming of the Shrew* simply celebrates Kate's submission, how does *A Midsummer Night's Dream* make us question such tactics in the play (or does it not question them and therefore concur with *The Taming of the Shrew*'s action)? If individual Shakespeare plays contain debates on many issues without resolution, the debates are multiplied when other Shakespeare plays treat the same issues with apparently different leanings. You may also consider comparing *The Taming of the Shrew* to *All's Well That Ends Well*, often described as a problem play or a romance. A primary consideration is that the later play dramatizes a female protagonist winning a husband through trickery and forcing him into a marriage he apparently disdains. What are the implications of this reversal, in gender terms, of *The Taming of the Shrew*'s story, and do important differences (or similarities) emerge when the tamer is a woman?

Sample Topics:

1. **Franco Zeffirelli's** *The Taming of the Shrew***:** How do Richard Burton and Elizabeth Taylor interpret the central characters, and how does Zeffirelli manage the difficult resolution?

Zeffirelli's film, in many viewer's eyes, has not aged well. Nonetheless, it probably remains the most commonly used film version in high school and college classrooms. Essay approaches that compare the film to the text of the play may do well to focus on what is predictably the most vital part of the film: the relationship between Petruccio and Kate.

You may start with outlining Burton's Petruccio and Taylor's Kate as they appear at the beginning. What do you make of Petruccio's impish chuckle, threadbare clothes, drunkenness, and occasional growling? The film overall seems to have a slapstick tone, but look for ways in which Petruccio is a genuinely threatening presence for a majority of the film. For example, the violence and disorder presented in the wedding scene may deserve especial attention, something reported in the play but not staged. Look at how the film represents the country house "torture" scenes and ask what balance is struck between torments kept and torments omitted from the text.

The nuances, however, might be mostly found in Kate. Look for evidence in Taylor's performance that may suggest ambiguous feelings, movements between outrage and acceptance, flashes of affection or optimism counteracting the outrage and anger she rightly feels.

To judge the relationship, closely read the first scene between the two (which turns into a farcical chase sequence), the country house scenes, and, of course, the equivalent action of 5.2 at the end. It is in this latter portion of the work that Zeffirelli makes his most interesting choices as a storyteller. Assess the nonverbal communication between Petruccio and Kate as the banquet begins (a moment of insight for Kate that seems to cement a transformation) and, finally, Kate's "submission" speech. The overall effect is subtle and mixed. What is the film finally saying about the relationship? It is far from clear. Certainly the film lacks what we might call the feminist undertones of the much earlier Sam Taylor 1929 version, which may seem odd and unexpected. A potentially strong essay could begin by characterizing the film's understanding of the relationship at the end then trace the relationship's development throughout the film.

2. **Bianca and Kate:** How does the play establish and pursue the opposition between the two sisters?

This essay could pursue a number of strong directions. You could argue that the two symbolically swap roles with Bianca asserting herself at the exact moment Kate concedes (5.2). This reading obviously arises from the conclusion (and needs to demonstrate) that Kate is actually tamed. If you feel the opposite is true, a contention that must equally be supported, then your essay can hinge on the assertion that the sisters collectively show the different ways an independent spirit existed within a marriage otherwise reflective of Elizabethan norms. Whichever course you pursue, you will likely want to begin by establishing the opposition between the two found in the play's early scenes (1.1 and 2.1, for example). You can also look for early signs of Bianca's unanticipated (by the men of the play) assertiveness early in 3.1, finding in 5.2 the full reverberations of this early boldness on her part. Do you imagine Bianca as someone who has simply woken up to the possibilities of her own authority now that she is married, or as someone who has cunningly and brilliantly manipulated the system and fooled everyone, including Kate, by exploiting the stereotype of the ideal Renaissance woman? Do you agree, as some have suggested, that Bianca, not Kate, emerges as the most clever and powerful woman in the play?

Bibliography for *The Taming of the Shrew*

Crocker, Holly A. "Affective Resistance: Performing Passivity and Playing A-Part in *The Taming of the Shrew*." *Shakespeare Quarterly*, 54, 2003: 142–59.

Friedman, Michael D. "'I'm Not a Feminist Director, but. . .': Recent Feminist Productions of *The Taming of the Shrew*." *Acts of Criticism: Performance*

Matters in Shakespeare and His Contemporaries: Essays in Honor of James P. Lusardi. Paul Nelsen and June Schlueter, eds. Madison, NJ: Fairleigh Dickinson UP, 2006: 159–74.

Newman, Karen. "Renaissance Family Politics and Shakespeare's *The Taming of the Shrew." Fashioning Femininity and English Renaissance Drama.* Chicago: University of Chicago Press, 1991: 33–50.

Parker, Patricia. "Construing Gender: Mastering Bianca in *The Taming of the Shrew." The Impact of Feminism in English Renaissance Studies.* Dympna Callaghan, ed. Basingstoke, England: Palgrave Macmillan, 2007: 193–209.

Pittman, L. Monique. "Taming *10 Things I Hate About You*: Shakespeare and the Teenage Film Audience." *Literature Film Quarterly,* 32, 2004: 144–52.

Wayne, Valerie. "Refashioning the Shrew." *Shakespeare Studies,* 17, 1985: 159–87.

TWELFTH NIGHT

READING TO WRITE

*T*WELFTH *NIGHT* offers a rich array of divergent essay topics. Of primary importance in defining a critical direction is which *Twelfth Night* do you see? Shakespeare's comedies contain elements of both light and darkness, doses of humor counterbalanced by scenes of tragedy and violence. *The Merchant of Venice,* for example, is formally a comedy, but it is almost impossible to imagine anyone today producing a frothy and slapstick stage or film production of it; the darker elements ultimately win out. On the other hand, *As You Like It,* though not without its share of wistfulness and sobriety, potentially demands a brightner and more affirmational tone in production. With the case of *Twelfth Night,* it is arguably a play in which Shakespeare apportions light and dark with almost clinical precision and evenness. Trevor Nunn's 1996 film version of the play (which factors into one of the topic strands suggested in the Compare and Contrast section) is comic, it ends happily, the problems presented in the play resolved. There is laughter along the way, as well as a good measure of camp and silliness. The film, in its own way, is true to the play. Tim Supple's 2003 film version of the play, however, is darker, consciously unfunny, even violent and menacing in segments. Still that film version, also in its own way, is similarly true to the play. In other words, as you absorb and then write about the work, be aware of the coexistence and interplay of sadness and mirth, of light and dark. The character of Feste, for example, embodies this duality.

It is important also to note that in *Twelfth Night* there are many puzzles and riddles that do not yield easily or without a conscious unraveling on your part. Confusion seems to be Shakespeare's primary theme in the play, and he invites you to try your luck. Take, for example, the following passage, delivered by Viola after receiving a ring from Olivia:

> I left no ring with her: what means this lady?
> Fortune forbid my outside have not charm'd her!
> She made good view of me; indeed, so much,
> That sure methought her eyes had lost her tongue,
> For she did speak in starts distractedly.
> She loves me, sure; the cunning of her passion
> Invites me in this churlish messenger.
> None of my lord's ring! why, he sent her none.
> I am the man: if it be so, as 'tis,
> Poor lady, she were better love a dream.
> Disguise, I see, thou art a wickedness,
> Wherein the pregnant enemy does much.
> How easy is it for the proper-false
> In women's waxen hearts to set their forms!
> Alas, our frailty is the cause, not we!
> For such as we are made of, such we be.
> How will this fadge? my master loves her dearly;
> And I, poor monster, fond as much on him;
> And she, mistaken, seems to dote on me.
> What will become of this? As I am man,
> My state is desperate for my master's love;
> As I am woman, –now alas the day!–
> What thriftless sighs shall poor Olivia breathe!
> O time! thou must untangle this, not I;
> It is too hard a knot for me to untie!
>
> (2.2.17–41)

This passage would be key to at least several essay topics. First, it is one of Viola's strongest speeches and could be used as part of a detailed analysis of her complex character. It would also be indispensable to a related but broader essay on the play's perplexing pattern of gender ambiguity—

Viola speaks these bewildered lines, after all, as she realizes Olivia has fallen for her. In either case, you would approach the passage hoping to peel away and reveal as many layers of confusion as possible.

The first thing to note is that Viola/Cesario has been the subject of Olivia's erotic gaze, a gaze that discomforts both (though for different reasons). "Fortune forbid my outside have not charm'd her!" hopes Viola. "She made good view of me; indeed, so much, / That sure methought her eyes had lost her tongue, / For she did speak in starts distractedly." Olivia's desire-filled gaze seems to have been barely contained, and its object, the ambiguous body of Viola/Cesario, beguiles Olivia as much as it does Orsino. There is a sense of passivity here, though, on Viola's part that contrasts with Olivia's active and penetrating vision. This culminates in the final, often-quoted lines of the soliloquy in which Viola essentially says that the situation is too difficult for her to resolve and she will let fate untangle the complex matter. In a sense, this is exactly what happens: As many have noted, the play is resolved through the miraculous and wonderful conventions of romance, a genre in which the dead can be returned to life and long-lost family members reunited (both of which events, through the figure of Sebastian, take place at the end of *Twelfth Night*). In a character study of Viola, you may want to think about her *agency,* a term used when talking about an individual's ability to control his or her own life and destiny. In some ways, especially at the start of the play, Viola is active and appears to have considerable agency, but does this lessen as *Twelfth Night* progresses?

To return to the passage, the middle lines form a knot that the reader, not time, must untie. Starting with the bold, blunt "I am the man," the dizzying changes in identification expressed by Viola/Cesario follow. She, not Orsino, is the man who Olivia loves. But "I am the *man*"[italics added]? Is Viola consciously playing with and distorting gender here, or is there a genuine sense of confusion in her words? The lines immediately following seem to suggest the latter as Viola attempts to restore order: Nothing can happen between Viola and Olivia, and the disguise is a cruel ruse for having caused so much trouble (note, nonetheless, how Viola displaces responsibility onto the disguise rather than the person who chose to wear it). At once, this attempt at establishing order is undermined. Viola bemoans how easy it is for a "proper-false" man to enchant a woman's heart with his looks. Though Viola identifies with the feminine ("our frailty is the cause, not we!"), it is crucial to note that she has also identified herself with the masculine figure in this movement, the "proper-false" man who is beautiful but untrustworthy. All of this makes a mockery of the line "For such as we are made of, such we be." Again, this seems another rhetorical effort to restore order, the implication being we are basically inalterable in our identity and character. Philosophers might call this an essentialist argument, meaning that we are a set and fixed product of nature. Traditionally, such things as one's gender would have been perceived in this way, but what emerges in this passage, and in *Twelfth Night* as a whole, is the sense of gender as a construction, as an unstable rather than solid, essentialist category. This sense of the uncertain, the unpredictable emerges most vividly in Viola's "And I, poor monster." Reflect on this concept on monstrosity and see if you can arrive at its implication and meaning, which will serve as an important central idea for either an essay on Viola specifically or gender confusion in general in the play. Do you see the monster simply as a comic device that can be vanquished by the play's conclusion or as something much more meaningful and far more transgressive? To focus on the disguise, after all, suggests the "problems" are merely at the surface level, but as you write about *Twelfth Night* look for ways in which these issues can be observed more deeply, both in Viola's fragmented identity—"poor monster"—and in the desire she sparks in those around her.

TOPICS AND STRATEGIES

Every essay requires a focus; you cannot write about everything in the play at once. As a specified focus evolves into a thesis, so observations develop into arguments. The starting point, nonetheless, always comes from a direct engagement of the text. The topic suggestions included here are geared toward helping you make the most of the budding ideas you will have as you read *Twelfth Night*. By no means should you feel limited to these topics, however.

Themes

When Feste observes that "Nothing that is so, is so," he provides an insight into *Twelfth Night*'s vision of the world (4.1.7). This is a play in which not merely surfaces—from Viola's clothes to Sir Toby's pretense of friendship with Sir Andrew—can deceive the mind and trick the eye, but so too can deeper, apparently more essential components of our identity, such as sexual desire, love, and self-knowledge. As a writer, make the most of the text's almost limitless play with instability and uncertainty. Embrace and exploit the confusion of the play and its characters, identifying that in its uncertainty and bewilderment might be found the play's most vital teachings. A thesis statement that begins from a point of uncertainty, one that paradoxically turns doubt into insight, is not necessarily any less desirable than a thesis statement that makes a bold and confident claim. By writing a carefully crafted thesis that justifiably acknowledges ambiguity and resists any summative or definitive conclusions, you will likely be perceived as an especially sensitive and alert student of the play. For example, the writer suggesting that love is rejected by the play would likely run into strong opposition. It may be true that Orsino's foppish and theatrical love is absurd and even foolish and that the play seems to confirm this by having Orsino paired not with the apparent source of his angst and suffering, Olivia, but with Viola. This observation advances the notion of love as false and fickle, but what of Viola's love for Orsino? As some have noted, it seems selfless, even self-sacrificing when Viola agrees to woo Olivia for the man Viola herself loves. More convincingly still, what of Antonio, whose love for Sebastian seems true and unyielding? At the very least, the play seems to demand nuanced and qualified thesis statements: "While the play seems to present much evidence for the mercurial and shallow nature of love, there are powerful contrary movements and forces present as well. The figure of Antonio compels us to note that love has many faces in *Twelfth Night* and that, while some of these facets of love are attractive yet insincere, others are truthfully represented. Like everything else in *Twelfth Night*, love cannot be reduced to one definitive truth or interpretation." After pointing out the contradictions at work in this theme and suggesting that these contradictions cannot be resolved, there is still one important move to make. Note how the final sentence in the example stands in for the solid claim one usually expects in a thesis statement. However, its claim is actually nothing more than saying uncertainty is certain in the text. Even when integrating elements of ambiguity and inconclusiveness into your essay, you must sound confident and authoritative—this is the key to successful academic writing. The body of the essay will then be an organized exploration of what the sample thesis calls the many faces of love in the play, from Olivia and Orsino's theatrical love to Malvolio's self-love to Antonio's pure devotion. Do not forget to frame the body of your essay with some reflections on how this theme cannot be definitively characterized, and what such indeterminacy or uncertainty might mean.

Sample Topics:

1. **Desire:** How is the play's representation of desire multifaceted and disorienting?

Building on the preceding discussion, an essay exploring this topic would encompass several prominent and distinct variations of desire in *Twelfth Night*. Viola's body as a shifting object of desire will most likely be central to the discussion. You might start with a consideration of Orsino's feelings for Viola, how she quickly wins his favor and intimacy. A careful look at 1.4 will be vital here; spend time, in particular, on Orsino's last speech in the scene. This can be paired nicely with a discussion of Olivia's attraction to Viola, closely reading 1.5 (lines 259–69, especially), for example. Identify what each of them sees in Viola and what it is about Viola's body that draws them into desire. The passage discussed in the Reading to Write section will be useful as a way of triangulating all of this, to demonstrate Viola's responses to her unique dilemma.

Now, alongside this central love triangle, Shakespeare places the character of Antonio and asks us to consider his desire for Sebastian as a source of contrast with (and, with its homoerotic undertones, as a source of comparison to) Orsino and Olivia's unstable desire for Viola. Despite Orsino's dramatic performance of his love for Olivia, he will end up paired with Viola, while Olivia, whose affections have been won by the disguised Viola, will happily be coupled with Sebastian, a man she does not know in the slightest, at the end of the play. By contrast, a careful study of Antonio's scenes (including 2.1, 3.3, and 3.4, lines 329–34 especially) can be used to reveal his fidelity and devotion to Sebastian as well as his bitter disappointment at Sebastian's perceived betrayal. What kind of character does Shakespeare create in Antonio? Why is it significant that this character rather than any other is ceded the moral high ground in the play? What do you make of the fact that Antonio ends up as one of the characters left out of the play's romantic machinations? Not paired off, he is arguably not embraced by the resolution.

2. **Festivity:** How is the play's title an important part of its thematic structure?

The life of people in the early modern period was intimately tied to the annual festivals and ritual celebration. The title of the play, *Twelfth Night,* of course references a holiday that took place on January 5. The festivities centered on the idea of disorder and the temporary cessation of ordinary behaviors and hierarchies. It is not difficult to see how the crossdressing Viola and the confusion she spreads emerge from such a festival mood. However, discussion of holiday disorder becomes a central debate in *Twelfth Night* rather than merely a catalyst for the chaotic. Excess clearly emerges as an important theme in the opening lines of the play with Orsino's speech on love. We see an excess of sobriety in Olivia's elaborate, ritualistic mourning and, of course, in Malvolio's severity. Orsino's melancholy love, as many critics have suggested, is not in opposition to but rather closely related to Olivia and Malvolio's grim excesses. At the other end of the spectrum is Sir Toby. He represents unbridled mirth, the holiday spirit at large. Do you think that Shakespeare seems to condemn this excess as much as he does the sober indulgences of Orsino, Olivia, and Malvolio? Examine the exchange between Sir Toby and Maria in 1.3, as well as the confrontation between Sir Toby and Malvolio in 2.3. Perhaps most important will be your interpretation of the trick Sir Toby plays on Malvolio. Closely read 3.4 and 4.2 to see if you believe Shakespeare wants us to sympathize with Malvolio and thus judge Sir Toby harshly—even Sir Toby himself appears to feel the joke has gone too far. You might want to follow this up with some examination of Sir Toby's trick on—

and general treatment of—Sir Andrew. For this, you might use 3.2 and 3.4, especially lines 163–73. One character who might be key to unlocking this theme is Feste. This fascinating figure, discussed in greater depth in the Characters section, can be characterized by the writer as a kind of hybrid or intermediary presence, someone who tempers his mirth with wisdom and wistfulness.

Characters

The characters in the play can be viewed as their thematic constructions. Orsino, for example, is the embodiment of hyperbolic love and self-indulgence. As is often said, he is more in love with being in love than with Olivia. His declarations of passion are highly stylized and frequently drawn from the commonplaces of Petrarchan love poetry, a popular Renaissance verse genre in which the poet reveled in his suffering at the hands of an unobtainable and "cruel" beloved. The woman existed largely as a disembodied catalog of impossibly beautiful features, not as a real flesh and blood human being. Instead she became a blank canvas on which the poet could paint the self-portrait of his own exquisite emotions. However, an essay outlining this rather superficial character might not receive the highest grade. If Orsino is the central focus of your essay, you must work to find complexities. Ironically, his most interesting lines come at the end of the play when he appears reluctant to acknowledge Viola's true name and gender while she is still dressed as a man. Has Orsino finally found out what real love is, only to learn that the object of his desire is Cesario not Viola? Similar considerations come into play when discussing Olivia. Cite, in your analysis, the reports we hear from Valentine (1.1.25–31) and the Captain (1.2.32–37) about Olivia's choreographed mourning, but be sure your essay engages the complexities of her desire, as discussed in the Themes section. In both Orsino and Olivia's case, complexity emerges from behind the early sketches we are given of allegorical figures who refuse to live. Look for changes in characters and evidence of personal growth, no matter how subtle, to provide the momentum for character analysis essays.

Sample Topics:

1. **Viola:** In what ways is Viola a fragmented character rather than a unified whole?

In some ways, as a character, Viola is the opposite of Orsino and Olivia. Though their affections will prove fluid and changing, Orsino and Olivia seem at first to be anchored firmly in reliable, if superficial, characterization. Viola, however, like the desire she generates in others, is volatile and unpredictable from the start. Emerging from a tempest, Shakespeare's signature device for signaling change and transformation, she is from the beginning like the sea she is pulled from. She reports early on that she would like to serve Olivia but a few lines later pledges herself to the service of Orsino, a man she has never set eyes on. Of course, she dresses as Cesario, but look for other ways to explore Viola's ambiguous identity and body. For example, Malvolio observes that Cesario seems to be in between boy and man. In gender and age, then, she occupies an ambiguous, uncertain space, as hard to define for Viola herself as for those around her. We have seen her (perhaps unconscious) confusion in the passage cited in the introduction, but what do you make of the equally intriguing story Viola tells to Orsino in 2.4? As you closely read this passage, note how Viola's identity splinters as she speaks.

2. **Malvolio:** Does Shakespeare want us to feel sympathy for the duped Malvolio?

It seems to be appropriate that Malvolio should be punished for his excess (though, interestingly, perhaps even hypocritically, we may not think the same way about Sir Toby, who, in fact, by the logic of the play is rewarded with the traditional gift of comedy, marriage). Is the disproportionate nature of his punishment, however, enough to alter our perception of him? An essay on this topic will likely begin with an account of Malvolio's early excess of sobriety, nicely summed up by Olivia's observation that Malvolio is "sick of self love" (1.5.77). As your analysis develops and grows more complex, consider the prejudices informing Malvolio's sullen superiority. In particular, you might want to establish early in the essay the idea of snobbery that will inform much of what Malvolio says and does during the play. Note the social condescension lacing his confrontation with Sir Toby and the other revelers in 2.3. Your essay could present a close reading of 2.5, in which Malvolio finds and misinterprets the trick letter. Again, look for the class fantasies fueling his false hopes. A similarly minded close reading of 3.4 could follow. Be sure to include in your essay what will most likely be the crux of your argument, consideration of Malvolio's anguish in 4.2 and his departure from the play at its close. Malvolio refuses to be embraced by the play's comic resolution, but is he justified in this, and how should we view him as he leaves the stage vowing revenge?

3. **Feste:** What is the role of Feste in the play's complex symbolic structure?

In Trevor Nunn's film version of *Twelfth Night*, Feste becomes central to the action, a pervasive presence who watches knowingly the misadventures of other characters. This is a clever and insightful piece of interpretation on Nunn's part as Feste, despite or perhaps because of his peripheral existence in the play, appears to be an axis of the work. As suggested in the Themes section, you may want to argue that Feste represents a kind of compromise between the forces of unchecked revelry and exaggerated sobriety that open the play. Is this moderate, balanced position, however, a little forced, the product of a reader's desire for harmony more than an accurate depiction of Feste's character? Certainly Feste plays the traditional role of Shakespeare's "wise fool," a character the dramatist employs often in different incarnations, and you can find helpful examples of and testimonies to this in 1.5 and 3.1. Perhaps more importantly, however, Feste exerts a powerful influence on the mood and tone of the play through his songs. These can be carefully studied to help you draw conclusions about Feste's overall significance and function in the play. These are songs of life, songs that blend light and dark themes and imagery to forge a sense of a reality that is more than mirth and sadness alone but pragmatically encompasses and understands both. The song that concludes the play is perhaps the most powerful example of this and perhaps invites us to step back from simplistic ideas of life as happy or sad, comic or tragic. As a final consideration, a sense of pragmatism or realism could be projected as the core of Feste's character rather than balance. After all, what do you make of Feste's apparently unapologetic confession of his role in Malvolio's gulling? Perhaps it can be said that Feste alone does not reject the excessiveness of the trick but rather recognizes in it the workings of "the whirligig of time," of the orderly disorder that governs all things in *Twelfth Night.*

Form and Genre

As with all of Shakespeare's comedies, *Twelfth Night* forces us to ask questions about the genre of comedy. How far can comedy's conventions be pushed before they break? How much tragedy can be contained within the borders of comedy without eclipsing the light and mirth of the genre? What exactly is a "happy ending"? What is required for one? What happens when a happy ending is qualified or not complete, when loose ends are not tied up? How do we feel when not everyone is invited to the feast of reconciliation and repair marking the comic closure? How valuable is comedy as an art form, as a way of representing and engaging human life? These and more questions loom large over all of Shakespeare's comedies and reflection on them can offer some of the greatest insights into the plays and Shakespeare's dramatic art.

Sample Topic:

1. **Comedy in *Twelfth Night*:** How satisfactory is the play's comic resolution?

The ending of *Twelfth Night* in some ways references the confrontation between Sir Toby and Malvolio in 2.3. Just as Malvolio attempts to assert order, Sir Toby resists, fighting back with the spirit of mirth: "Dost thou think that because thou art virtuous there shall be no more cakes and ale" (2.3.103). The fifth act of the play, likewise, presents a conflict between forces of order (here the actions of the play and its characters conform to our expectations of how a comedy should end) and disorder (the elements of the text that resist this submission to conformity). An essay that defines this conflict will likely attempt to argue that the forces of disorder, of the anticomic, either prevail or radically undercut the comic conclusion of the play. One can certainly still argue that the play has a comic resolution, but doing so possibly results in an oversimplification of the conclusion. You risk relying on stating what is apparent, what is already visible on the surface of the work, and this is not usually the best position from which to start. However, uncovering and addressing the disruptive elements of the text offers a potentially stronger direction, as you assert that things are not as they seem in the text.

You may want to begin by marshalling the evidence against your point, showing the elements of order and traditional comic reconciliation. It is always a good idea to show you can see and anticipate other sides of an argument, but with this approach it will be particularly useful as the disruptive and conservative elements are tightly and closely interwoven throughout. Among these conservative elements are, first and foremost, the union of the couples and the miraculous incidents that allow for the apparently happy joining of Orsino and Viola and Sebastian and Olivia. Viola is revealed to be a woman, and Sebastian is revealed to be alive; fate (in the guise of the dramatist) appears to have engineered a perfect resolution in keeping with social and aesthetic norms. This line of thinking is summed up by Sebastian's claim that "nature" has returned to its natural "bias" (5.1.253), that the "unnatural" dangers presented by a woman loving a woman have been avoided and all is right in the world. Look for ways in which Olivia tries to make similar points as well. Yet are we supposed to believe a single word that Sebastian says in this speech? Is saying that nature has fixed everything really enough to make it so? You will find some textual evidence related to this consideration in Orsino's final lines (5.1.371–75). Is this attempt to enforce order enough to suppress the countless moments and episodes of chaotic free play that form the core of the play?

Another consideration is those characters left out of the feast: Antonio, Malvolio, and Sir Andrew. How do these loose ends—and Malvolio is a particularly problematic one—also threaten and undercut the comic movement? In the end, is *Twelfth Night* not a comedy because Shakespeare inserts too much distance between the optimistic words of his main characters and the spirit or tone of the play itself?

Compare and Contrast

In *Twelfth Night,* Shakespeare established intricate connections and parallels among his characters, as a result, presenting the writer with numerous directions in pursuing compare and contrast essays. For example, for all their differences, Malvolio, Olivia, and Orsino are plagued by the same repression and self-absorption. Sir Toby and Malvolio are different aspects of the same person or type. Sir Andrew, Malvolio, and Antonio experience a common exclusion from the play's resolution. There are sharp distinctions and polarities present as well. Antonio's devotion to Sebastian is in opposition to the ephemeral and amorphous desires of every character except perhaps Viola. Feste's nuanced and pragmatic sense of lived experience contrasts bluntly with the excesses of Malvolio and Sir Toby.

The play also presents many compare and contrast possibilities in conjunction with other Shakespearean comedies. Two particularly viable opportunities lie in juxtaposing *Twelfth Night* with *As You Like It* and *The Merchant of Venice.* On the surface, *Twelfth Night* and *As You Like It* have much in common with their crossdressing and sexual confusion. Yet in what ways are the two works different? In particular, discuss how the two plays use a similar motif—crossdressing—to create subtly but meaningfully distinct effects. You may want to consider how the two plays approach the confusion created by crossdressing in different ways. Perhaps explore the idea that *As You Like It* is more playful, focused on the possibilities and opportunities of instability, while *Twelfth Night* is occupied more with the psychological anxiety and long-term problems of disorder. The differences between Rosalind and Viola will be key here, of course. Think, too, about the symbolic differences between the conclusions of the two plays, with *As You Like It*'s resolution celebrating

202 Bloom's How to Write about Shakespeare's Comedies

comic excess while *Twelfth Night*'s ending offers an altogether paler pretense of the comic.

If *As You Like It* and *Twelfth Night* seem a natural pairing, perhaps one of the most intriguing "coincidences" in all of Shakespeare occurs between *Twelfth Night* and *The Merchant of Venice.*

Sample Topics:

1. **Compare Antonio of *Twelfth Night* to Antonio of *The Merchant of Venice*:** What resonance is suggested in comparing the role and function of these same-named characters?

> For this topic, you may find it helpful to consult the *The Merchant of Venice* chapter in this volume. There you will find more on that play's Antonio as well as an overview of recent critical discussion of Renaissance homosexual and homosocial love. Perhaps because the characters have so much in common, the task of asserting a key difference offers the most challenge and potential reward (though you do not want to suggest the similarities are unimportant). After making your claim of difference in a strong thesis statement, begin perhaps by summing up what the characters actually have in common. This is important, and though the reader may well have a clear sense of it from the beginning, a detailed consideration of their commonality will be helpful nonetheless and set the stage for the more complex and unexpected contemplation of difference. It may be difficult to talk clearly about the kind of love each Antonio feels for his respective beloved. Nonetheless, it seems possible to assert that there is a gap worth exploring and considering between the wistful, almost mournful longing of *The Merchant of Venice*'s Antonio and the much more explicit and tangible desires of *Twelfth Night*'s Antonio. You may also want to consider at length the idea of selflessness. Each play's Antonio provides the most authentic and sincere example of love, but amid the gold digging and superficiality of *The Merchant of Venice,* this is mild praise. Look for ways in which that play's Antonio demands a kind of "interest" on his generosity to Bassanio and almost to the

end, consciously or not, acts as an obstacle to the coupling of Bassanio and Portia. Look for ways in which *Twelfth Night*'s Antonio is given much less power in the play he inhabits and how he emerges, finally, more alienated but also more noble than his namesake in *The Merchant of Venice.*

2. **Comparing Shakespeare's *Twelfth Night* to Trevor Nunn's 1996 film adaptation:** In what ways does Nunn produce his own distinct version of the play?

A good approach to this essay might be to focus on Nunn's use of the comic. As discussed in the Form and Content section, there is much in *Twelfth Night* that tempers the apparently joyous coupling of the four central lovers. However, look for ways in which Nunn's version of the play erases these problems or manipulates them to fit more neatly into the comic spirit a popular audience might expect. Look for elements throughout the film that stress the comic. For example, what do you make of the schoolboy-like Sir Toby and Sir Andrew? Perhaps make use of scenes like the fight between Cesario and Sir Andrew to show how farce is an important part of Nunn's palette. Perhaps, not surprisingly, you will find much material in the film's closing scenes. For example, how are the departures of Sir Andrew, Antonio, and Malvolio handled tenderly enough to soften the blow of their final absence? Most importantly, though, what do you make of Nunn's handling of the gender concerns that continue to haunt the close of Shakespeare's play? For example, consider why Nunn stages a grand ball at the end of his film, complete with Viola in a lavish ball gown.

Although the 2003 Tim Supple film version is much harder to access, a strong essay arises from a consideration of its departures and reinventions as well. The most likely approach to this film version would be the opposite of the preceding suggested approach to Nunn's film. In what ways does Supple stress the dark and tragic tone latent in Shakespeare's play? His Orsino is no fop, for example, but rather a dignified and even masculine figure from the start. Consider the role of violence in the film,

too, from the opening scenes of gunfire to the brutal Cesario/
Sir Andrew knife fight. Note, also, how the character of Sir Toby
becomes a genuinely threatening presence. Examine in particular bleak scenes such as the film's interpreting Malvolio's
imprisonment as torture—complete with hood over his head.
Moreover, Supple's treatment of the lovers' confused dalliances
is more subtle than Nunn's, less giddy and comic, while the revels are much more riotous and abusive. Why does Supple push
so hard for this grimmer, more realistic interpretation? Do you
feel it is too great a departure from the spirit of the play, or do
you believe that such tensions and concerns are already contained in and suggested by the work?

Bibliography for *Twelfth Night*

Gay, Penny. "*Twelfth Night*: Desire and Its Discontents." *As She Likes It: Shakespeare's Unruly Women.* London: Routledge, 1994: 17–47.

Greenblatt, Stephen. "Fiction and Friction." *Shakespearean Negotiations.* Berkeley: University of California Press, 1988: 66–93.

Osborne, Laurie E. "Twelfth Night's Cinematic Adolescents: One Play, One Plot,
One Setting, and Three Teen Films." *Shakespeare Bulletin: A Journal of Performance Criticism and Scholarship,* 2008 Summer; 26: 9–36.

Schalkwyk, David. *Shakespeare, Love and Service.* Cambridge, England: Cambridge UP, 2008.

Tassi, Marguerite. "'Sportful Malice,' or What Maria Wills: Revenge Comedy in
Twelfth Night." *The Upstart Crow: A Shakespeare Journal,* 2007–2008 (27):
32–50.

THE TWO GENTLEMEN
OF VERONA

READING TO WRITE

THOSE FAMILIAR with Shakespeare primarily through his legend and a few major works often believe that his plays have been revered since they were penned, that his reputation was established at once and that all his works must have met with no shortage of continuous praise, even veneration, from audiences and critics alike. Of course, this is not the case at all. There is a significant number of plays that have had difficult lives despite their author's seemingly unchecked success over the centuries. It can be interesting to trace the critical legacy of an individual text and see how, perhaps, it was battered and bruised by critics for generations, only to be met with critical reappraisal and reevaluation, often occasioned by a shift in thinking or values. The play had not changed, but the world and the times had; each age has its own fresh, new Shakespeare as a result. Like *All's Well That Ends Well* and *The Winter's Tale*, *The Two Gentlemen of Verona* has been frequently condemned over the ages. Arguably, however, it might be suggested that the play has never really received the kind of critical reevaluation awarded to the other two texts. *The Two Gentlemen of Verona*, in many ways, continues to languish at the edges of Shakespeare's contemporary existence, a play whose problems have not yet turned into puzzles that audiences or critics seem particularly eager to unravel.

Historically, there are several associations with the play of which an essay writer needs to be aware. First, it is an early work, but, more tellingly, it is typically referred to as an immature work; the latter description implies that Shakespeare had not yet arrived at the imaginative heights that would mark his later work, and the play is understood to reflect this. Often it is seen as light in its concerns and sloppily constructed, especially in regard to the dramatist's sketching of his characters. Second, countless critics have been baffled and appalled by Valentine's offer of Silvia to Proteus at the play's close. It is interesting to see the uniformity of response to this gesture among critics ranging from the eighteenth to the twenty-first centuries: disgust. In the case of reaction to *The Taming of the Shrew,* one is able to make the case that the misogyny we witness is simply the result of fundamental differences in ideas about gender relations between the early modern world and our present time. It can certainly be argued that Shakespeare intended Petruccio's cruelty to be seen as extreme even to early modern audiences, but it nonetheless represents core Renaissance ideals of a man's right to authority over women. Kate's final speech relinquishing her assertions of power over her husband (if taken at face value) is then simply a restoration of order and harmony; it is an untenable moral outcome today, but it represents the basic principles (even though potentially in a burlesque form) of Shakespeare's day. In contrast, it seems as though there has never been anything but disgust for Valentine's treatment of Silvia, going back even as far as the earliest surviving commentaries on the play. Even in an age that had a different understanding of gender relations than we generally have today, Valentine gratuitously breaches basic ethical standards. So, we are left to ask, why would Shakespeare choose to present such an outcome? Why would he compromise the integrity of his play with such a repellent resolution? Arguably, even in his apprentice phase as a playwright, he could not make such a thoughtless and damaging mistake. The absurdity of Valentine's actions can be seen as an essential part of the play's discourse on human folly and infidelity, something that Shakespeare is in control of as a theme in his text. Valentine's gesture was potentially intended to be viewed as implausible and deeply unsettling. At the very least, the play challenges us to respond to rather than dismiss its difficulties.

These challenges reside in and begin with the play's language. In this passage, Proteus delivers a soliloquy in which he first tries to articulate why he is willing to abandon his deep friendship with Valentine and love of Julia in exchange for a newfound obsession with Silvia.

> Even as one heat another heat expels
> Or as one nail by strength drives out another,
> So the remembrance of my former love
> Is by a newer object quite forgotten.
> Is it my mind, or Valentinus' praise,
> Her true perfection, or my false transgression,
> That makes me reasonless to reason thus?
> She is fair; and so is Julia that I love,—
> That I did love, for now my love is thaw'd;
> Which like a waxen image 'gainst a fire
> Bears no impression of the thing it was.
> Methinks my zeal to Valentine is cold,
> And that I love him not as I was wont.
> O! but I love his lady too-too much,
> And that's the reason I love him so little.
> How shall I dote on her with more advice
> That thus without advice begin to love her?
> 'Tis but her picture I have yet beheld,
> And that hath dazzled my reason's light;
> But when I look on her perfections,
> There is no reason but I shall be blind.
> If I can check my erring love, I will;
> If not, to compass her I'll use my skill.
>
> (2.4.185–207)

The first thing to note is that this is a soliloquy, a speech uttered by a character alone onstage. The typical function of a soliloquy is to reveal to the audience a character's intentions that, for any number of reasons, need to be kept secret from the other characters. What is striking in this example, however, is that Proteus actually reveals virtually nothing about his motives because he does not understand them himself. Instead, what we have is a character facing bewilderment and uncertainty over a sudden change of mind and heart. Proteus attempts to frame his thoughts and observations in a rational manner and yet repeatedly stumbles over the fact that reason is incapable of accounting for these experiences. In *A Midsummer Night's Dream*, such changes will be explained by the use of magic and potions, but here there is nothing but the realization of a self suddenly and radically disconnected from its own values and identity. The tension between active self-reflection and radical loss of self-control causes the central rupture of the passage when Proteus asks what "makes me reasonless to reason thus?" The concept of reason here seems to implode in this line, splintering into multiple uses of the word *reason* throughout the passage. The term can refer to reason as an intellectual process but also to reasons as methods of accounting for and explaining the link between cause and effect. In both senses of the word, however, the emphasis is on the failure of reason to provide a reliable explanation of or insight into one's thoughts and actions.

This passage could be used in a variety of essays. It would prove important, when paired with another soliloquy from Proteus moments later at the beginning of 2.6, for any character study of the speaker. Equally, the passage establishes itself as one of numerous moments in *The Two Gentlemen of Verona* central to the issue of mutability or infidelity (not only to others but to oneself, as it is part of the play's apparent attack on the idea of a coherent entity that could be called the self). Moreover, an analysis of the theme of mutability in this individual play presents the opportunity to plot out a compare and contrast essay that looks at the theme in other texts (*A Midsummer Night's Dream* and *Much Ado about Nothing* would be especially effective companion texts, though the writer would probably want to pay close attention to distinctions between the texts as well). In these other plays, Shakespeare explores sudden changes of heart, particularly in regard to romantic love. However, *The Two Gentlemen of Verona* appears to be the most radical of the three plays mentioned here because the other two at least offer potential and tentative explanations of the shifting heart (magic in *A Midsummer Night's Dream* and the power of social pressure and opinion in *Much Ado about Nothing*), while *The Two*

Gentlemen of Verona makes no effort to provide sound reasons for sudden and violent breaks from reason.

TOPICS AND STRATEGIES

Every essay requires a focus; you cannot write about everything in the play at once. As a specified focus evolves into a thesis, so observations develop into arguments. The starting point, nonetheless, always comes from a direct engagement of the text. The topic suggestions included here are geared toward helping you make the most of the budding ideas you will have as you read *The Two Gentlemen of Verona*. By no means should you feel limited to these topics, however.

Themes

Many of the themes available to the essay writer addressing *The Two Gentlemen of Verona* reflect some aspect of the play's obsession with mutability, with the shifting and changing nature of the human psyche. As you explore any particular theme in the play, demonstrate how the chosen theme also connects with the broader patterns and interests of the play. Finally, for those who would like to approach the theme of mutability itself, note that this may be most realistic only for longer essays or shorter ones where depth is willingly sacrificed for breadth.

Sample Topics:

1. **Gender:** For all the instability and flux witnessed in the play, can we say that the one constant in *The Two Gentlemen of Verona* is the suppression of women?

   A writer approaching the theme of gender must recognize that, like everything else in the play, gender discourses in *The Two Gentlemen of Verona* are fluid. The embodiment of shifting gender is seen in Julia's disguise as a page; certainly a writer might use this as a concrete, exterior emblem of the kinds of inner metamorphoses the characters are vulnerable to. There is, too, the somewhat embarrassing representation of Julia early in the play, dithering emotionally over a letter from Proteus, finally and rashly tearing it up though her wish was to read it (1.2.45–130). It is possible to say the episode is a stereotypical portrait of female histrionics, but is it rather just part of a broad pattern in which everyone in the play dithers emotionally? Pay special attention to scenes in which two women talk (Juliet and Lucetta as well as Juliet and Silvia), especially the exchange between Juliet and Silvia around 5.4.45. Can we characterize the relationships between women here? Is there a kind of stability to them in this notoriously unstable play?

There is also the matter of Silvia's much-discussed silence at the end of the play. Note how she is treated by the various male figures populating the stage in the final act. How do they interact with Silvia and she with them? What political statements might the play conceivably be making through this odd and unnerving action and silence? For more on this, see the discussion of Julia in the Characters section.

2. **Love:** Is the play entirely cynical about the possibilities of faithful love?

Perhaps key to this topic is the appreciation of different kinds of love witnessed in the play. There is no doubt that if we focus on male heterosexual desire, the play resoundingly tells us that such feelings and emotions are ephemeral and shifting. When it comes to men in love, the play tells us to look for the truth by combining the qualities and emotional states associated with the names of the two central male characters: Valentine/love and Proteus/shifting. You may wish to trace such an unstable view of love from the conversation about love that takes place between Proteus and Valentine in 1.1, through Proteus's severe declarations of fidelity to Julia (2.2), Valentine's own embrace of love on meeting Silvia, and then the scenes of Proteus's sudden reversal in 2.4 and 2.6. The broad strokes of your argument here will no doubt establish how reliably inconsistent these two are, though you may wish to find an additional point of entry (such as the idea of self-awareness or lack of on the part of the pair) for your analysis.

To complicate things further, however, amid this inconstancy are other kinds of love not so easily dismissed by the play. Famously, of course, there is the relationship between Lance and his dog, Crab, apparently based on the deep and unrelenting dedication of man to dog. Pay close attention to how these scenes from the secondary plot are juxtaposed with those of the central plot featuring Proteus and Valentine (see the Compare and Contrast section for more on this). Equally, consider how the female characters might be incorporated into a discussion of love, studying not just their attitudes to the men they love but also, in the case of Julia and Silvia, to each other in times of need. Another form of love featured in the play might be called homosocial love, the (typically) nonsexual, idealized devotion of a man to his male friend often imagined in Renaissance literature (see the chapters on *The Merchant of Venice* and *Twelfth Night* for more historical and theoretical discussion of this theme). Can we argue that the two men finally privilege their friendship with each other over the women of the play, and that this mutual regard and affection are sincere? Is anything these two men do or say credible after we have seen them vacillate so wildly and so often during the course of the play? Although they may apparently privilege their friendship over their heterosexual loves, is there any indication that such a decision could have any pretensions to permanence?

3. **Identity:** What does the play suggest about the construction of human identity?

An essay based on this topic can essentially bundle strands from the previously discussed topics on gender and love with other discourses from the play to talk broadly about identity. What will distinguish this essay from the preceding pair of topics is the reach of the conclusions you draw. Proteus's name here may likely become a philosophical symbol for the overarching way in which the human mind, spirit, and body are deconstructed and reconstituted over and over again; a passion for one woman and friendship for one man can evaporate in an instant and be replaced by even more violent passions in an entirely new direction, while a woman's body can be transformed into a young man's (just as the convention of the English stage in Shakespeare's time was to cast young men as the female characters).

Traditionally people speak of a person's identity, the self or the I, as a fixed entity, something concrete and singular. Poststructuralist thinkers in the late twentieth century and beyond have made much of challenging such unities and have suggested that long-held beliefs in the cohesion of the self are illusory. It seems that Shakespeare had reached that conclusion far, far earlier.

Characters

Character studies may be most effective when dealing with works in which Shakespeare has etched out deep, psychologically complicated characters (a Hamlet or a Lady Macbeth, for example). Writing character analysis of figures that are not necessarily fully formed characters, as can justifiably be argued of Proteus and Valentine, for example, presents certain challenges but can still be a rewarding path to a strong essay. The challenge is to recognize that such an essay will merge character analysis with thematic analysis; the characters in a play such as *The Two Gentlemen of Verona* do not live and act so much as they represent. Perhaps the best approach to adopt, then, is to understand the likes of Proteus and Valentine as commentaries on humanity that need to be decoded and understood in order for the message to be related through your analysis to your reader. Equally, as the characters are assigned dialogue and speak to one another, the ideas that each character embodies symbolically converse with another character's possible emblematic meaning in the text through the juxtaposition of similarity and difference.

Sample Topics:

1. **Lance:** Does Lance emerge as a foil to the inconstancies of Valentine and Proteus?

A good way to frame an essay on Lance is through the character's function. Lance is a clown, and his scenes are comical. However, paying close attention to Lance's presence in 2.3 and 4.4, assess how he may serve a more serious role within the philosophical framework of the play. How would you characterize his bond with Crab? How must it be distinguished from the wavering of Proteus and Valentine? How does this difference influence the philosophical discourses on love and identity in *The Two Gentlemen of Verona*?

2. **Julia:** Can any claim be made to the existence of feminist sympathies in the play through the figure of Julia?

It is important to understand that, while it can be productive and exciting to couch essays on Shakespeare in the language of modern-day feminism, the concept is anachronistic in this context. You must demonstrate in any essay pursuing this topic that you are sensitive to the historical nuances of applying contemporary theoretical terms to a play many centuries old. In short, you need to show the reader that you understand that Shakespeare's was a very different world when it came to gender politics, but that, nonetheless, as a writer you naturally bring your own modern interests and sensibilities to the play, and that such insights are important to the continued life and vitality of Shakespeare's work.

This particular play's gender discourses have not simply become problematic to later audiences; the treatment of Julia and Silvia (especially the latter) has caused difficulty and concern from all but the beginning of the play's life. This oddity makes it possible for us to talk about gender and the female characters in the play in somewhat more ambitious terms than usual: Does Shakespeare allow his women to be treated so outrageously because he wants to use excess as a means of stimulating sympathy? Alternatively, does he treat them so outrageously because, apparently even by early modern standards, he is a chronic misogynist? Although you should always be cautious when making claims about authorial intent, always ready to place conditions on your own tentative conclusions, this play's idiosyncrasies invite strongly worded questions as well as strongly worded answers.

Although Julia could be the central focus of a strong essay, the play's two main female characters could be treated in a single essay as two closely related or even overlapping female presences. In either case, the relationship between the two characters, as seen, for example, in 4.4 and 5.4, is particularly important. Julia is interesting, too, because although the female characters seem to represent an emotional stability that is beyond the two male leads, Shakespeare also gives us notable examples of mutability from Julia too. In the world of the play, the line dividing stability from instability is ever being redrawn. Because these characters can be seen more as functions than as psychologically real creations, what role does Julia and/or Silvia play in the work's conversation about either love or identity? Remember that for every moment of fluctuation for Julia, something concrete seems to emerge as well: Her decision to pursue Proteus makes her active and decisive, though her chosen disguise simultaneously exemplifies the indeterminacy that saturates the play.

Form and Genre

One of the most compelling questions that can be asked about one of Shakespeare's comedies seems to be "How much of a comedy is it?" Selecting such a question for an essay topic is strong for several reasons. It calls for a close reading of a particular sequence of the text (the final scene in which the comedy is "resolved," plus any additional scenes, of course, that warrant sustained attention). This concentrated focus on a piece of text, if done well, working with the details of the play's conclusion in order to assess how much of the comic spirit truly shines on the play at hand, will add complexity and distinction to your argument. This approach necessitates a close reading of the final scene and an appraisal of how well these problems have been overcome and the loose ends tied up. Typically, the problems of a resolution in Shakespeare's comedies tend to fall into several categories, ranging from issues that are apparently resolved but, after closer inspection, the intensity of the earlier obstacles overpowers the forces of reconciliation Shakespeare employs at the play's close. Both modes are present in *The Two Gentlemen of Verona*, though each plays out in unique ways.

Sample Topic:

1. **Comic form and *The Two Gentlemen of Verona*:** How does the play's obsession with mutability finally disrupt the comic drive of the play?

The final line of *The Two Gentlemen of Verona* is at odds with the overwhelming philosophical thrust of the play. When Valentine claims that the four central lovers will soon wed with "One feast, one house, one mutual happiness" (5.4.170), he is attempting to conclude the play with an emphasis on wholeness and completeness, of unity where before there had been only fragmentation and dissolution. The lovers hope that the shifting ground of the self has now settled and that the four fluid individuals have re-formed into some solid and reliable shape as two faithful, mutually devoted, and well-matched partnerships. However, does the play's earlier talk of fluid identities challenge this possibility?

Moreover, there is the primary consideration of Silvia's treatment by Valentine, Proteus, and the other male characters who arrive onstage during 5.4. As an example of protean affections, this issue can be included in an essay focused principally on shifting identities and the comic outcome of the play, but it could also be used in a more political essay on the comic form, one that attempts to understand how social problems may unhinge the play's resolution.

Compare and Contrast

Many critics have suggested that *The Two Gentlemen of Verona* can be put to best use in making comparisons with later plays, seeing the early formation of Shakespeare's most common comic themes and charting their development and maturation in the subsequent plays. This is a rewarding approach and a useful avenue for the writer. Questions like "How does the theme of crossdressing develop in Shakespeare's comedies?" open up numerous possibilities. Obviously you can go to mature comedies that were produced toward the end of the first decade of Shakespeare's career (*As You Like It* and *Twelfth Night*) or focus on another relatively early comedy with *The Merchant of Venice*. With the former, you will probably find it easier and more productive to talk about ways of distinguishing Shakespeare's use of crossdressing rather than finding similarities (remember that useful rule that if the two subjects you are comparing look broadly more alike than different at first glance—and in this case they do—than the essay should probably gravitate to highlighting the evident contrasts. If the two subjects appear more different at first glance, then explore what an examination of certain similarities reveals). For example, it could be argued that in *The Two Gentlemen of Verona* Shakespeare shows a clear interest in using crossdressing as part of a philosophical discussion of fluidity and identity. However, by the time he writes *Twelfth Night*, Shakespeare is using crossdressing as the singlemost prominent symbol of fluid identity.

Another theme present in *The Two Gentlemen of Verona* is the issue of inexplicable human behavior. Shakespeare, throughout his career, seems drawn to the dramatic possibilities of the absence of motive. This is unorthodox and has gotten him into trouble over the years. For example, in *The Winter's Tale* Leontes flies into a sudden and unaccountable rage of jealousy that leads directly to his wife's death. There is no spark visible in the play, just a spontaneous eruption of violent passion. To many critics over the centuries this has been an example of failure—we expect characters to behave in ways that make sense, otherwise the representational value of the piece, how well a work of literature can talk about human behavior and what degree of light it can shed on the human condition, is judged poorly. However, Shakespeare at times seems to have disagreed on this point, fascinated often by characters who act wildly and without logical cause—they simply become what they become. Probably the most famous example of this in Shakespeare's canon is the malignant Iago in *Othello*, a villainous character who embarks on a murderous and vindictive plan without any clearly or plausibly defined cause. Though Iago supplies the audience with excuses and reasons, none seems in the least bit compelling or convincing, and we are left with the terrifying sense that Iago simply is the embodiment of evil, and that people can simply be bad. This view is frightening and goes against much well-documented social theory, of course, but this is the psychological nightmare that Shakespeare envisions. Interestingly, the disconnection of reason and action, as we have seen, begins in the comedies and begins vividly, of course, in what may be his first comedy, *The Two Gentlemen of Verona*.

The writer can certainly find great pairings or groupings of texts among these and other plays, but one theme stands out as a particularly promising subject for compare and contrast analysis: love. In one way or another, all of Shakespeare's comedies are about love and romantic relationships, but a number of the plays are nothing less than philosophical, lyrical debates on the theme of love. *As You Like It*, for example, would make for a strong companion text for *The Two Gentlemen of Verona*; your essay could possibly suggest that the romantic teachings of Rosalind are the perfect antithesis of Shakespeare's cynical (if you agree they are cynical, of course) sketches of Proteus and Valentine. This is just one of many pairings of texts useful for exploring the theme of love in Shakespeare's comedies.

Sample Topics:

1. **Compare *The Two Gentlemen of Verona* and *A Midsummer Night's Dream***: In what ways do these early comedies form a dialogue on love? What is the outcome?

   As these two works are roughly contemporaneous, written at roughly the same moment in or stage of Shakespeare's career, the discussion would stress not the idea of Shakespeare's dramatic evolution but rather the idea of a "snapshot" of Shakespeare's creative thinking at one moment in time. With these two texts, you have more than enough material to make solid and compelling claims about what Shakespeare seems to have been thinking and valuing when he began his writing career.

A possibly suitable framework for such a comparison might look at the two male leads in each play: Demetrius and Lysander and Proteus and Valentine. Though a possible differentiation between the two depictions of inconstant love might be the role of magic, it is possible to complicate this by recognizing that Demetrius's first major change of heart comes before the play when he stops loving Helena and falls for Hermia. Also, what do you make of the fact that part of the comic resolution of the play relies on Demetrius being left in his enchanted state in order to neatly pair off the lovers? Look for broader ways to characterize the inexplicable and unstable nature of love in both plays. For example, critics often talk about the almost indistinguishable qualities of the four Athenian lovers in *A Midsummer Night's Dream,* the fact that there seems to be no real logic to favoring a Hermia over a Helena or a Demetrius over a Lysander. Because *A Midsummer Night's Dream* is probably the more complicated text, the challenge will be to devote equal discussion to each play (unless you signal specifically in your thesis the intention and justifications for a particular focus on one play over the other).

Finally, you might also consider using these two texts in an essay about gender politics. This aspect of *The Two Gentlemen of Verona* was discussed in the Themes section, but there is plenty in *A Midsummer Night's Dream* to almost match the grotesque treatment of Silvia at the close of the play she inhabits. You would do well to consider her fate alongside that of Hippolyta, the Amazon prisoner of war turned wife to Theseus, or the notorious humiliation of Titania by her husband, Oberon. A strong essay could be produced on the humiliation of women by men in early Shakespeare (and, of course, *The Taming of the Shrew* could be integrated into the discussion as well). An interesting angle to take might be to assess what the play seemingly wants us to feel about these allusions to violence and callousness.

2. **Comparing Shakespeare's two plots in *The Two Gentlemen of Verona*:** What is said by the conversation Shakespeare

establishes between the "high" or primary and "low" or secondary plots of the play?

It is a common device in Renaissance drama to mix scenes of a high plot with parallel scenes of a low plot. High plot references class issues and refers to the main story line with its typical focus on aristocratic or well-to-do characters, while the low plot features servants and clowns facing their own troubles and dilemmas. Although these respective plots may never significantly mingle with each other in many scenes, there is often a mirroring effect established by their mutual presence, in which the low plot resembles, parodies, or burlesques the main plot. Another example of this in Shakespeare would be *Love's Labour's Lost,* in which a comical group of clowns and pedants ridiculously pursue their own amorous adventures in scenes that alternate with the apparently loftier (though, in actuality, no less ridiculous) romantic plans of a king and his lords. In that play, Shakespeare's primary intention behind the mixing of high and low plots is laughter. While the Lance scenes in *The Two Gentlemen of Verona* are genuinely funny (perhaps among the most hilarious in all of Shakespeare), an essay writer can effectively and justifiably look for more significant, more resonant conclusions to draw from the juxtaposition of high and low plots in the text. Much of the material from the essay on love discussed in the Themes section would be integrated into a essay on this topic. Of course, the emphasis is going to be on making the two plots respond or talk to each other, or, perhaps more exactly, talk about each other. Does the low plot join in the attack on love (witnessed in Shakespeare's portrayals of the unsteady Valentine and Proteus) by also mocking love when a man devotes himself passionately to his dog? Or, as is often suggested, does Shakespeare actually use these low scenes to suggest an alternative vision of love, one self-sacrificing and authentic by comparison? In other words, does the low plot end up being, morally and emotionally, higher than the high plot?

Bibliography for *The Two Gentlemen of Verona*

Brooks, Harold. "Two Clowns in a Comedy (to say nothing of the Dog): Speed, Launce (and Crab) in *The Two Gentlemen of Verona*." *Essays and Studies: Collected for the English Association.* London: John Murray, 1963: 91–100.

Carroll, William. "'And Love You 'gainst the Nature of Love': Ovid, Rape, and The *Two Gentlemen of Verona*." *Shakespeare's Ovid: The Metamorphoses in the Plays and Poems.* A. B. Taylor, ed. Cambridge, England: Cambridge UP; 2000: 49–65.

Collington, Philip. "'Like One That Fears Robbing': Cuckoldry Anxiety and The *Two Gentlemen of Verona*." *The Premodern Teenager: Youth in Society 1150–1650.* Konrad Eisenbichler, ed. Toronto, ON: Centre for Reformation and Renaissance Studies; 2002: 245–69.

Fudge, Erica. "'The Dog Is Himself': Humans, Animals, and Self-Control in The Two Gentlemen of Verona." *How To Do Things with Shakespeare: New Approaches, New Essays.* Laurie Maguire, ed. Malden, MA: Blackwell, 2008: 185–209.

Hunt, Maurice. *Shakespeare's Religious Allusiveness: Its Play and Tolerance.* Aldershot, England: Ashgate, 2003.

Smith, Bruce. *Homosexual Desire in Shakespeare's England: A Cultural Poetics.* Chicago: University of Chicago Press, 1991.

INDEX